RIVER OF MY ANCESTORS:

THE RIO GRANDE IN PICTURES

RIVER OF MY ANCESTORS:
THE RIO GRANDE IN PICTURES

NOËL FLETCHER

Fletcher & Co. Publishers
www.fletcherpublishers.com

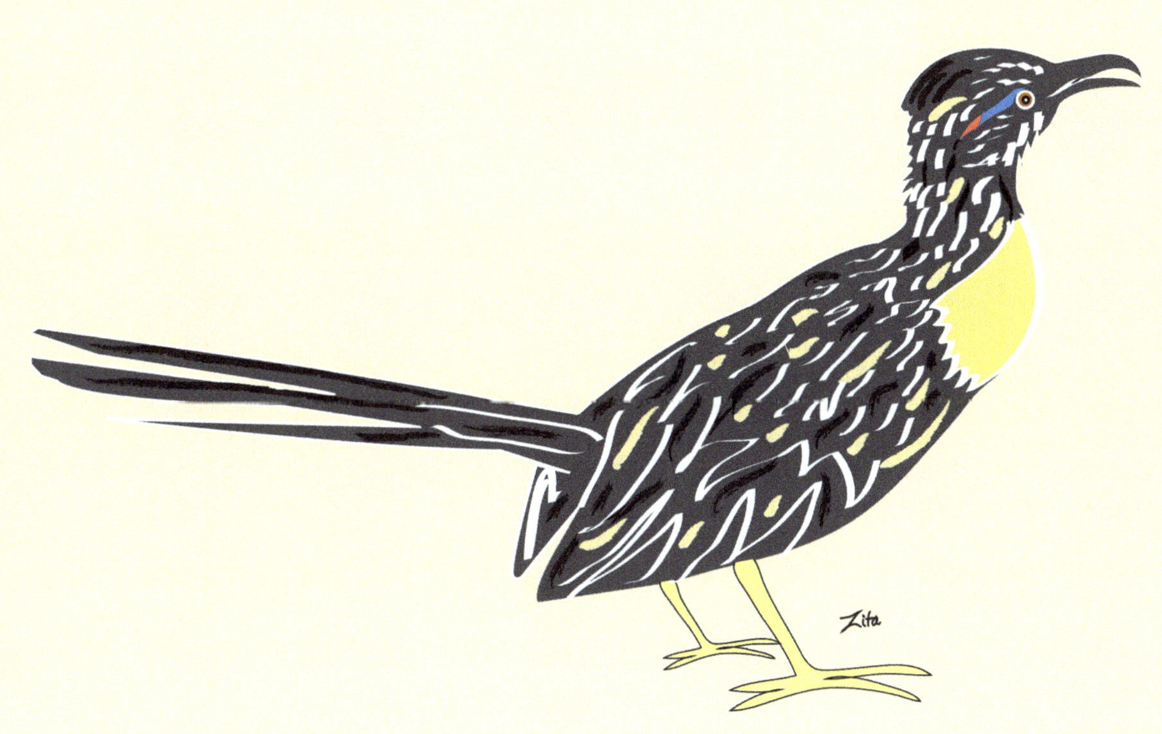
Zita

ISBN-10: 1941184049
ISBN-13: 978-1-941184-04-2

© 2015 Fletcher & Co. Publishers LLC.
All photography © Noël Fletcher (unless otherwise attributed).

All rights reserved. No part of this publication may be reproduced, distributed, or transmitted in any form or by any means, including photocopying, recording, or other electronic or mechanical methods, without the prior written permission of the publisher, except in the case of brief quotations embodied in critical reviews and certain other noncommercial uses permitted by copyright law. For permission requests, see: www.fletcherpublishers.com.

Cataloging-in-Publication data for this book is available from the Library of Congress.

Library of Congress Catalog Number: 2015901899
Fletcher & Co. Publishers LLC
www.fletcherpublishers.com
Cover and graphic design by Zita Steele

First Edition
Printed in the United States of America

Note: I would like to acknowledge that Native Americans have lived along the Rio Grande and used its waters for centuries before Europeans arrived in the region. The Native Americans also made numerous contributions to the history of New Mexico. This book focuses on the history and experiences of my Spanish family.

Contents

Dedication

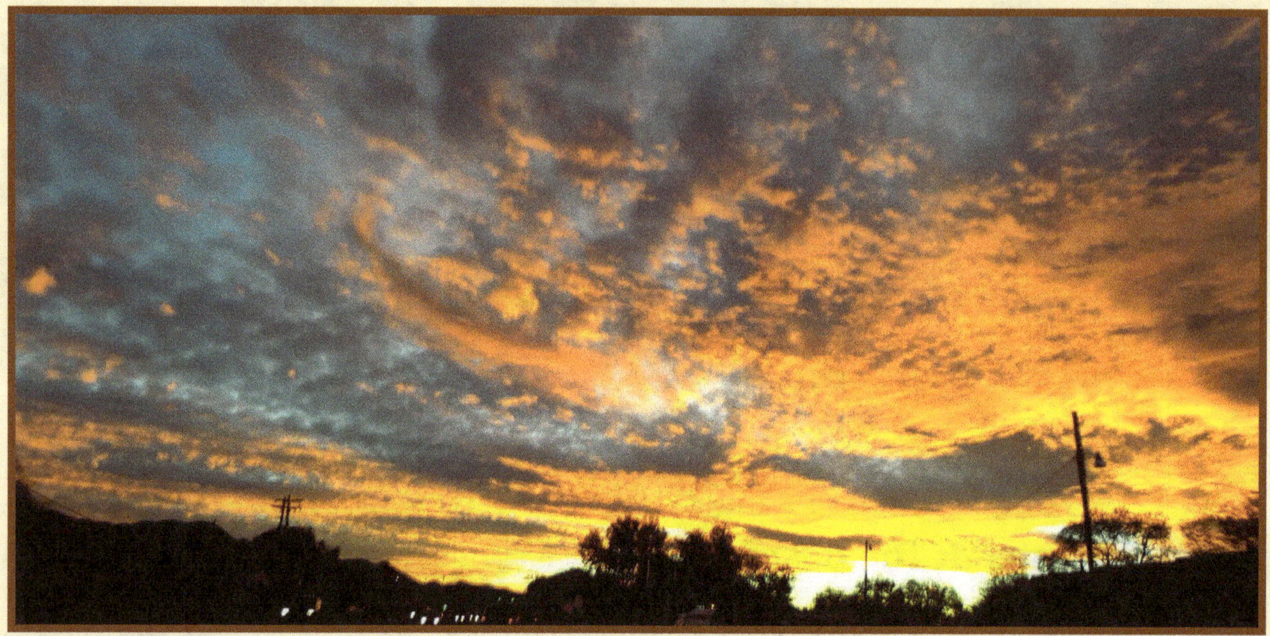

A magnificent sunset my daughter and I witnessed while traveling home from a photo expedition. Photo by Zita.

Dedico este libro a mi queridisima hija, Zita.

I have fond memories of our adventures when these photos were taken...fueling up with coffee and sweets for our excursions; driving white-knuckled amid strong wind gusts along that lonely highway to Socorro; finding the snake coiled on the ground outside our car door along the Bosque; getting the creeps as we approached the suspension bridge at the Rio Grande Gorge; passing through steep curving roads in pitch-black canyons at night; and sneaking around the irrigation ditches trying to approach elusive sandhill cranes...

I'm grateful for your sound artistic judgment and keen eye. When I couldn't make up my mind about which photo to include from a series, you had the deciding vote.

You always have been—and will remain—my inspiration!

Chapter 1: History

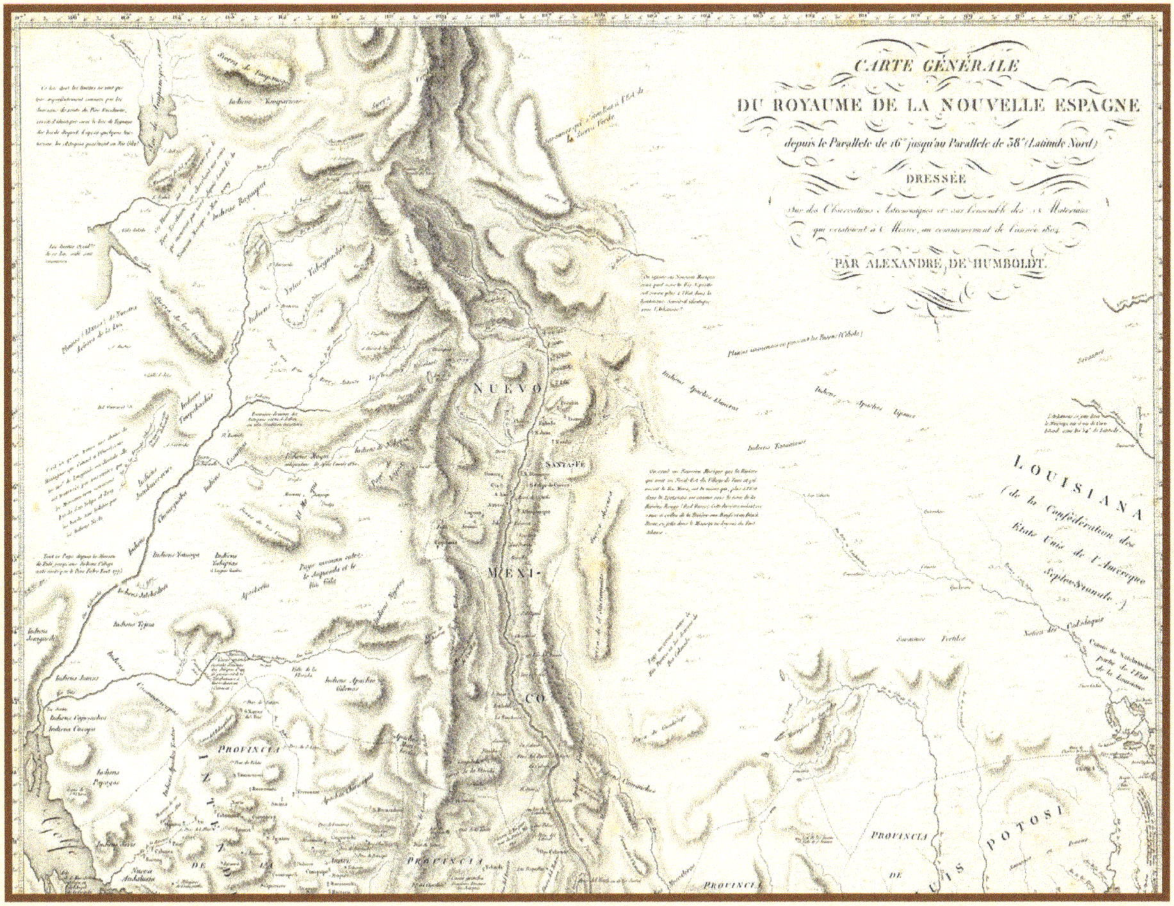

"Geographical and Physical Atlas of New Spain" by Baron Alexander von Humboldt (1827). Courtesy La Biblioteca Nacional de España.

Snaking along the base of canyons and through volcanic ridges, the waters of the Rio Grande for centuries have provided a lifeline for my Hispanic family and others in windswept New Mexico. El Morro, a massive monument in New Mexico, became a camp along an early highway used by Spanish explorers, clergy, and officials who would govern the land claimed by Spain and give the Rio Grande its name.

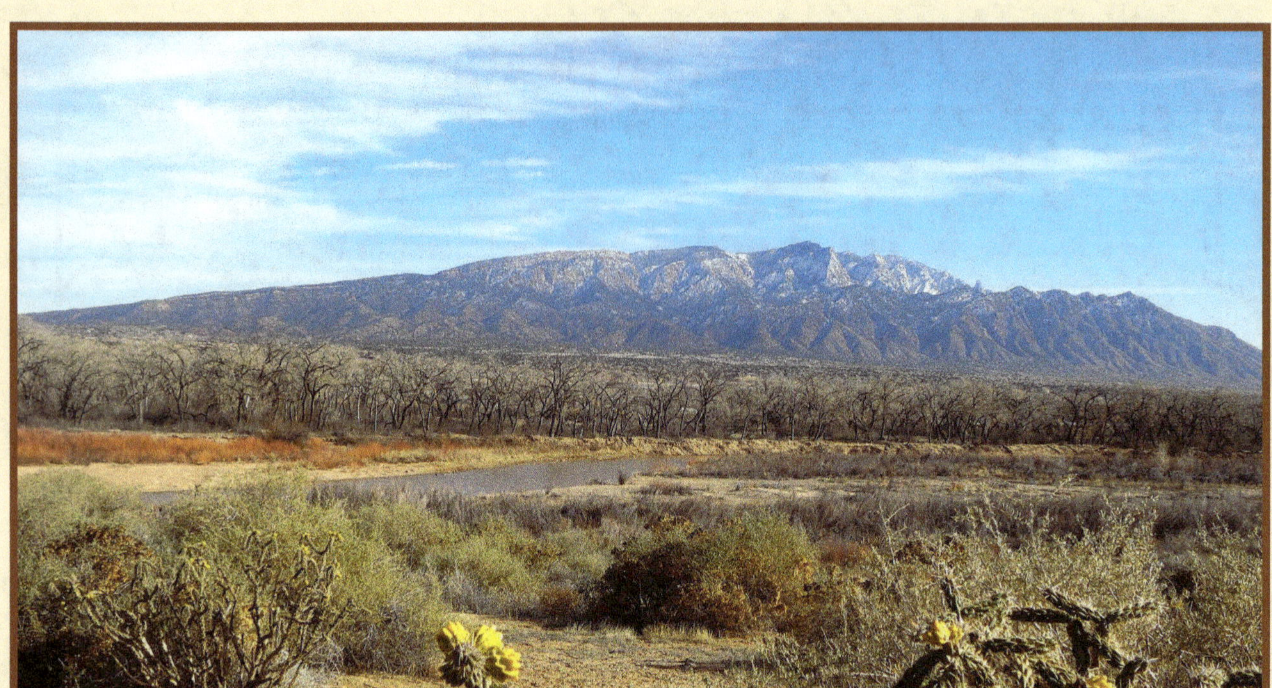

A winter view of the Rio Grande. This area in Bernalillo is where explorer Francisco Vázquez de Coronado is believed to have established his headquarters during the cold months before continuing his explorations in the spring of 1541. This view of the snow-capped Sandia mountains and barren cottonwood trees along river is probably very similar to what Coronado saw here since the area has changed little during the centuries.

The Rio Grande provided a byway for Spanish conquistadors during expeditions into the New World. The Spanish followed the river to create a route, much of which is known today as "El Camino Real."

During his search for the Seven Cities of Gold (Cibola), explorer Francisco Vázquez de Coronado, 500 soldiers, and 2,000 Mexican Indian allies established a large camp near present-day Bernalillo, N.M. They spent the winter of 1540–41 there along the banks of the Rio Grande before resuming a journey of some 800 miles into the wilderness that took them into present-day Kansas.

The influence of the Spanish conquistadors is present today. In addition to the way of life they forged along the Rio Grande, they also left a spoken legacy. The form of the Spanish language spoken in New Mexico is archaic, with words from the 1500s and 1600s. This language remained without change due to the isolation of the Spaniards in New Mexico. Spanish-language scholars continue to study the archaic Spanish found in New Mexico.

In contrast, the Spanish spoken in nearby Arizona, Texas, and California has been influenced by Mexican dialects.

Conquistadors trekking through desert plains from 1519 through 1589 gave the mighty river various titles, including "Rio del Norte" and "Rio Bravo". But Juan de Oñate is believed to have named the river "Rio Grande" when he and bands of soldiers followed the river upward from El Paso, Texas in 1598 into the rugged territory known today as New Mexico.

My Ancestors

My family has played an important role in New Mexico. My ancestors were among the first Spanish settlers who came to the region. In 1605, ancestors of my Candelaria grandfather (a soldier and his two brothers) accompanied Oñate during his exploration up the Rio Grande through present day New Mexico.

Pausing during their journey, the Spanish stopped to rest at a spring at the base of a massive sandstone cliff called El Morro, which later became a national monument. There, my ancestor Joseph de la Candelaria carved his name alongside Oñate's. During the late 1600s, my grandmother's family, the Pereas, joined Diego de Vargas in Spain's reconquest of Santa Fe, N.M.

Named "Holy Faith" in Spanish, Santa Fe is oldest city in New Mexico. Its tributary of the Rio Grande (the Santa Fe River) provides the city with nearly half of its water supply.

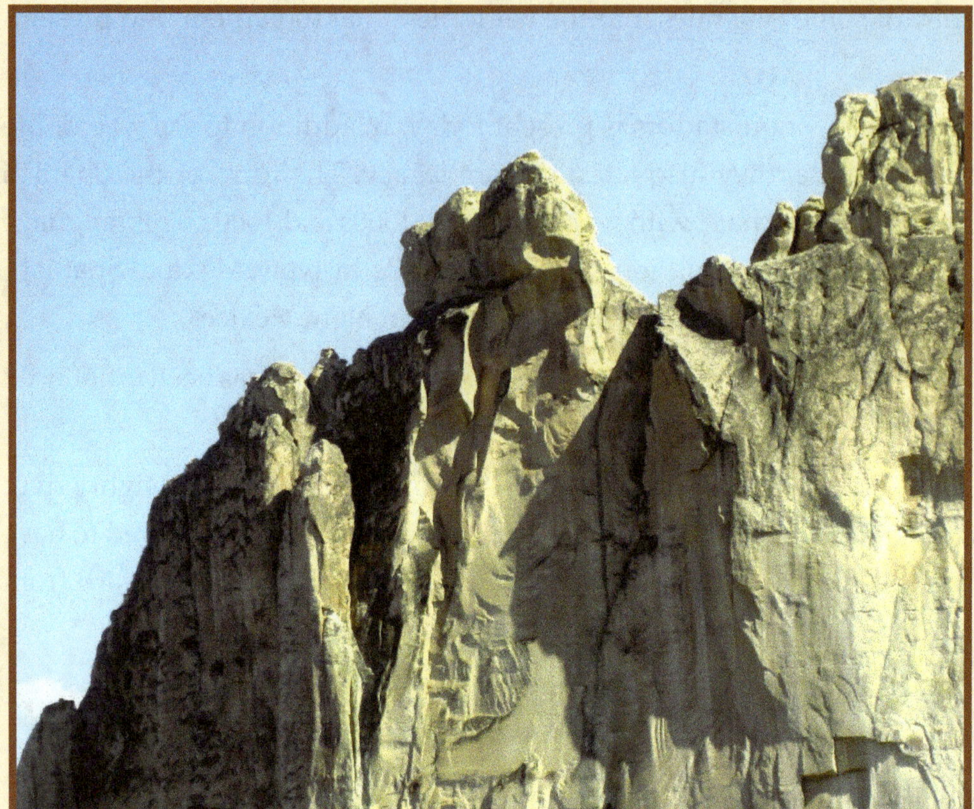

The sandstone cliff in what is today called El Morro National Monument in western New Mexico. Photo by Zita.

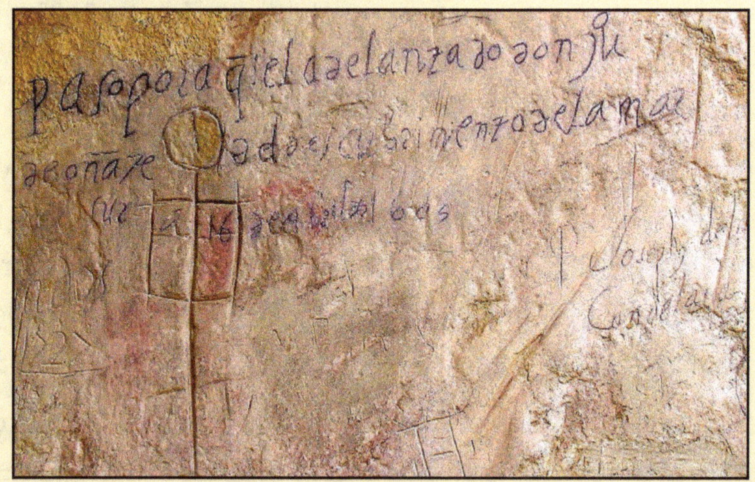

The signature of Juan de Oñate (left, photo courtesy Wikimedia Commons) that he carved in 1605 into the side of El Morro. My relative, Joseph de la Candelaria, carved his signature alongside Oñate's (lower right).

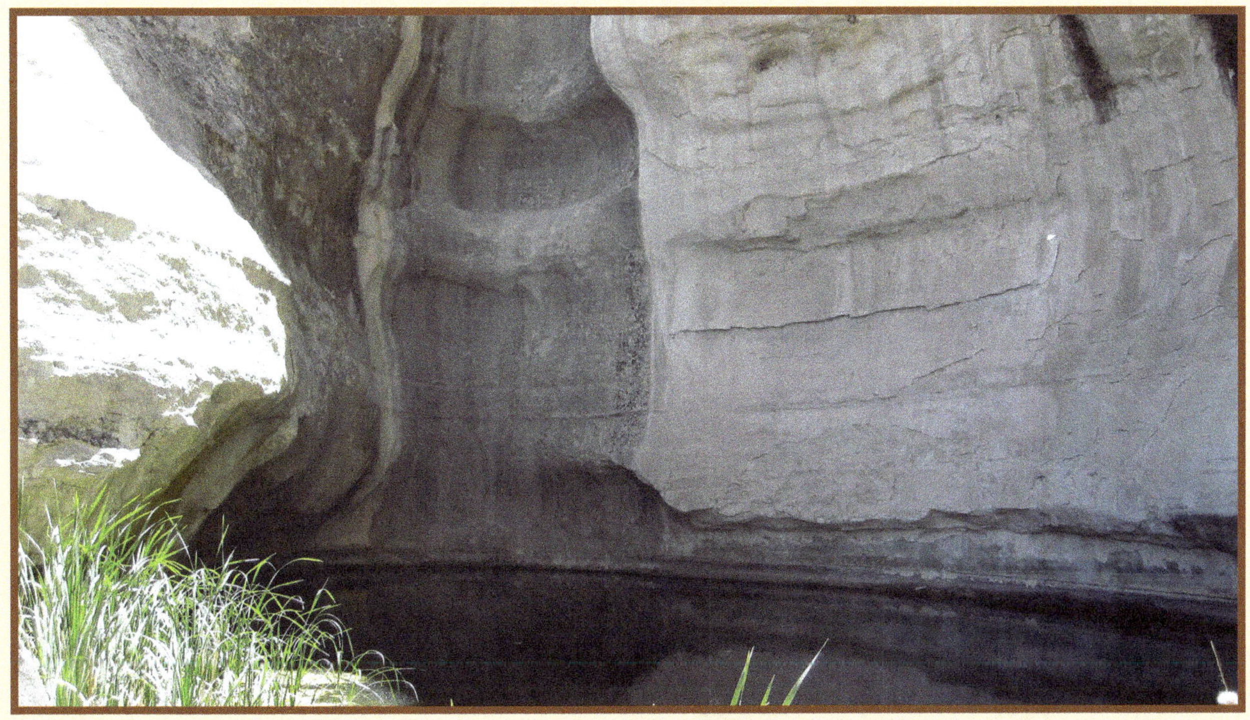

A pond provided refreshment that made El Morro (Inscription Rock) a popular rest area in the desert. Photo by Zita.

Various members of my family established ranches and homes throughout the state of New Mexico, including in Corrales, Albuquerque, Santa Fe, and Santa Rosa. They were highly influential in politics, social development, and trade along the Santa Fe Trail as well as in California, Colorado, Texas, and Mexico.

My relatives, particularly the Pereas, relied on the Rio Grande to sustain their haciendas and various commercial enterprises in New Mexico's central valley. My great-grandfather, Abenicio Perea of Corrales, was the Mayordomo (chief irrigation officer) on the board for the main *acequia* system there. Referred to in my family as Papá, Abenecio was also a sheriff. Along with other members of the important Perea clan, he had major land holdings and was a prominent cattle and sheep rancher. His family formed the Perea Brothers, an influential mercantile company that traded goods in the mid-1800s along the Santa Fe Trail between the East Coast, California, and Mexico.

Growing up, I spent much time with my Perea relatives. I recall hearing stories from my grandmother about cousin Jose Leandro Perea, known as the Sheep King of New Mexico. Don José Leandro was described as a man of "perseverance, industry and spirit," with vast holdings of sheep, cattle, and horses, who relied on the Rio Grande to make his living. His son Pedro and my other relatives made important contributions to New Mexico.

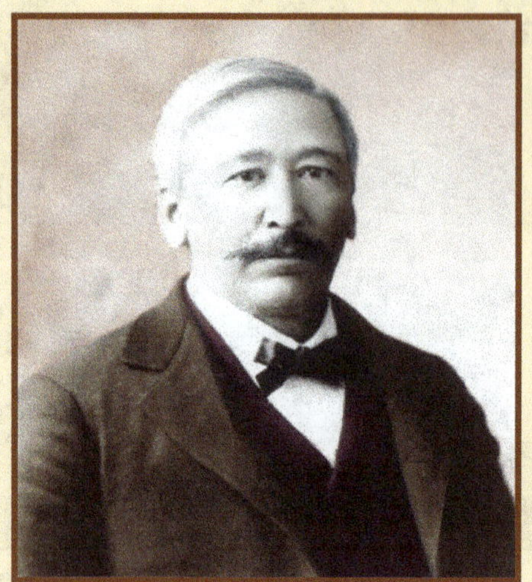

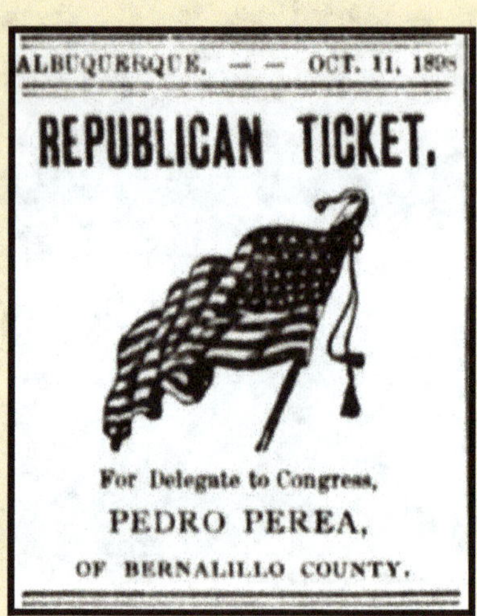

ALBUQUERQUE. — — OCT. 11, 1898

REPUBLICAN TICKET.

For Delegate to Congress,

PEDRO PEREA,

OF BERNALILLO COUNTY.

Pedro Perea (1852-1906). Photo courtesy the U.S. Congress (left) and a campaign ad (right) from the *Albuquerque Daily Citizen* newspaper on Oct. 11, 1898.

Pedro Perea was a successful rancher, businessman, banker, and contender for Territorial governor. He was elected as a Republican delegate to the U.S. Congress from the Territory of New Mexico before it became a state. He was credited by the *Albuquerque Daily Citizen* newspaper in 1989 for helping "establish the public school system in New Mexico, and has proven a good friend of the territorial university."

His cousin Col. Francisco Perea also was a Republican Territorial delegate to Congress. Col. Francisco was the first Republican Hispanic-American member of Congress in U.S. history. Francisco used his political influence to keep New Mexico on the Union side during the Civil War. He served as a lieutenant colonel and formed at his own expense Perea's Battalion, which consisted of some 500 Hispanic men, in order to defend New Mexico against a Confederate surge.

In addition, Francisco's battalion fought in Apache Canyon during the Battle of Glorieta Pass, a decisive battle dubbed the "Gettysburg of the West," whose successful outcome for the Union forced the Confederates out of New Mexico.

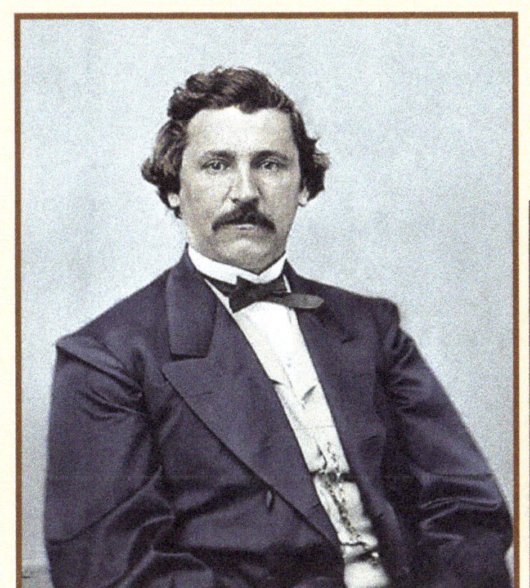

The Hon. Francisco Perea (1830-1913), left. Photo courtesy the U.S. National Archives and Records Administration.

Col. Francisco was a strong supporter and friend of Abraham Lincoln. He was among the delegates who nominated the U.S. President for a second term and witnessed Lincoln's second Inaugural Address.

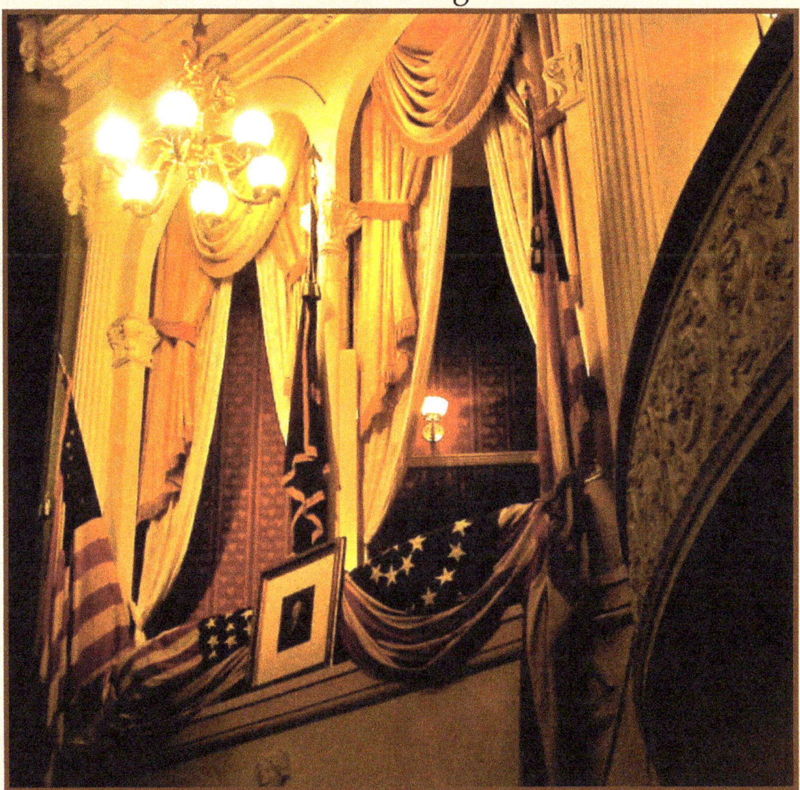

The box in Ford's Theatre in Washington, D.C., where Abraham Lincoln was assassinated April 14, 1865. Photo by Zita.

Col. Francisco also was in Ford's Theatre attending the three-act play "Our American Cousin" when the President was assassinated. He was seated in the orchestra pit directly under the box when Lincoln was shot.

"I heard the shot fired by [John Wilkes] Booth; it sounded like the report of a small pistol, not loud, but loud enough to make the theater in an instant as quiet as the grave," Francisco recalled in a Feb. 12, 1909 interview with the *Albuquerque Morning Journal.* "The confusion and grief that swept over the city that night is something I shall never forget. It was terrible."

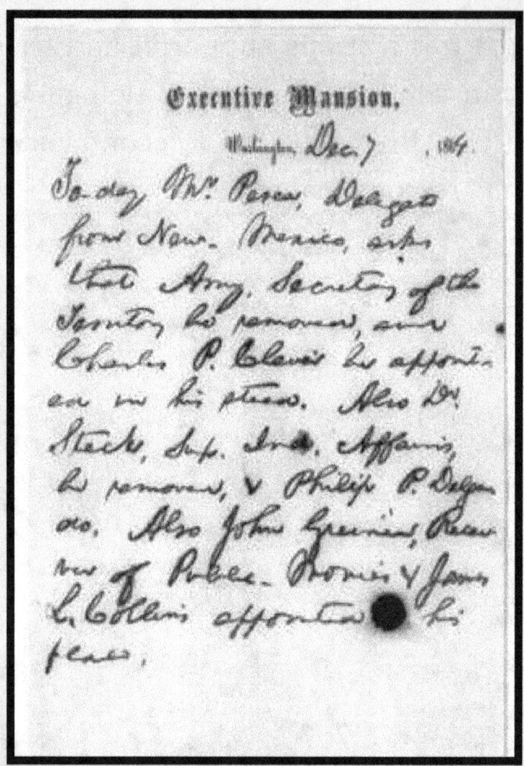

Executive Mansion,
Washington, Dec. 7, 1864.
To-day Mr. Perea, Delegate from New-Mexico, asks that Arny, Secretary of the Territory be removed, and Charles P. Clever be appointed in his stead. Also Dr. Steck, Sup. Ind. Affairs, be removed, & Philip P. Delgado. Also John Greiner, Receiver of Public Monies & James L. Collins appointed in his place.

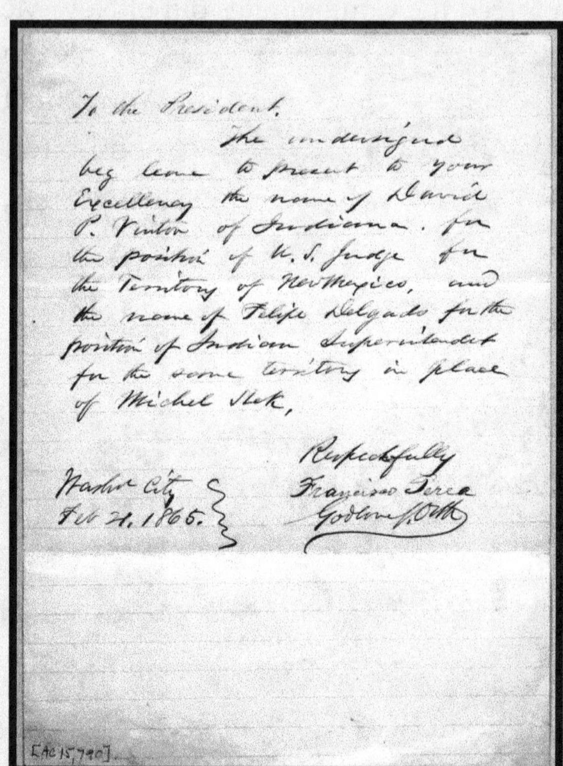

To the President.
The undersigned beg leave to present to your Excellency the name of David P. Vinton of Indiana, for the position of U. S. Judge for the Territory of New Mexico, and the name of Felipe Delgado for the position of Indian Superintendent for the same territory in place of Michel Steck,
Respectfully
Francisco Perea
Godlove S. Orth
Washn City
Feb 21, 1865.

Abraham Lincoln memo (left) about Francisco Perea and New Mexico, Dec. 7, 1864, from the Abraham Lincoln Papers at the Library of Congress. One of Francisco's letters to Lincoln (right).

Col. Francisco was a leading rancher and trader who ran mule trains along the Santa Fe Trail into Missouri. His family owned much land throughout the state, particularly along the Rio Grande and its tributaries.

José Leandro's other son, Jesus Maria, relied on the Rio Grande to irrigate his winery, where he produced thousands of gallons of wine yearly in the 1880s and cultivated a grape named El Paso from seeds imported from Spain. According to the *Dodge City Times,* he also had over 400,000 head of Merino sheep, of which he sold 40,000 one year in Dodge City, Kansas. Irrigation from the river was essential to another relative, Maximo Perea, who farmed over a thousand acres of wheat near Alameda, N.M.

About the River

The Rio Grande spans nearly 2,000 miles in length. Running in a north-south route from the mountains of southwestern Colorado through New Mexico to Texas, it forms a natural border between the United States and Mexico. The river rises at 12,800 feet above sea level at its origin in Colorado. It traverses mainly at high altitudes in New Mexico through canyons, mesas, and valleys before descending to 1,800 feet along Big Bend National Park in Texas before finally flowing out into the Gulf of Mexico. Due to ever-changing sandbanks and rapids, the Rio Grande is heavily silted and has a limited navigation history. In the mid-1800s, steamships sailed mainly at its mouth near Texas and the Gulf of Mexico. Today recreational boating, such as whitewater rafting and kayaking, occur in some areas—such as in northern New Mexico where the river passes through the 800-foot deep Rio Grande Gorge. Rapids and river-flow levels remain unpredictable. A 74-mile stretch of river through the Rio Grande Gorge is designated as a protected National Wild and Scenic River System. In addition, the Rio Grande numbers among 14 American Heritage Rivers designated by Presidential order for protection, revitalization, and preservation.

During the 1800s and early 1900s, flash flooding from mountain snowmelts in the spring and summer rainstorms was an ever-present danger due to a lack of dams to control water levels. A river flood in the Rio Grande valley occurred in 1903 in the Spanish community of Alameda, where another branch of my family lives. This flood destroyed an important community church, forcing the locals to build a replacement much further downstream.

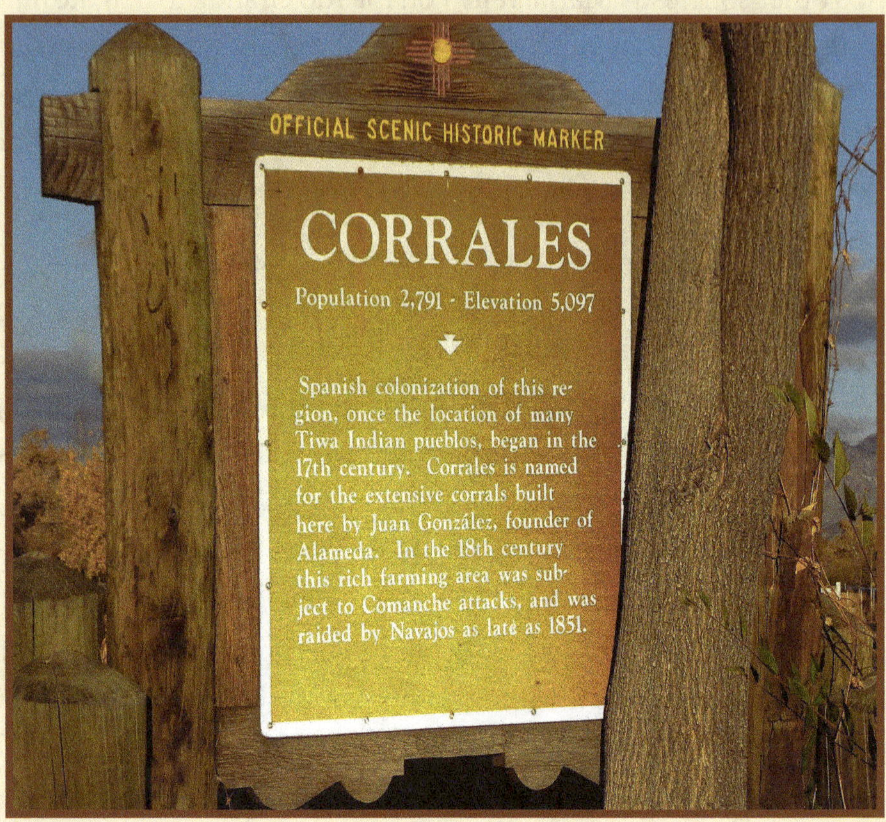

My grandmother was born 1906 in Corrales, N.M.—six years before New Mexico became a state. New Mexico had been a U.S. territory since 1850.

I recall listening to her stories about crossing the treacherous waters of the Rio Grande by horse-drawn wagons in the absence of bridges. My grandmother, as a child, once even fell into the Rio Grande while sitting on the buckboard of a wagon. She turned around to look at the back of the wagon and lost her balance as it lumbered through the river.

Fortunately, her father, Papá, was riding alongside on his Arabian horse and pulled her up into safety.

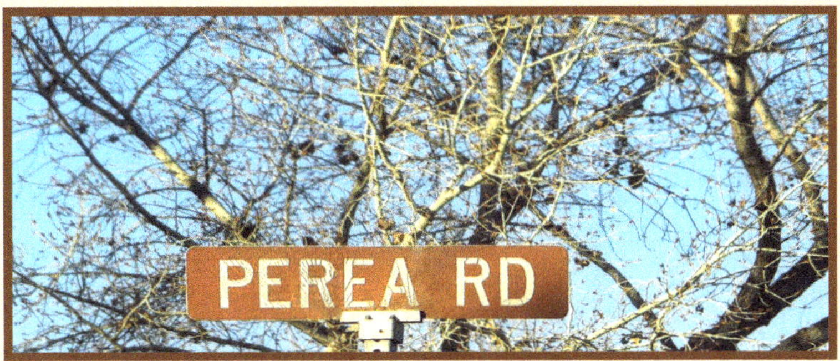

One of three streets named after the Perea family in Corrales, N.M.

River of Life

Water always has been a precious natural resource in the desert. It is vital to the farms and ranches that arose along both sides of the Rio Grande and its 12 key tributaries. The Spanish settlers created a vast network of irrigation ditches called *acequias,* which still exist and are used today. The brownish waterways, fed by melting winter snow from the Rocky Mountains and summer rains, provide nourishment for crops, orchards, and livestock.

The Rio Grande is a central part of New Mexico's ecosystem. Its native fish include gizzard shad, red shiner, river carpsucker, bluegill, mosquitofish, flathead catfish, and brown trout. Other species include German brown trout, rainbow trout, and northern pike. There is abundant wildlife within the river's surrounding Bosque (woodlands), marshes, ponds, meadows, and farmlands. New Mexico has nearly 500 different birds on its state bird list. Cottonwood trees along the Bosque provide habitats for owls, hawks, ring-necked pheasant, falcons, flycatchers, and woodpeckers. Ducks, quail, doves, sparrows, finches, mockingbirds, and geese as well as migratory birds—such as sandhill cranes and bald eagles—gather around the shorelines of the Rio Grande and in nearby areas with lush vegetation.

Mammals who make their homes along the Rio Grande include bats, rodents, skunks, raccoons, river otters, beavers, deer, elk, bighorn sheep, and coyotes. In the Middle Rio Grande Valley alone, there are three types of turtles, nine lizard species, and 13 different kinds of snakes.

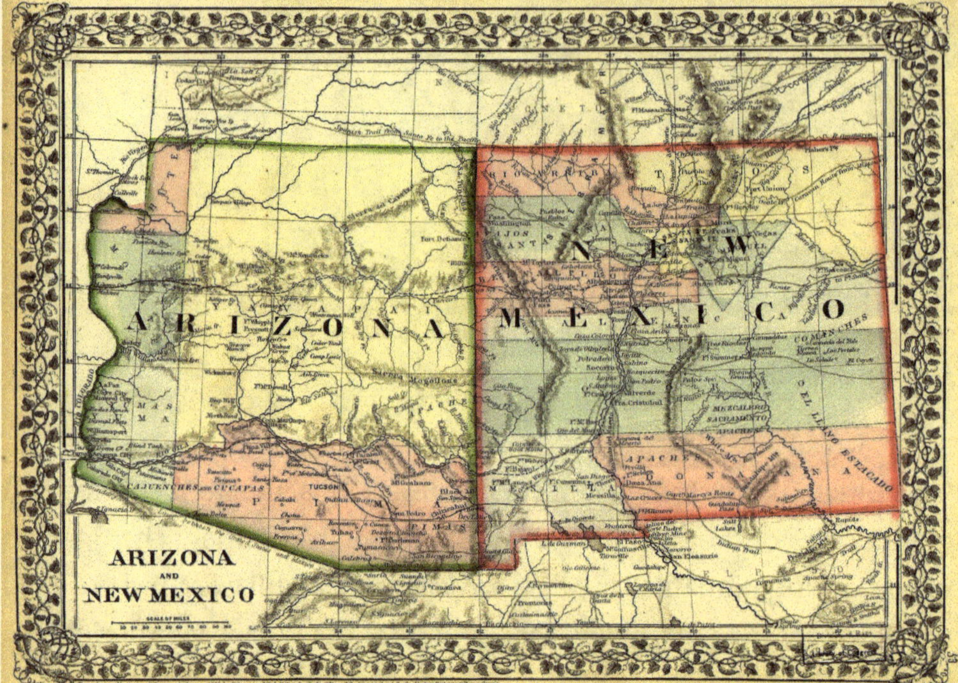

Map of the U.S. territories of Arizona and New Mexico (1867) by Samuel Augustus Mitchell.

New Mexico ranks the 4th highest in the United State (after California, Texas, and Arizona) for having native richness of plants and animals, according to a report by The Nature Conservancy based on an analysis of more than 21,000 species. Various shrubs, grasses, trees, and cacti are found along the Rio Grande as it passes through mountains, across high desert terrains and into river valleys. Despite its sluggish appearance, the Rio Grande continues to be a vital resource to those who live amid the arid climate of New Mexico, where surface water is precious and life is harsh in the rugged environment.

My ancestors overcame many obstacles as they struggled to carve out lives for themselves in a vast wilderness. In addition to the difficulties of frontier life they faced social barriers including racism and discrimination. Through their hard work, tenacity, and enterprise, they achieved success while helping others who lived along the banks of the mighty Rio Grande. Generations later, the Rio Grande remains a source of life and inspiration for people today.

Chapter 2: The River

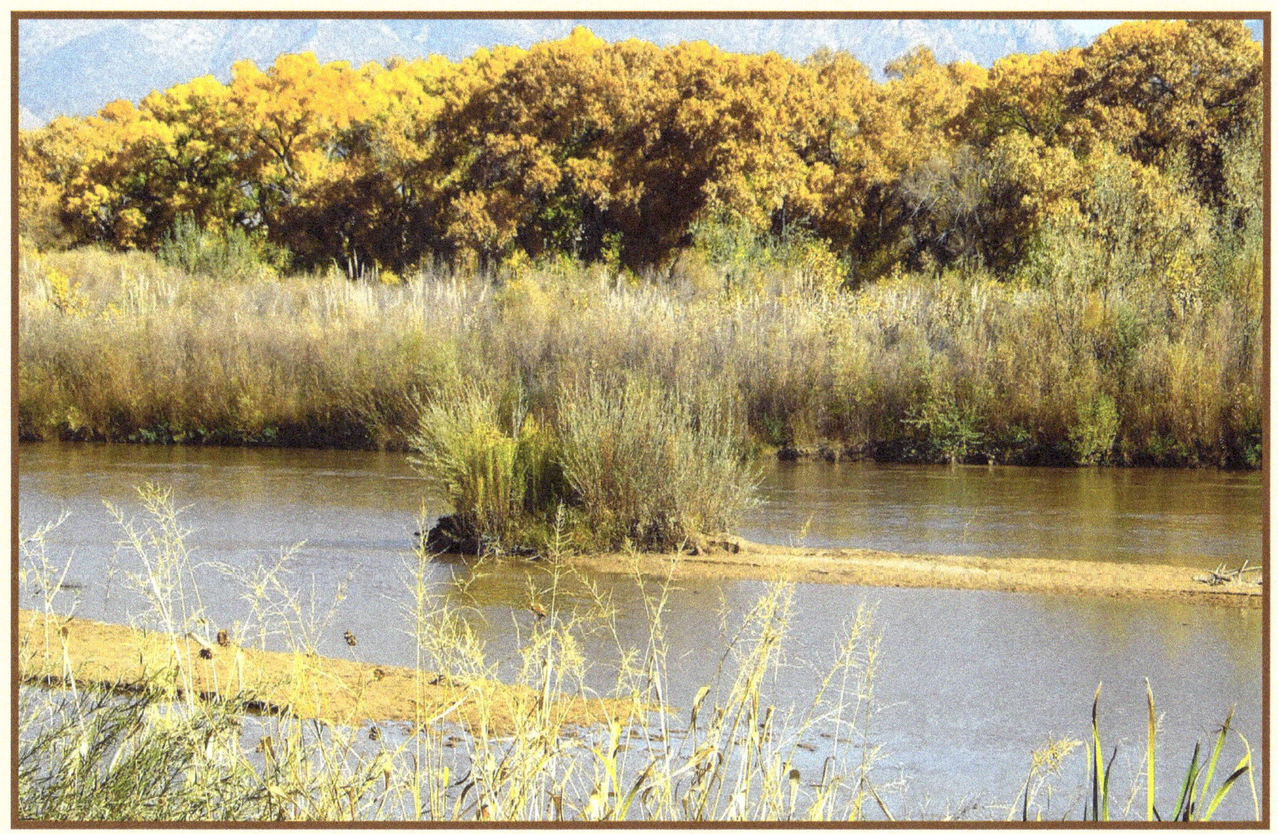

Sandbars are regular features of the Rio Grande and contribute to its unique character.

The Rio Grande meanders through craggy mountains and high desert valleys. Between low banks, the river expands and contracts as it travels through waters flanked by sandy soil. The Rio Grande runs through the entire length of the state of New Mexico.

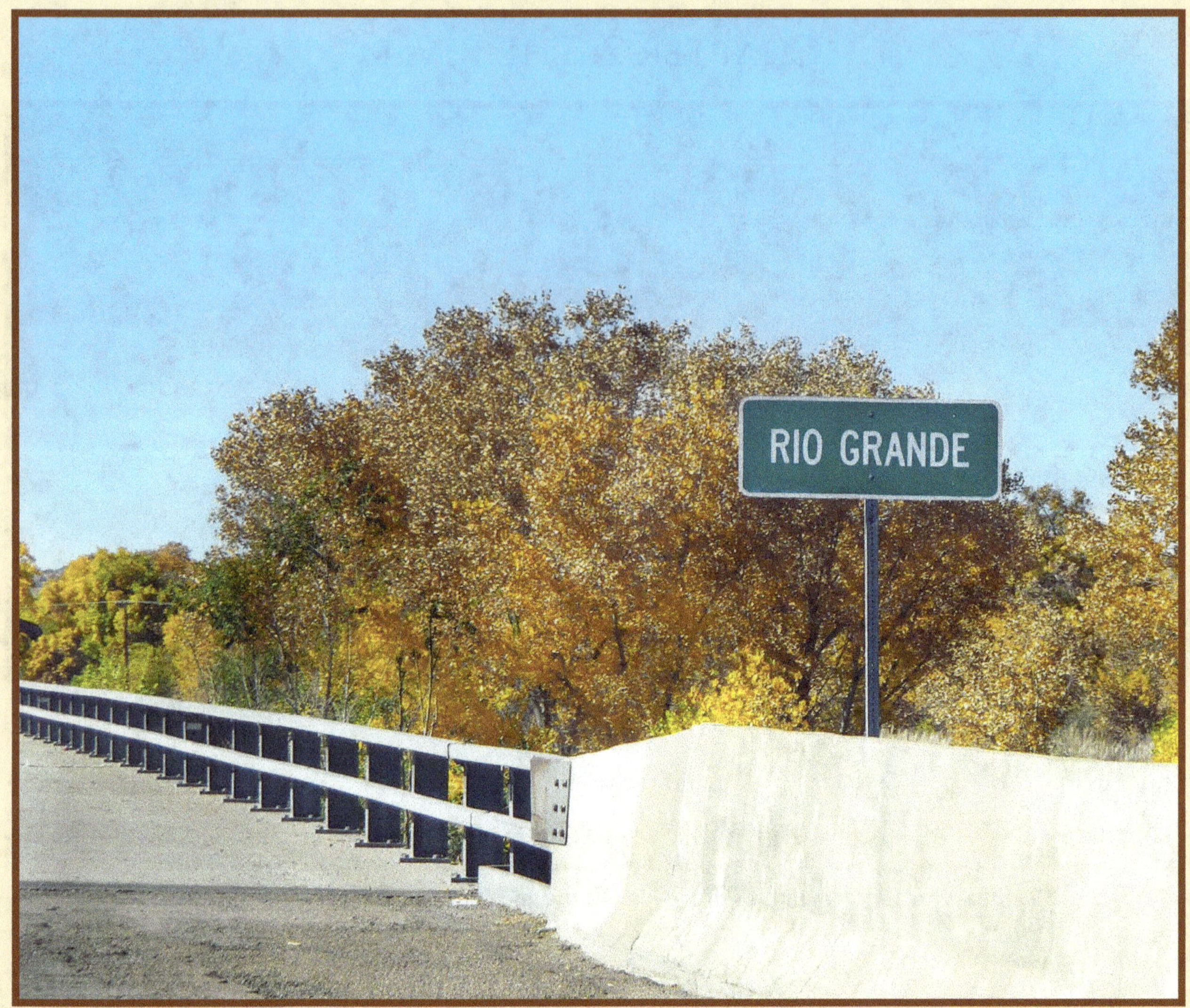

A typical type of bridge over the Rio Grande, with cottonwood trees bordering both sides of the riverbanks.

Cottonwood trees, which range in height from 40 to 90 feet tall, grow all along the Rio Grande from Mexico to southern Colorado. The cottonwoods provide an important natural habitat for wildlife.

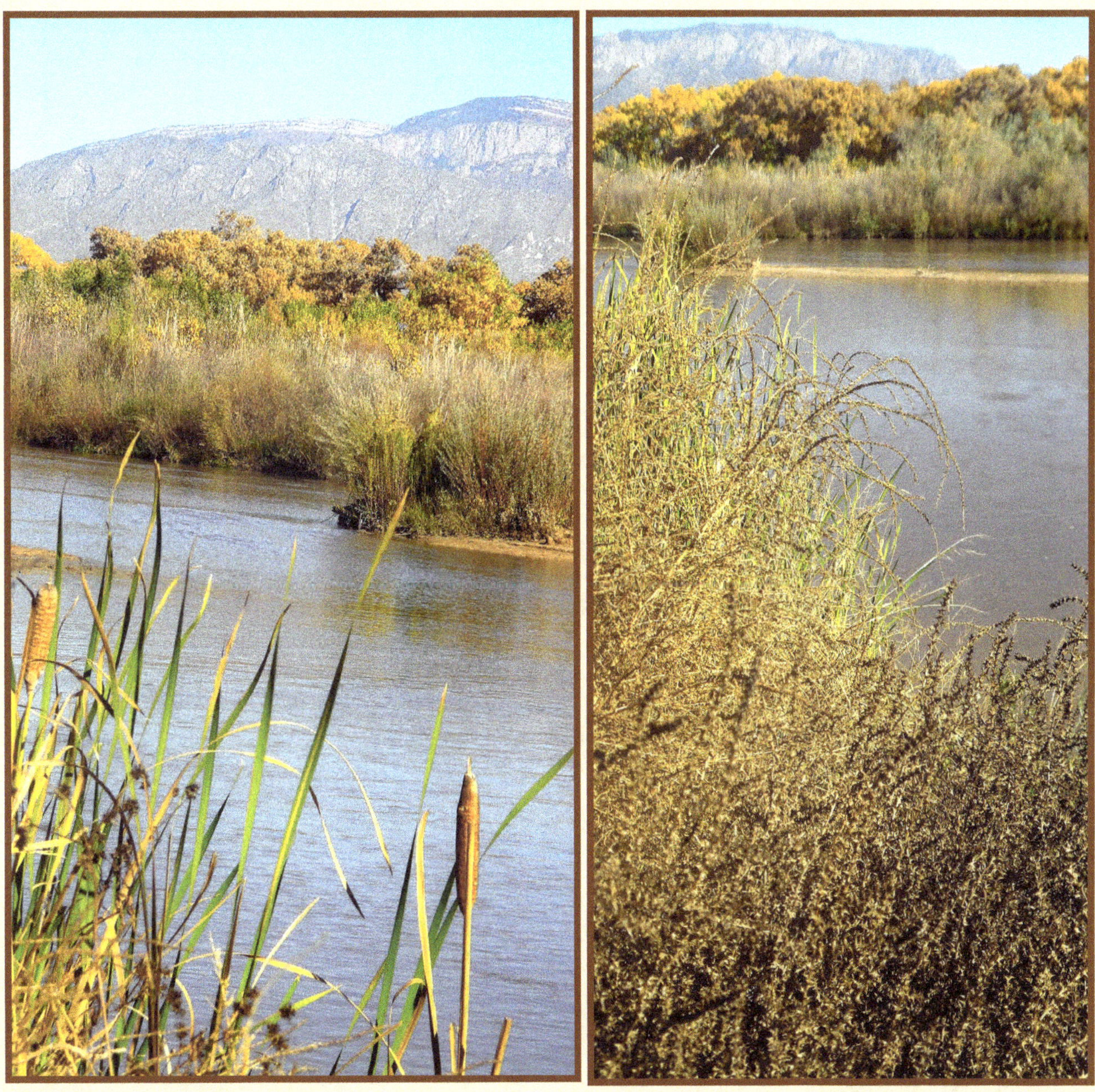

The following photos show different views of the Rio Grande. The Sandia Mountains rise in the background.

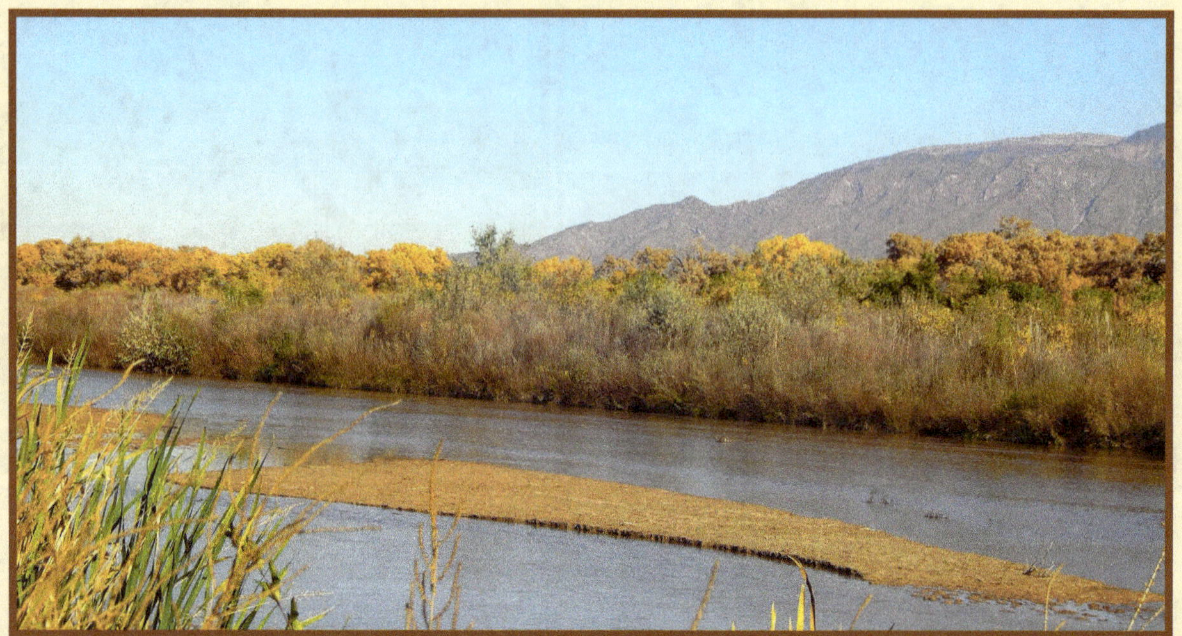

Movement of the water flow in the Rio Grande can vary between 2,500 and 4,000 cubic feet per second, depending on the time of year and the weather. The normal flow averages 2,500 cubic feet per second.

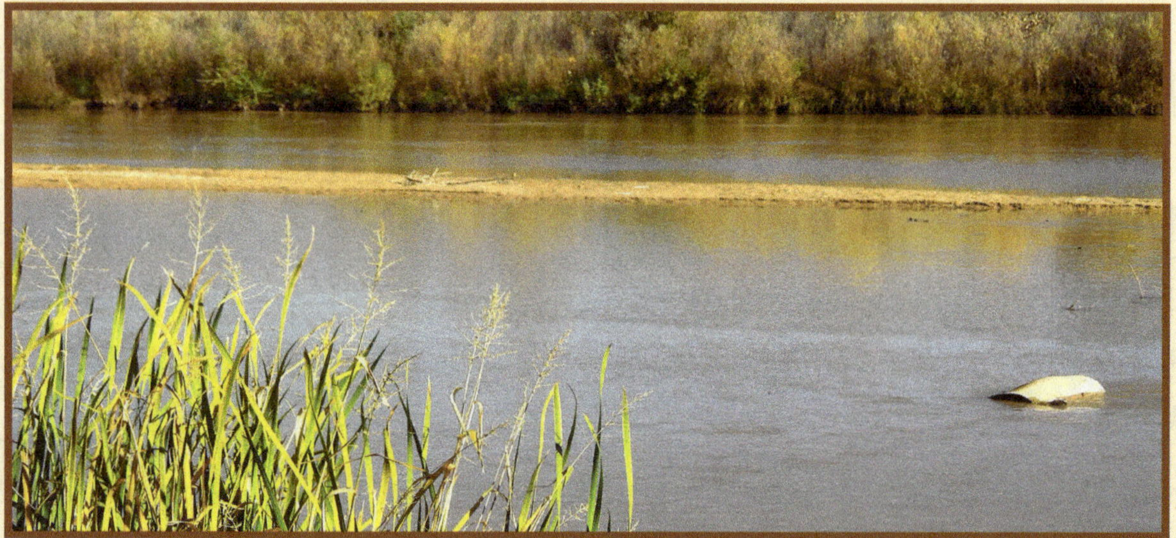

Shifting sandbars are a common feature of the river. They take shape, disperse, and form again further downstream.

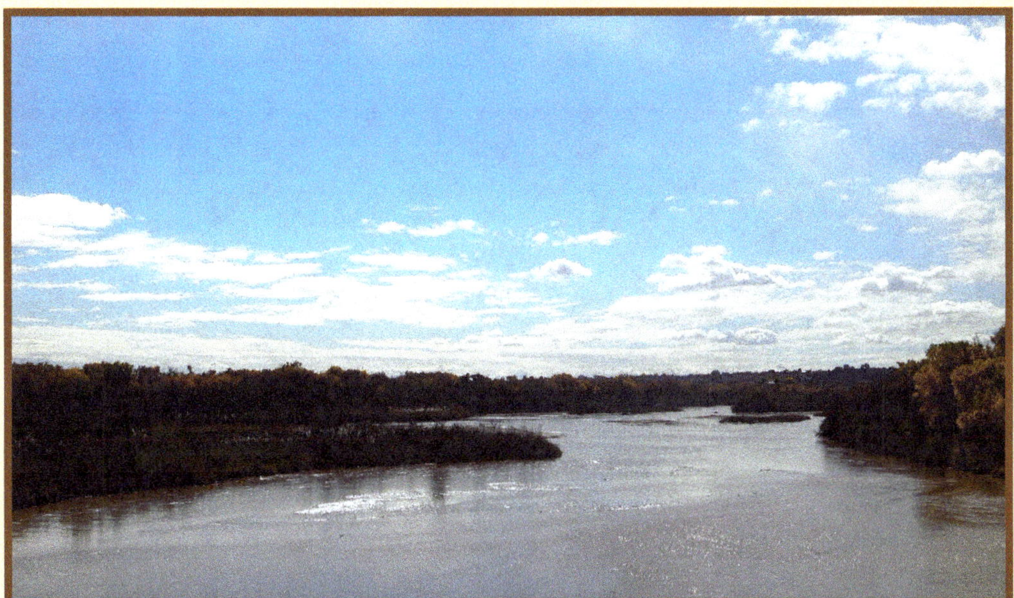

A turquoise blue sky stretches above the Rio Grande. From the 1600s through the early 1900s, before dams were built to control water flows, the course of the Rio Grande shifted due to flooding.

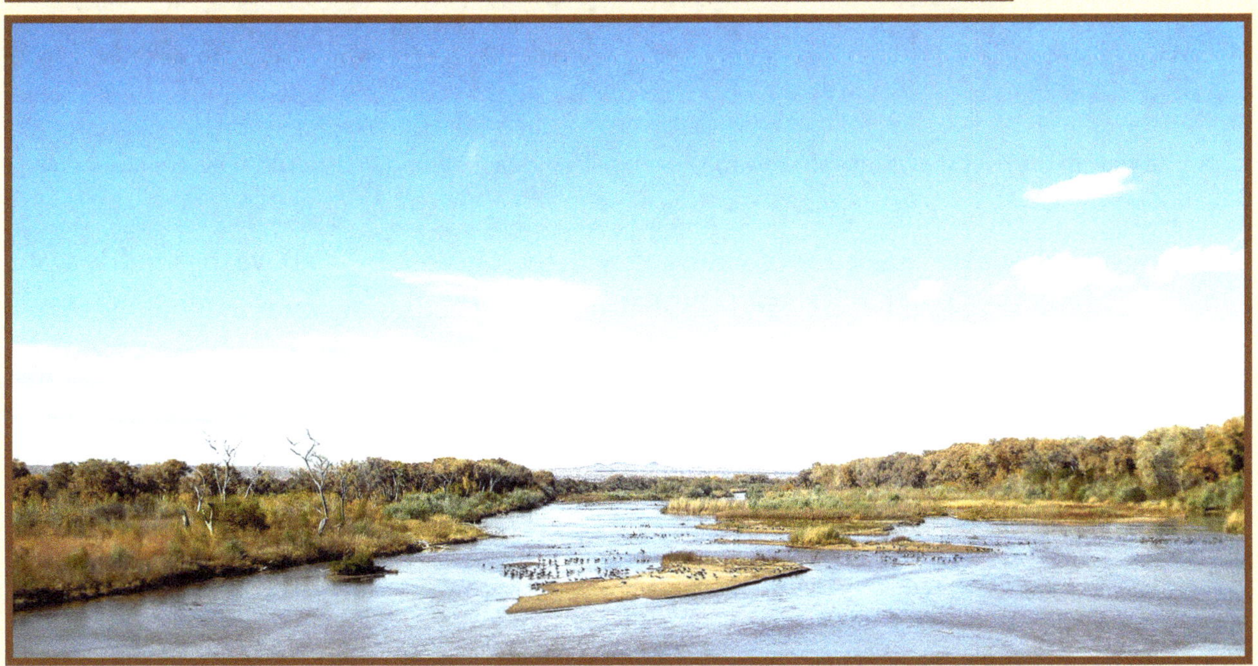

Canadian geese enjoy a sunny autumn afternoon swimming in the water and resting upon sandbars. Photo by Zita.

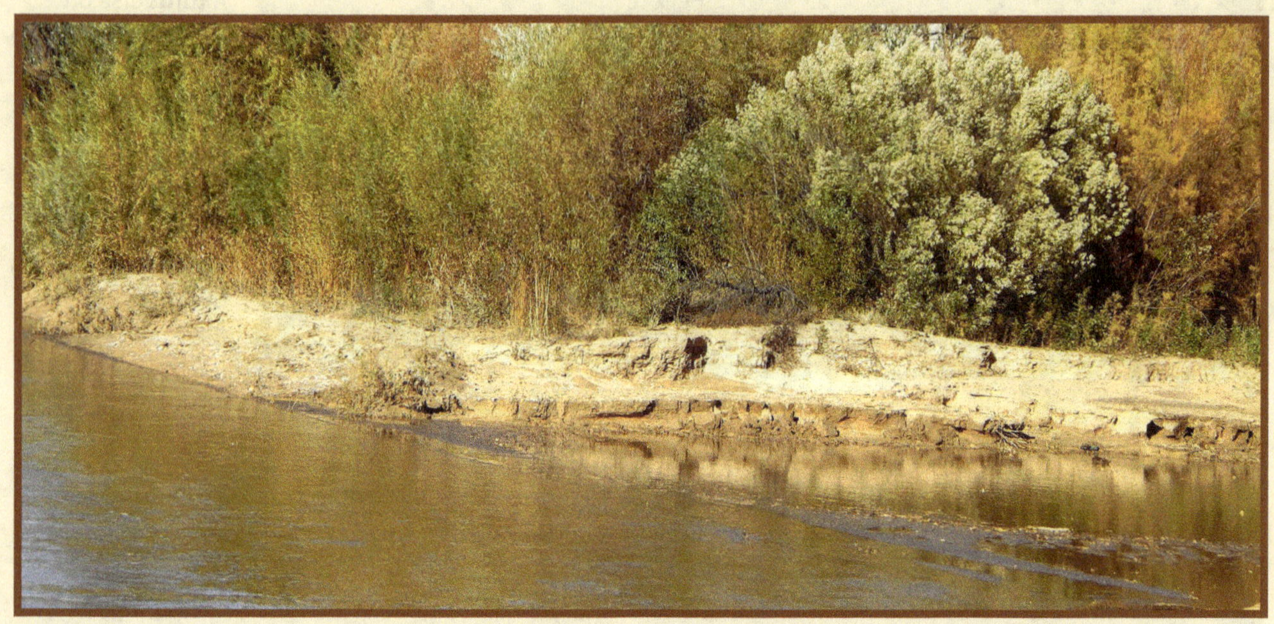

A side view of the river shows how shallow the water is at sandbanks along in the central Rio Grande valley.

At times, rattlesnakes can be seen swimming with their heads rising above the muddy water. Snakes swim not only in the Rio Grande, but also in other bodies of water in New Mexico.

When my siblings and I were young, we swam in mountain streams and large irrigation ditches. We were instructed to avoid grabbing onto anything floating nearby in the water, even if it looked like driftwood, because it could be a snake.

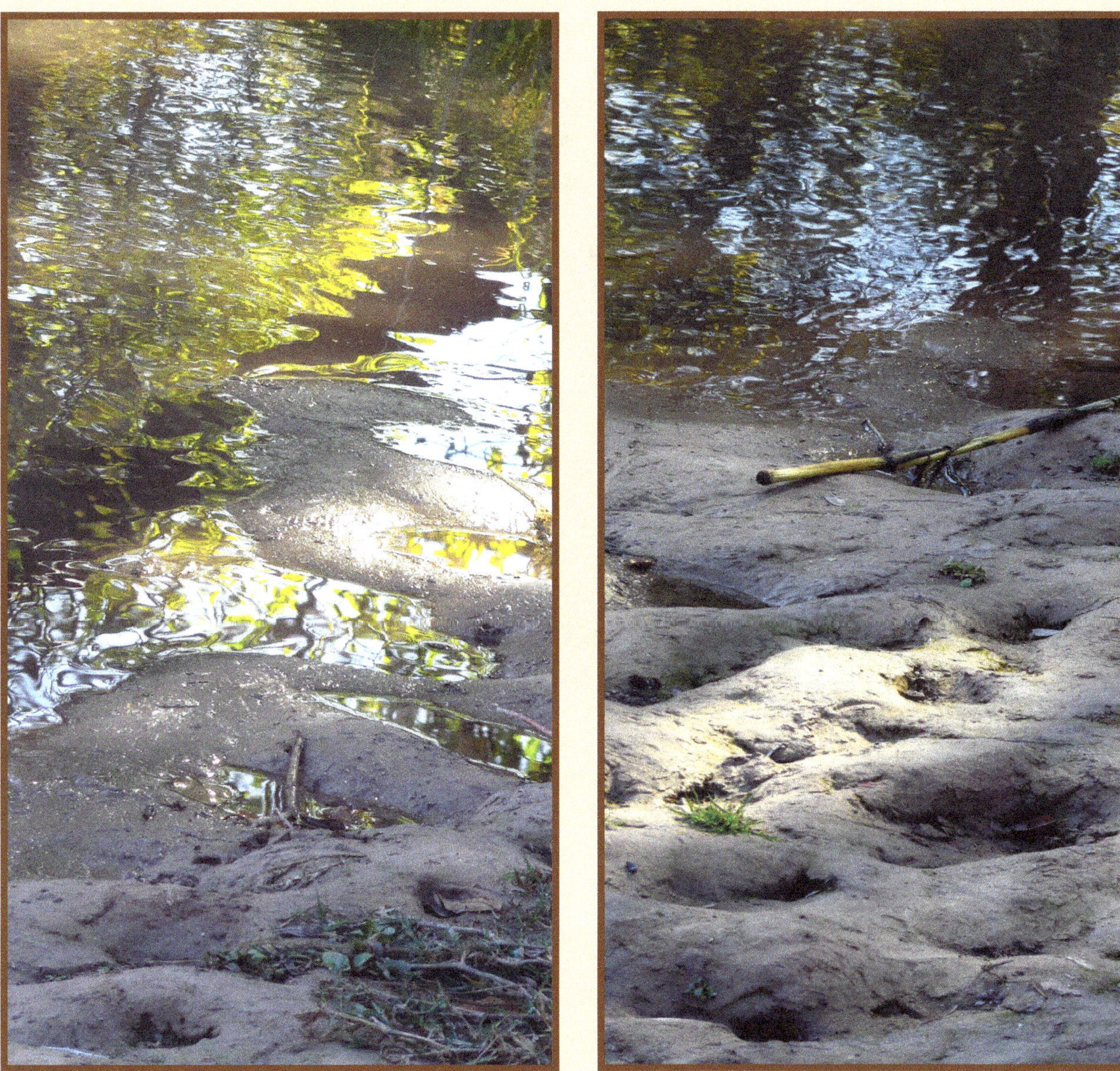

This series of photos shows mud formations along the riverbanks.

I was taught from an early age to be wary of the mud around the river. The elders in my family always warned the children that the river had quicksand.

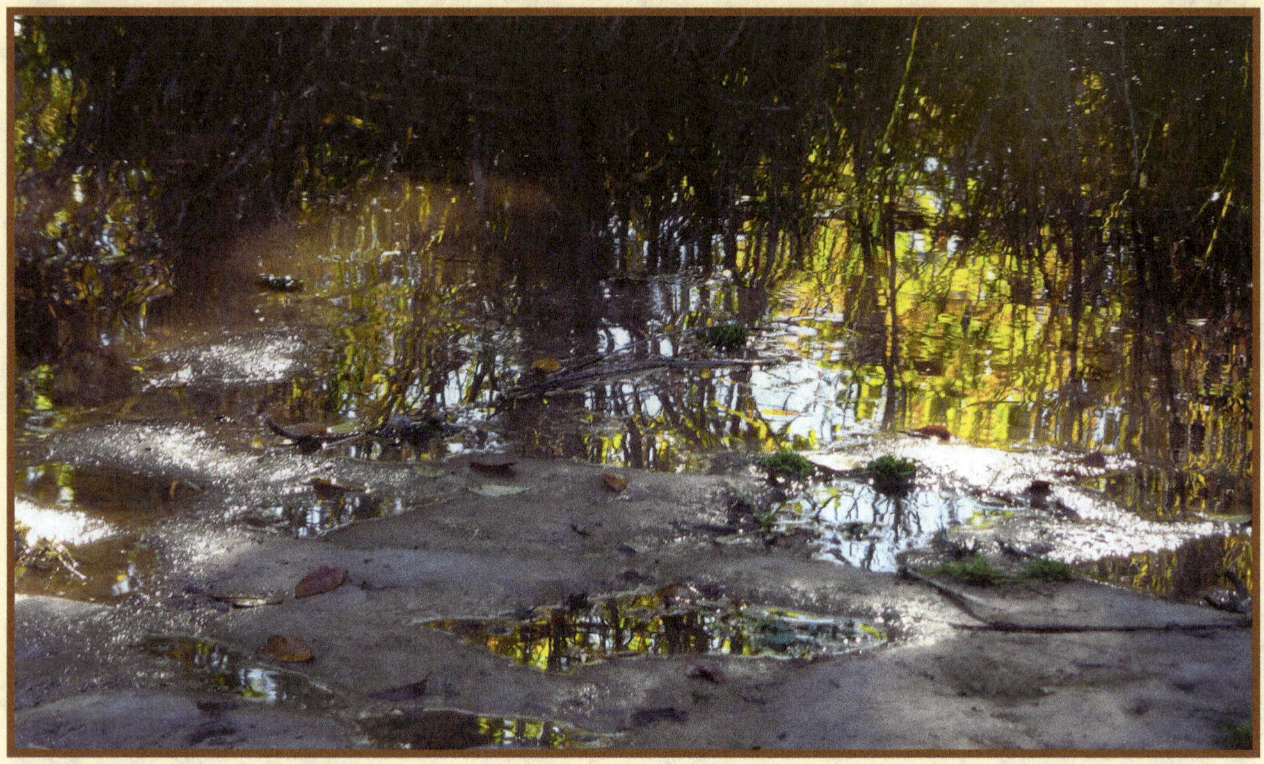

We also were instructed that even though the river may look shallow or dry on the surface, appearances could be deceptive due to hidden dangers below the surface— such as quicksand or strong undercurrents. No one in my family ever swam in the Rio Grande. Emergency officials warn people in the summer to avoid walking or swimming in the river due to drowning. People who venture into the river can sink in quicksand or become swept away by the sudden, fast-moving water.

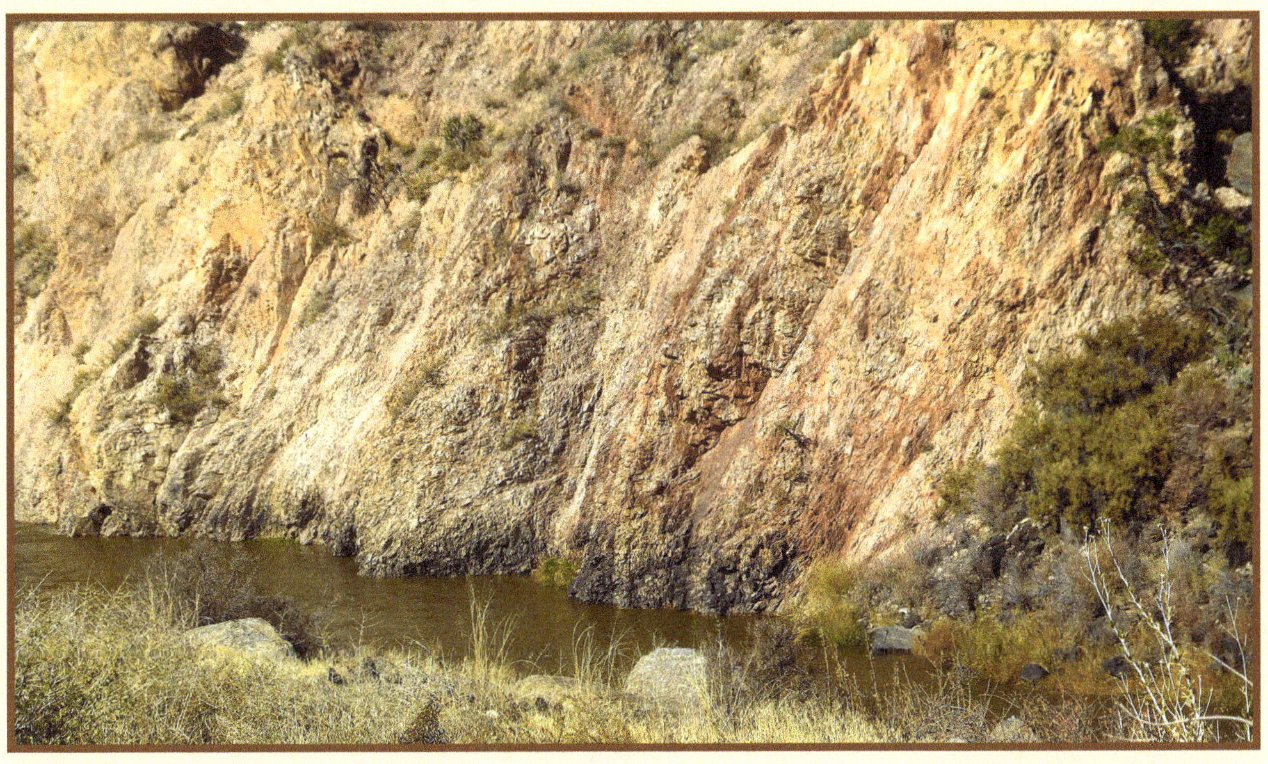

The Rio Grande cuts a narrow passage through canyons in northern New Mexico.

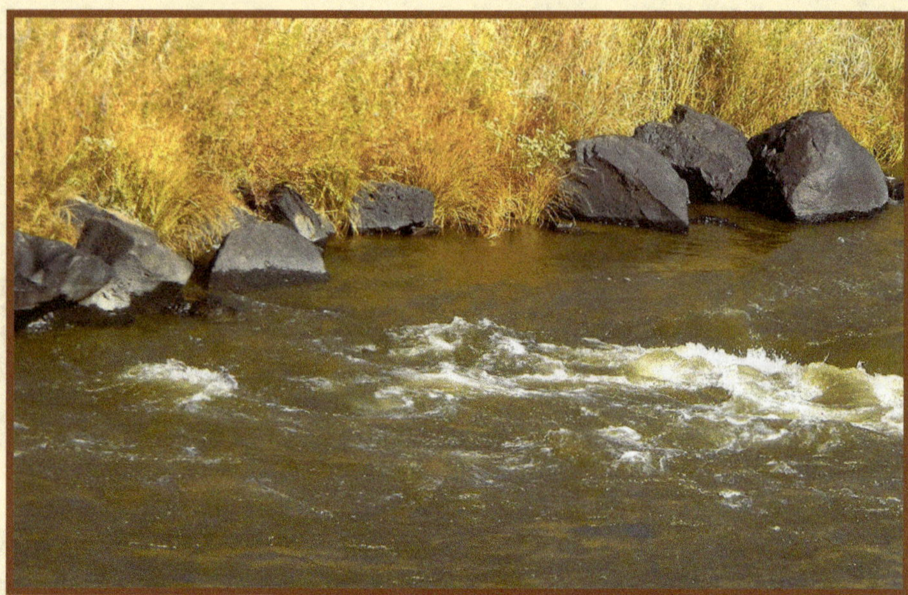

Heavy summer rains and flash floods can send boulders tumbling down mountainsides into the river and onto highways.

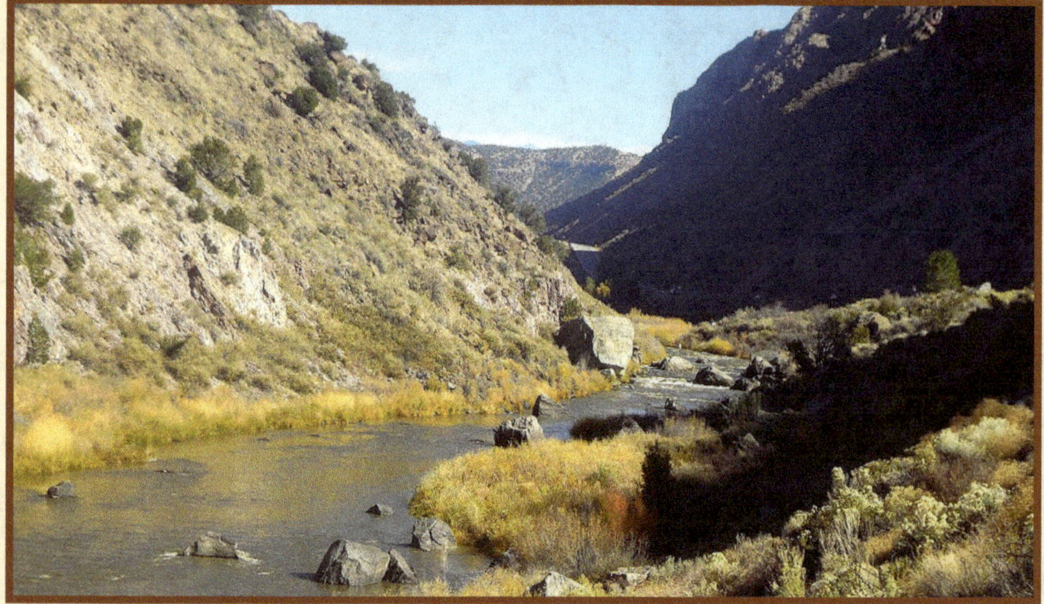

Turbulent rapids along the Rio Grande in Northern New Mexico are popular for whitewater rafting.

Boulders in and around the northern, mountainous areas of the Rio Grande present challenges for people venturing into the water on kayaks, rafts, and canoes.

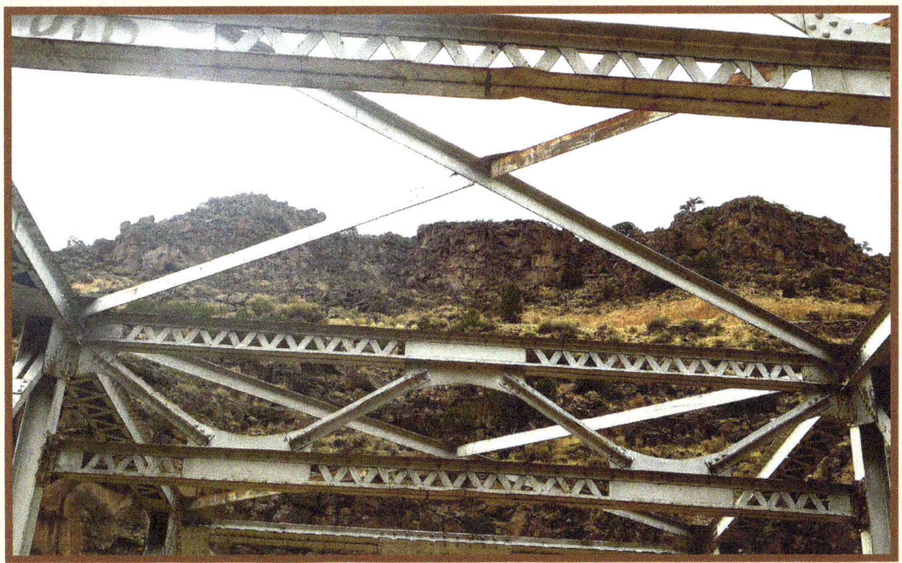

Basalt cliffs overlook the top of John Dunn Bridge, which provides a river crossing at the northern entrance of the Rio Grande Gorge.

The John Dunn Bridge was built in 1908 by Dunn, a former stagecoach driver, at the bottom of a steep winding road through the canyons.

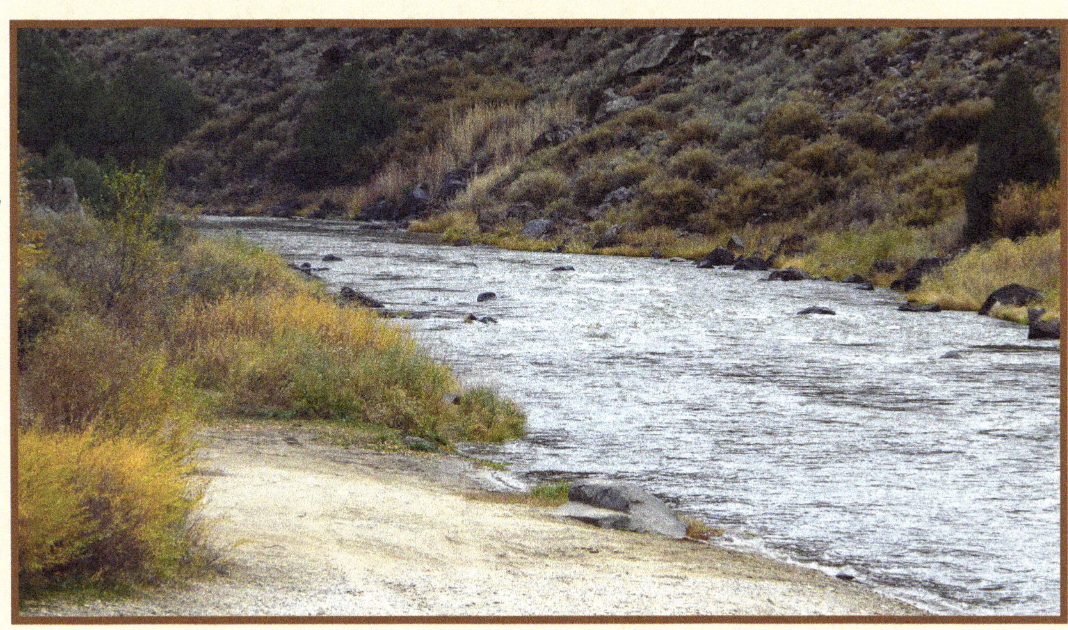

This area around the John Dunn Bridge is popular for rock climbing, hiking, and fishing. It also provides a starting point for boaters seeking adventure on the dangerous river rapids through the gorge.

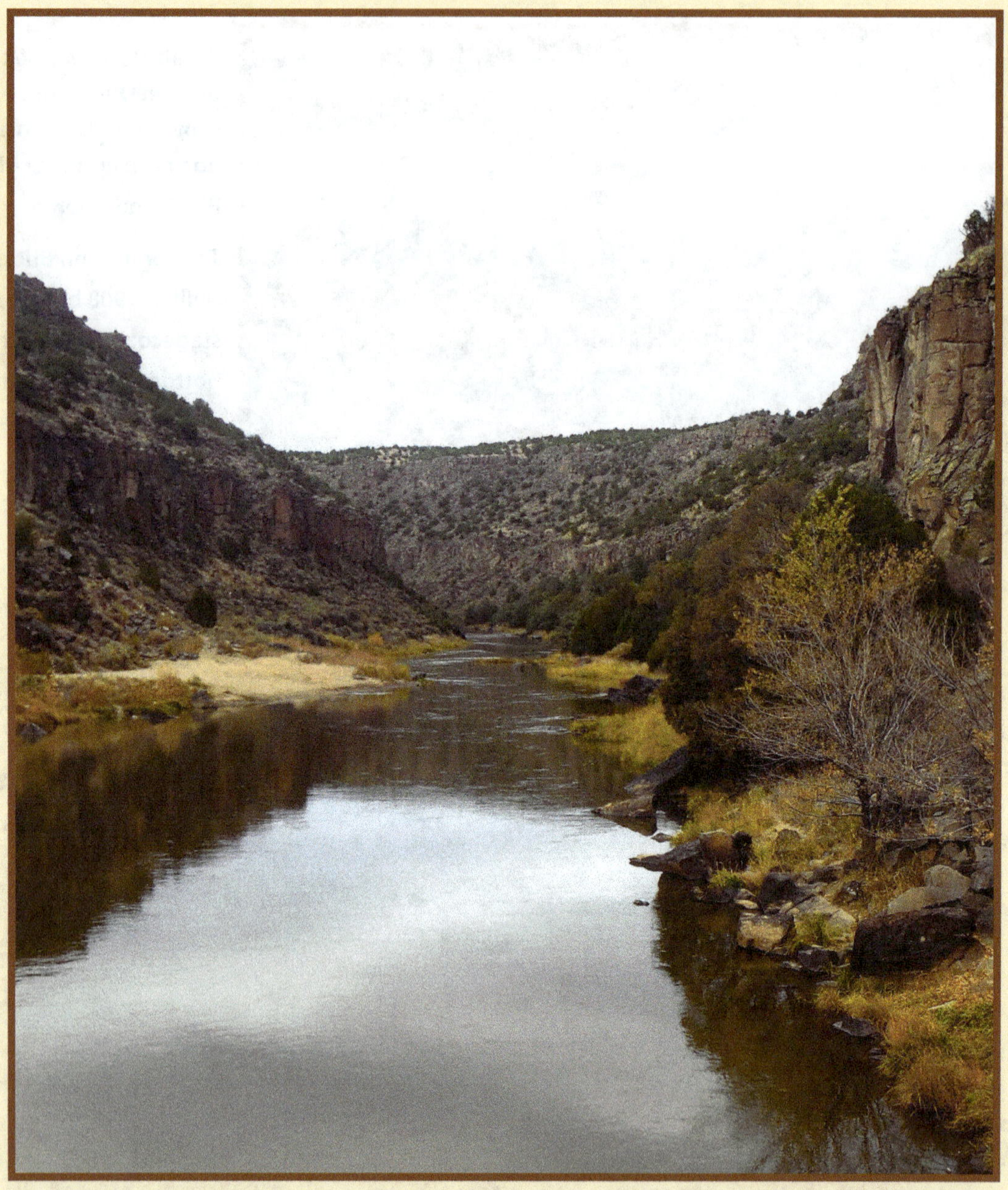

A view from the John Dunn Bridge over the Rio Grande before it traverses into the gorge, a famed volcanic plateau near Taos, N.M.

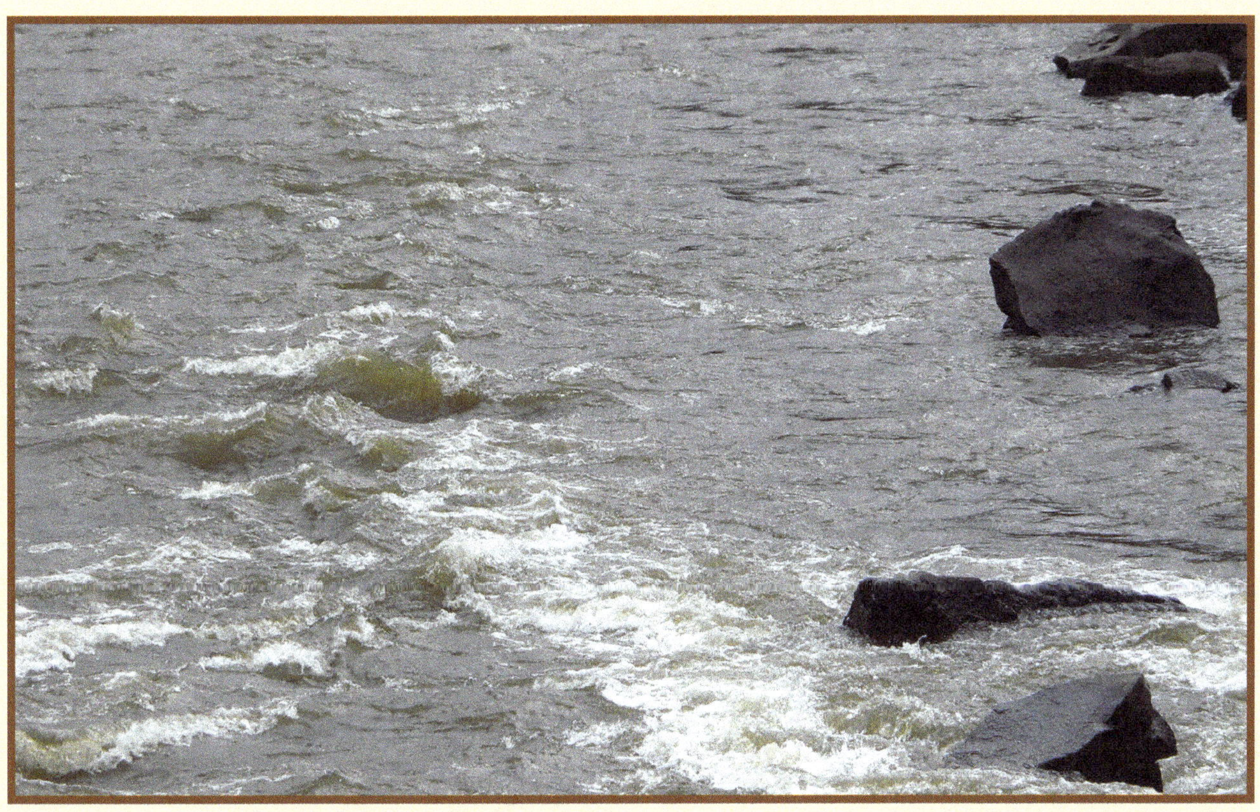

Because the river appears slow and narrow, people underestimate the force of the underwater currents. There have been numerous accidents related to boating and swimming. Even people who are considered experts on the river have met their death in the dangerous waters.

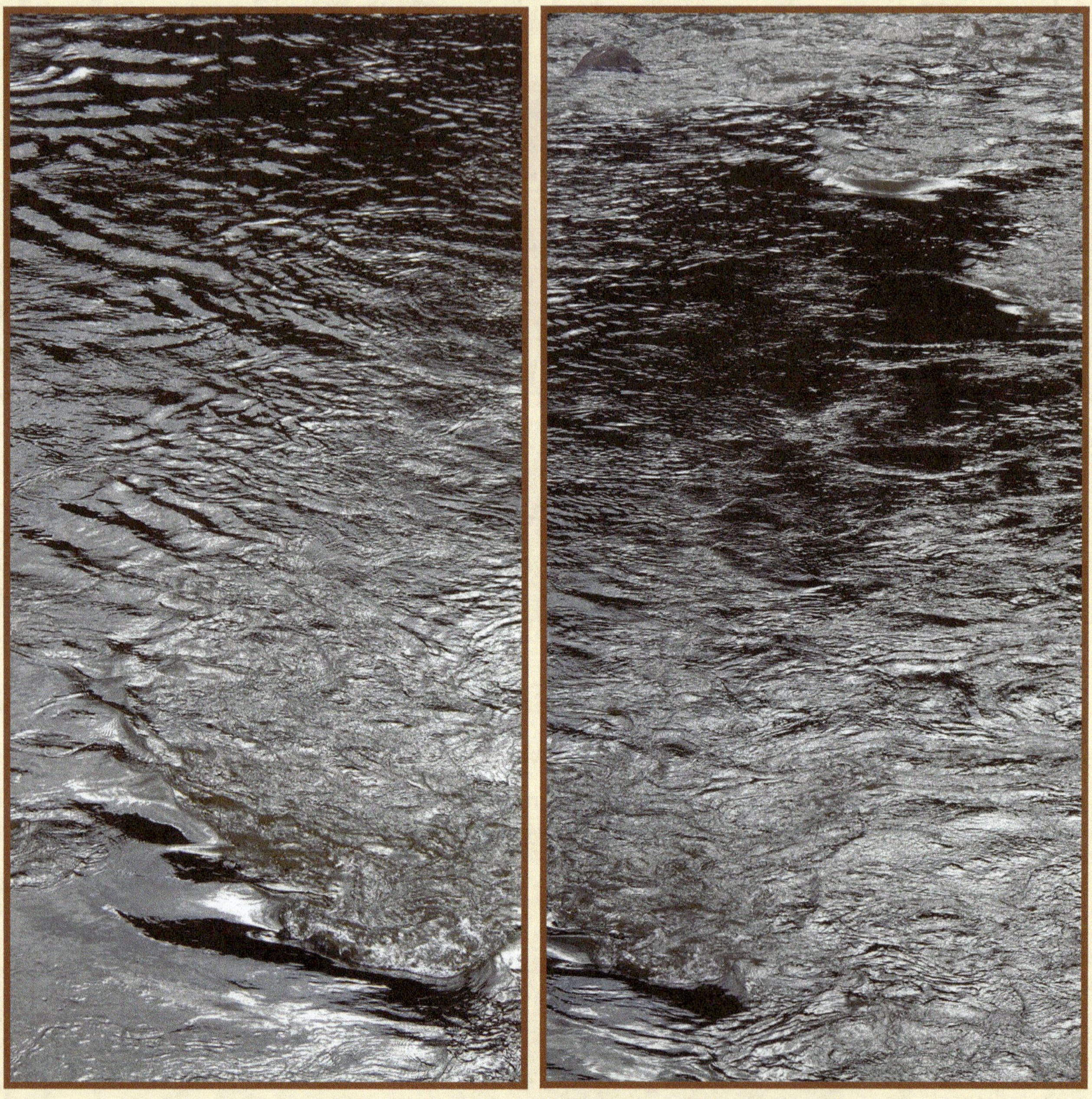

Currents are visible in the treacherous waters of the Rio Grande.

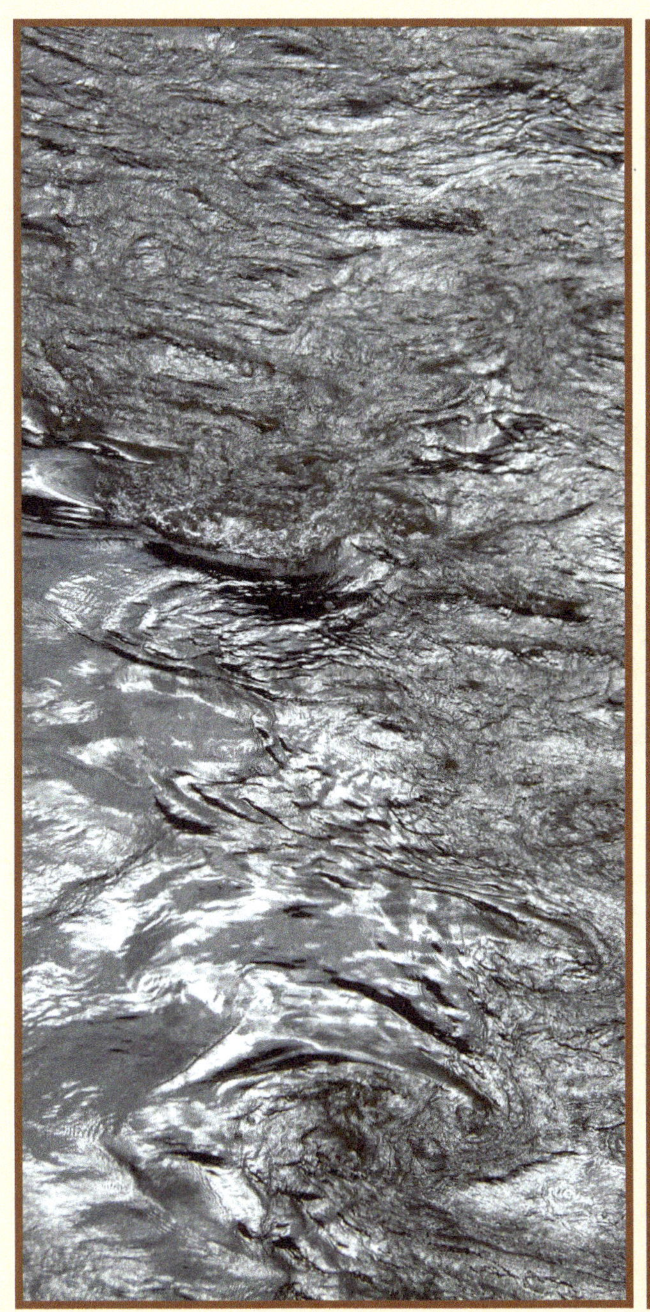

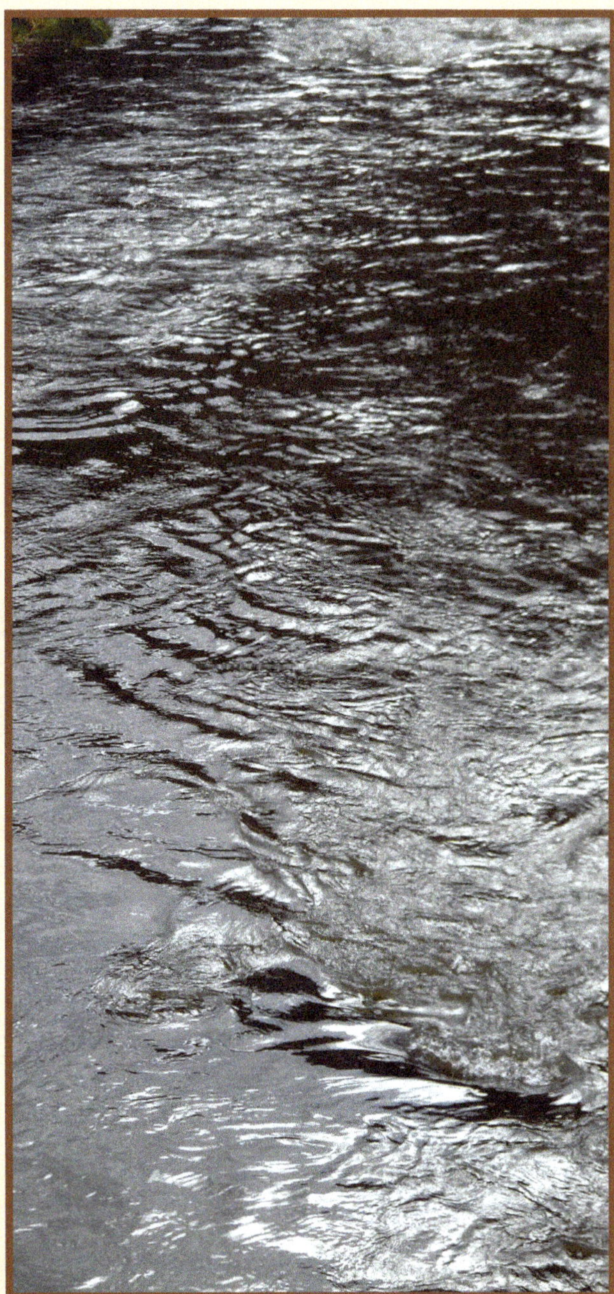

Chapter 3: Las Lomas

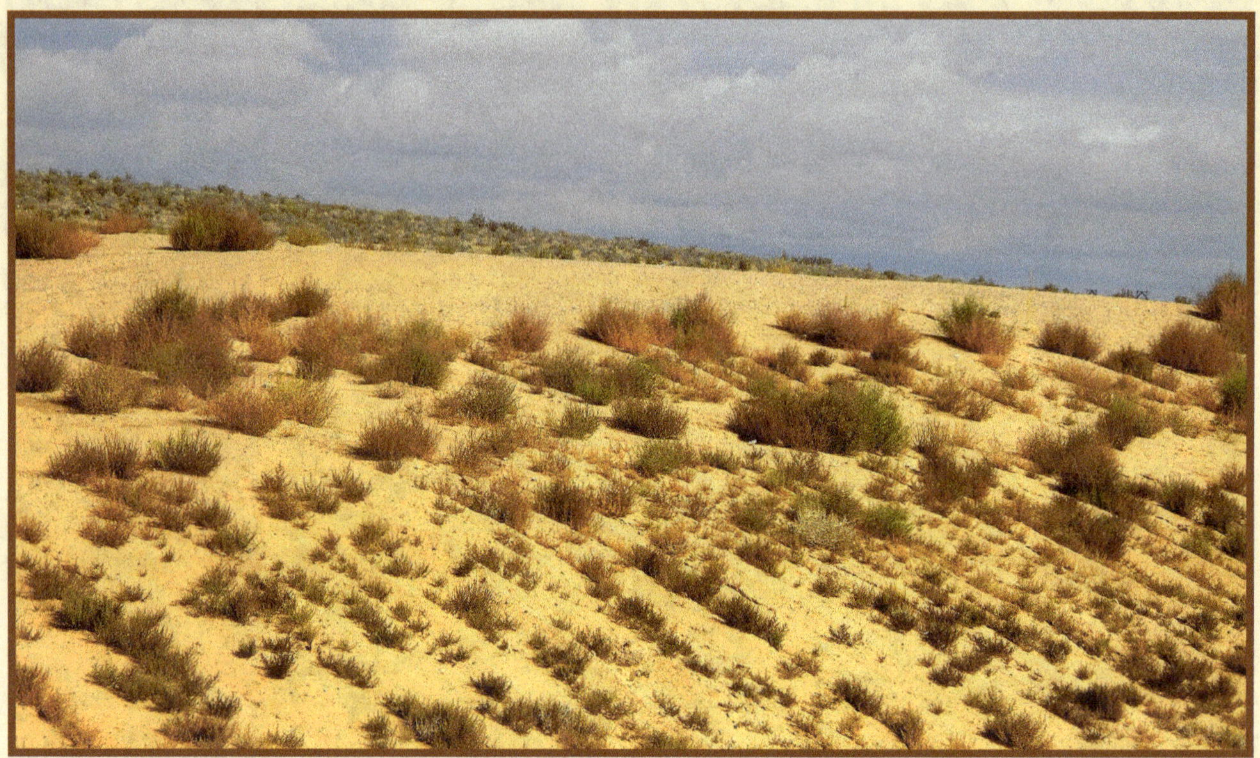

The hills (Las Lomas) rise adjacent to the farms, fields, and wetlands that flank the Rio Grande in the Central Valley of New Mexico.

Hillsides such as this one, located between Bernalillo and Corrales, are among typical sights I used to see during my childhood as I accompanied my grandparents to boisterous Perea family gatherings.

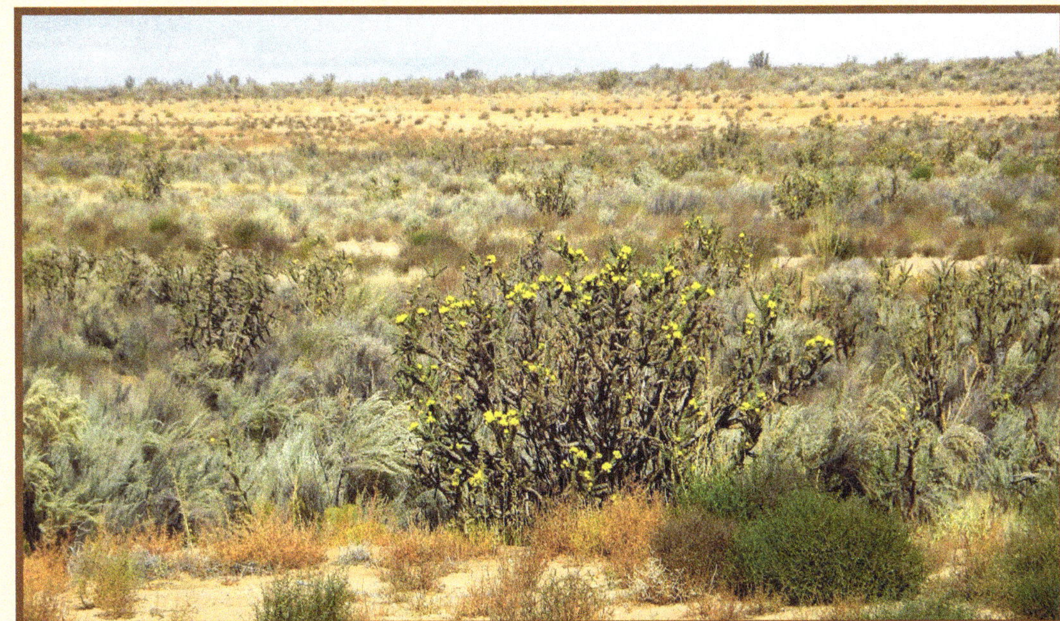

Rolling hills appear in the high desert around the Rio Grande.

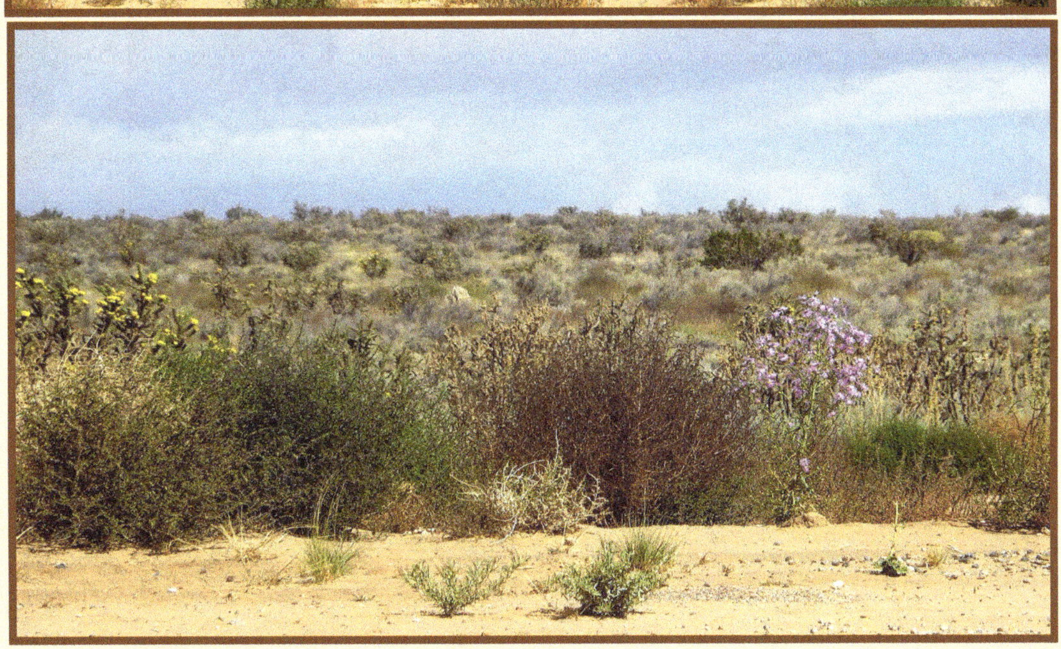

The bright colors of yellow cactus blossoms, green and rust tumbleweeds, and purple flowers of desert aster create a vibrant beauty in a desolate landscape.

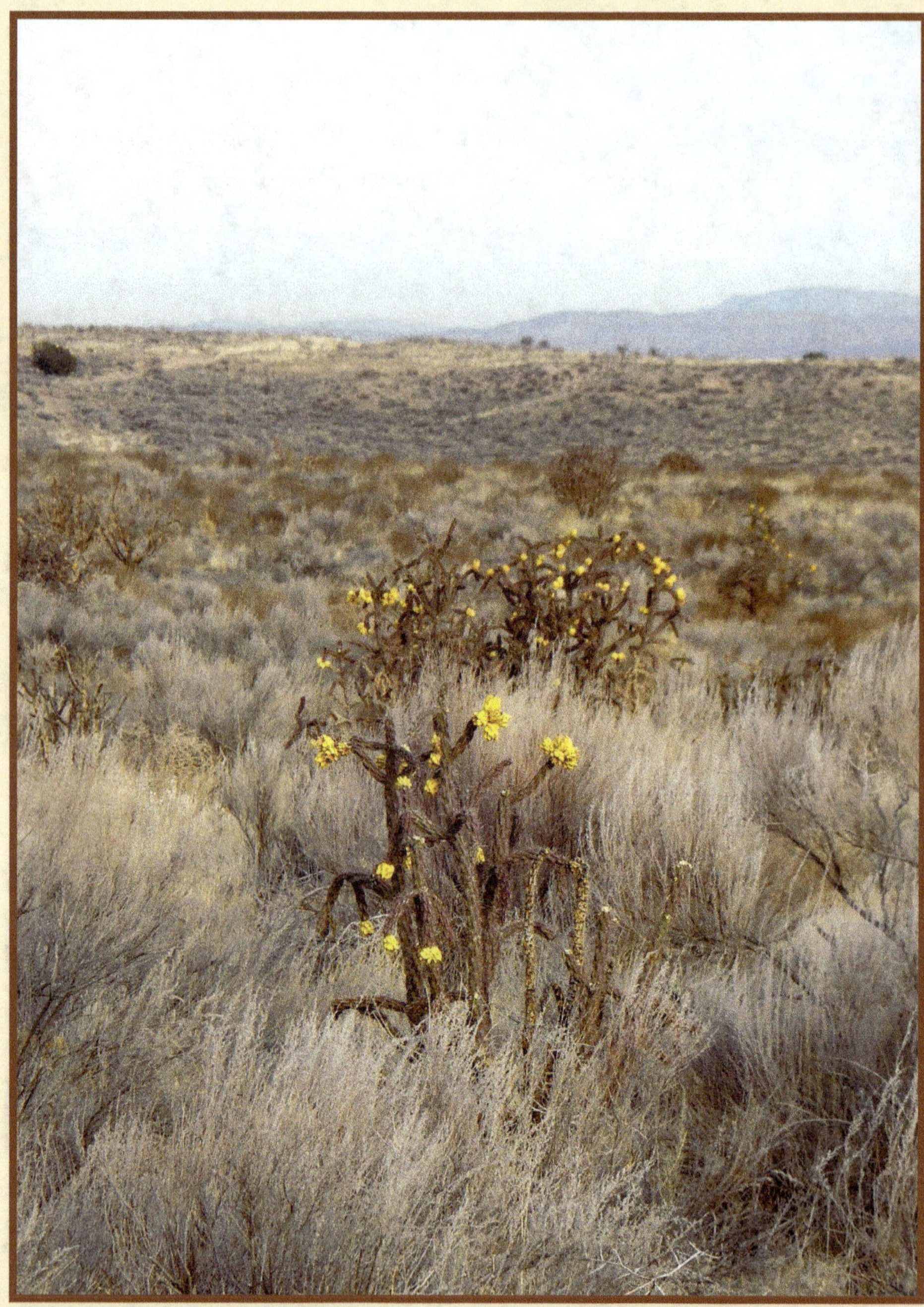

Desert sagebrush and cholla cactus on the mesa are common in New Mexico.

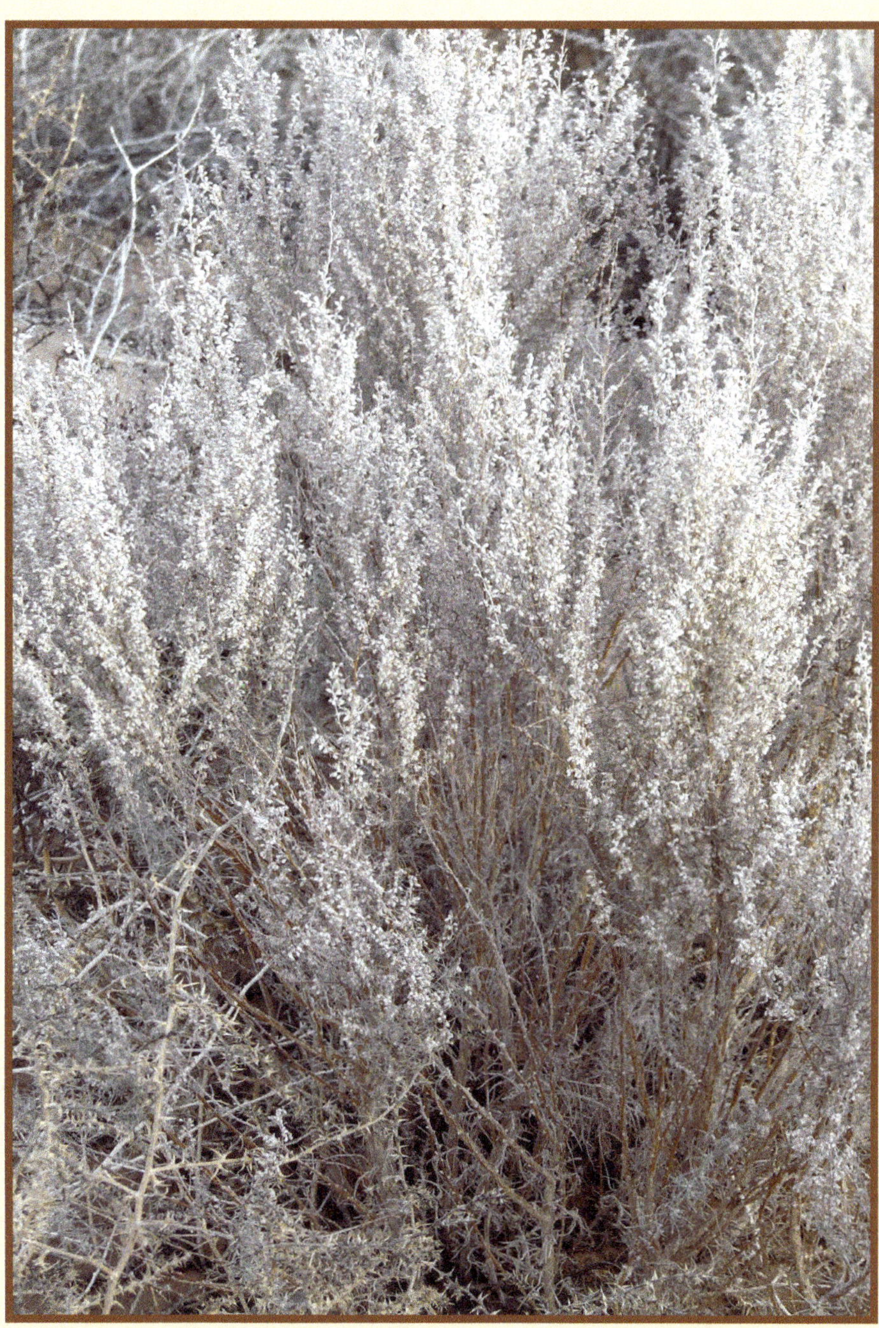

A closeup view of sagebrush.

The earth beneath the plants is also home to animals such as prairie dogs and jackrabbits as well as snakes and lizards. The larger hole in the ground, center, has fresh earth around its entrance, which has been kicked outside by its occupant. When walking on the mesa, it is important to look at the ground before you take a step. In the hot summer months, snakes seek shade under brush and rocks. As autumn approaches and temperatures drop, snakes prefer to sun themselves out in the open under warm rays.

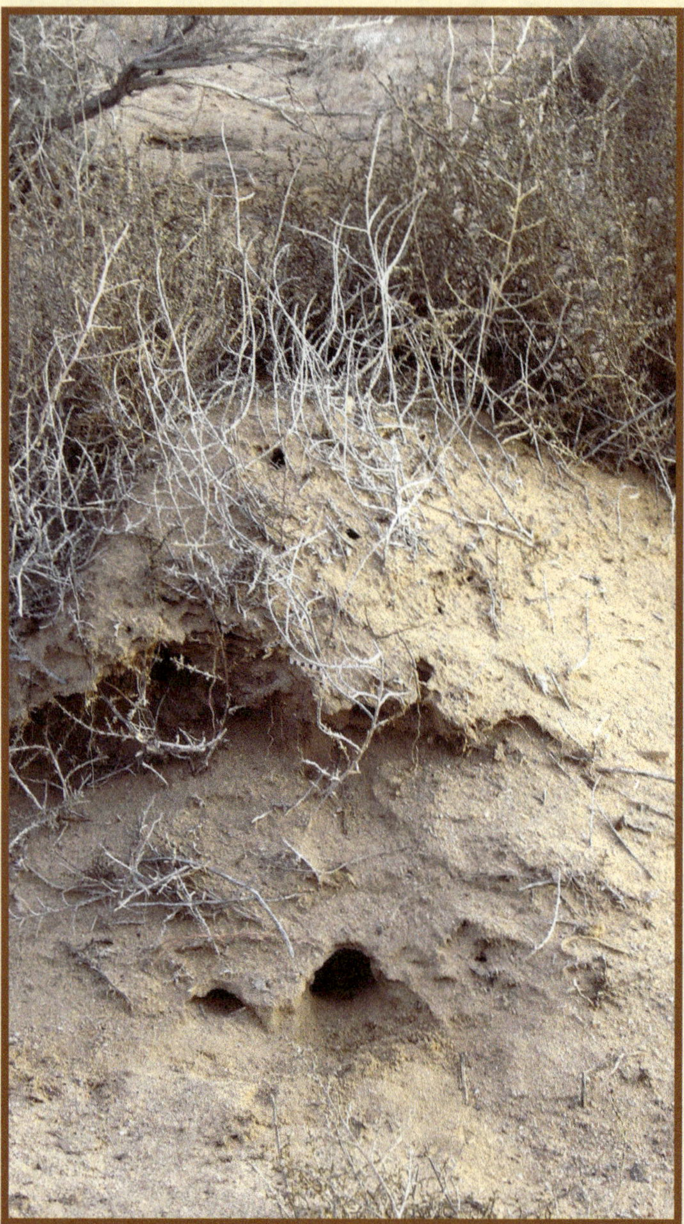

Holes in the ground under sagebrush and tumbleweeds where desert creatures live.

One sunny October afternoon, my daughter and I came upon a rattlesnake while walking the dog along a trail near alfalfa fields by the Rio Grande. We thought that snakes would have been hibernating by that time, but that wasn't the case. The dog went over to sniff what appeared to be a stick. We weren't far behind the dog when we realized that the dog was only a few inches from touching a rattler. About 4 feet long, it was warming itself on the concrete side of a ditch. The alarmed snake raised its body up a foot from the ground. We yanked the dog away and ran as fast as we could in the opposite direction. Rattlesnakes are known to chase people. We were fortunate the snake did not follow us!

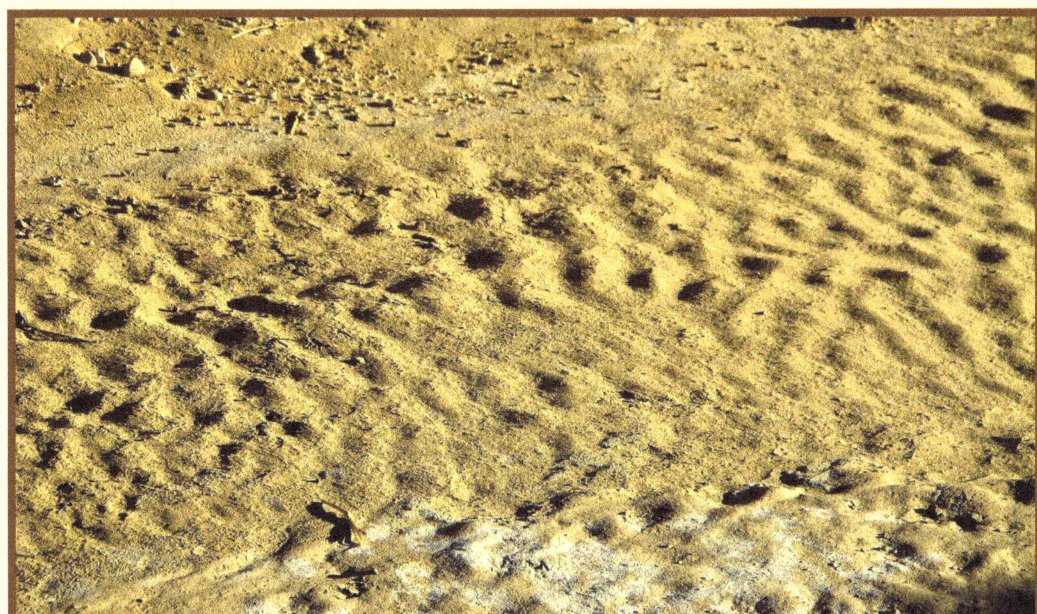

Patterns of rain and wind appear in the sand.

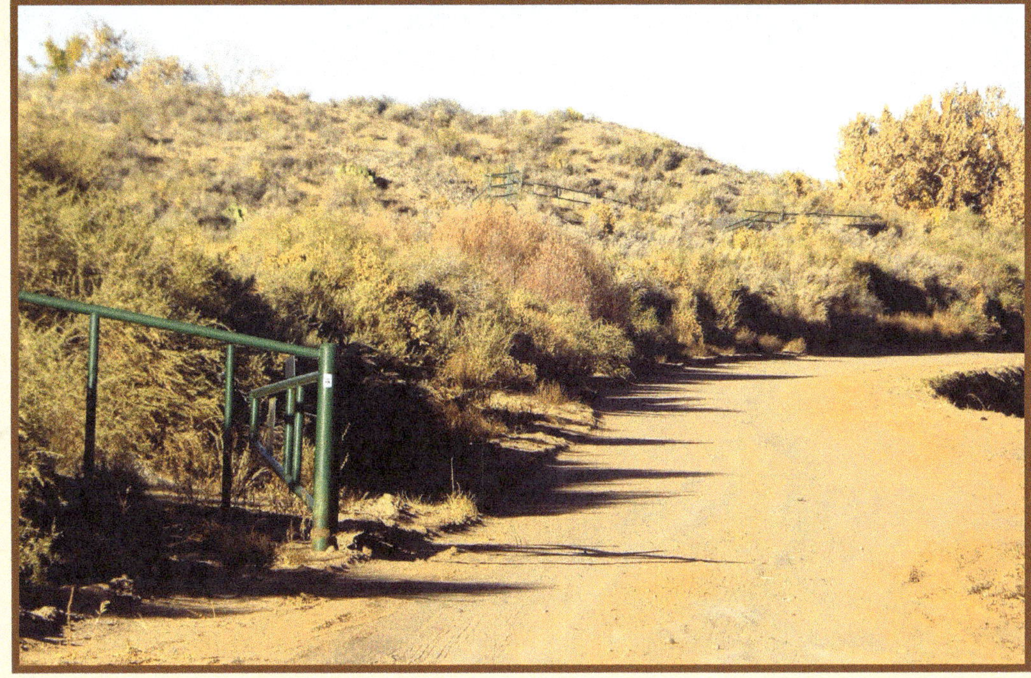

My grandmother rode horses with her family members along these hills outside of Corrales. She had many fond memories of her childhood on Papá's ranch.

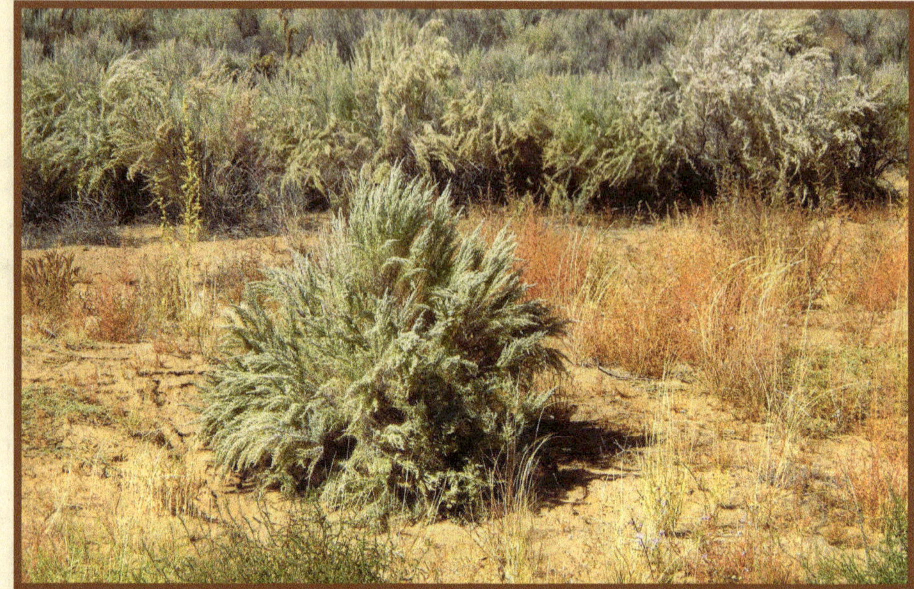

A lone sagebrush stands in the soil of Las Lomas.

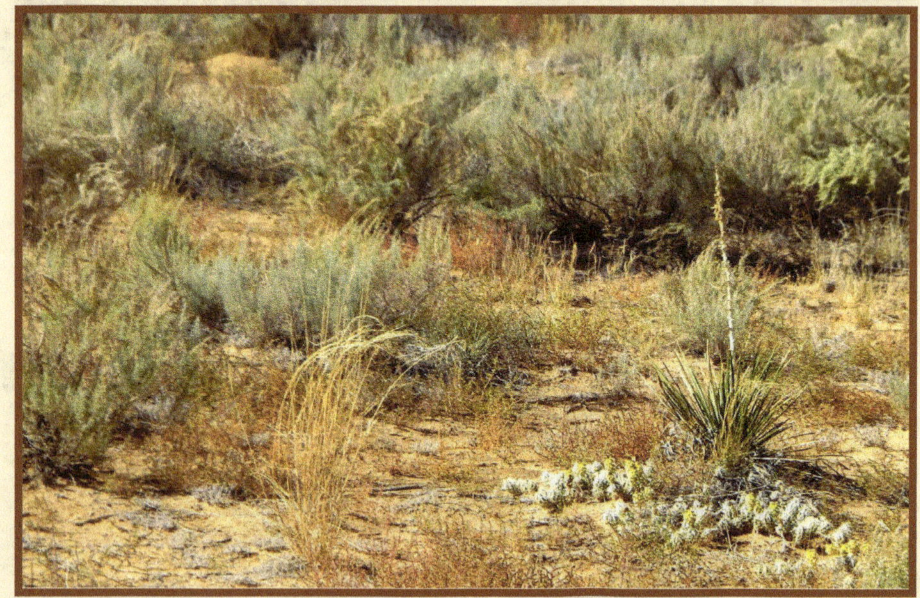

A yucca (right) is surrounded by a small cactus cluster.

The state flower of New Mexico is the white bloom of the yucca. Native Americans and Spaniards used the roots of one type of yucca to make a shampoo and hair thickener called *amole.*

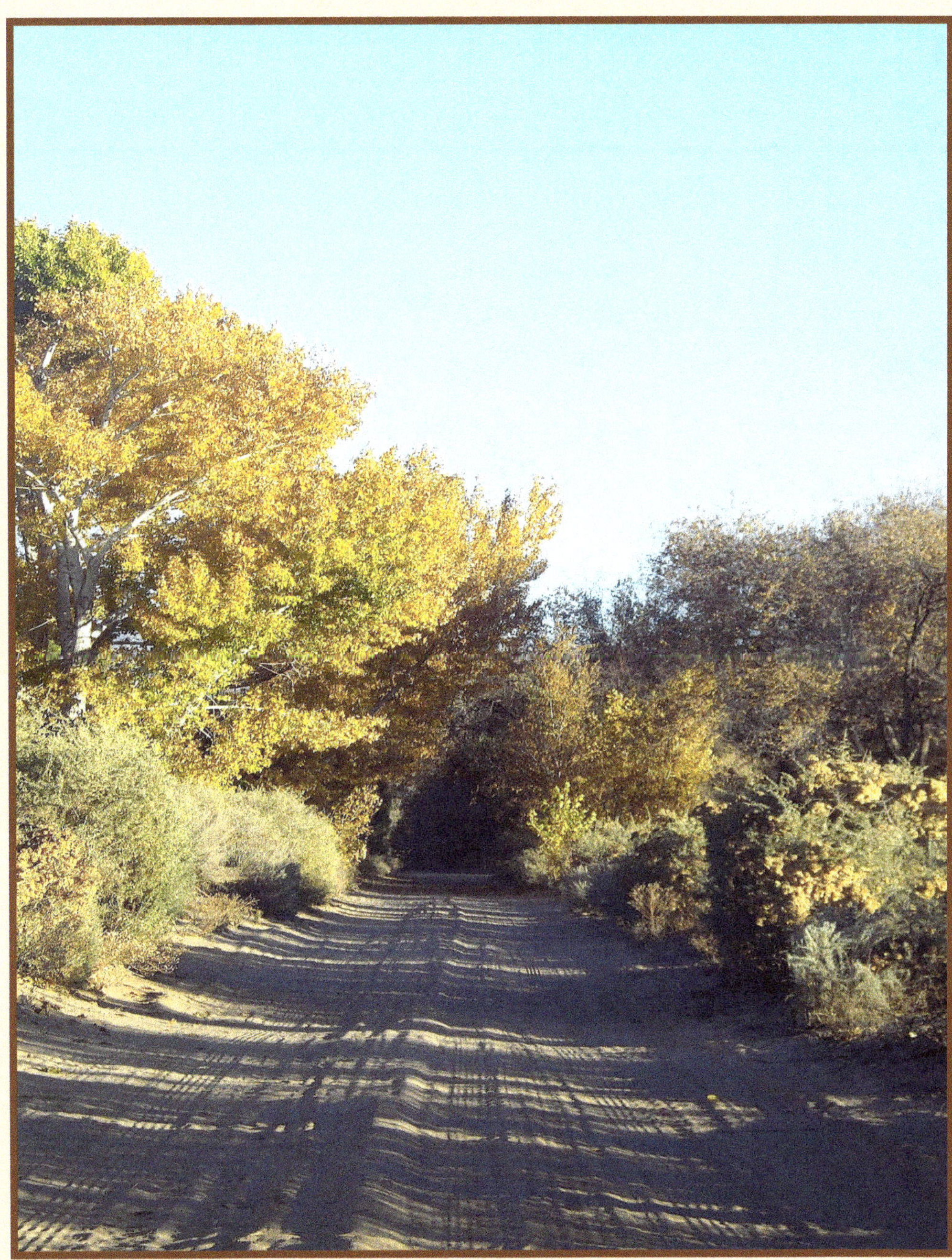

An isolated road near Las Lomas leads to the former location of my Perea family's hacienda and ranch.

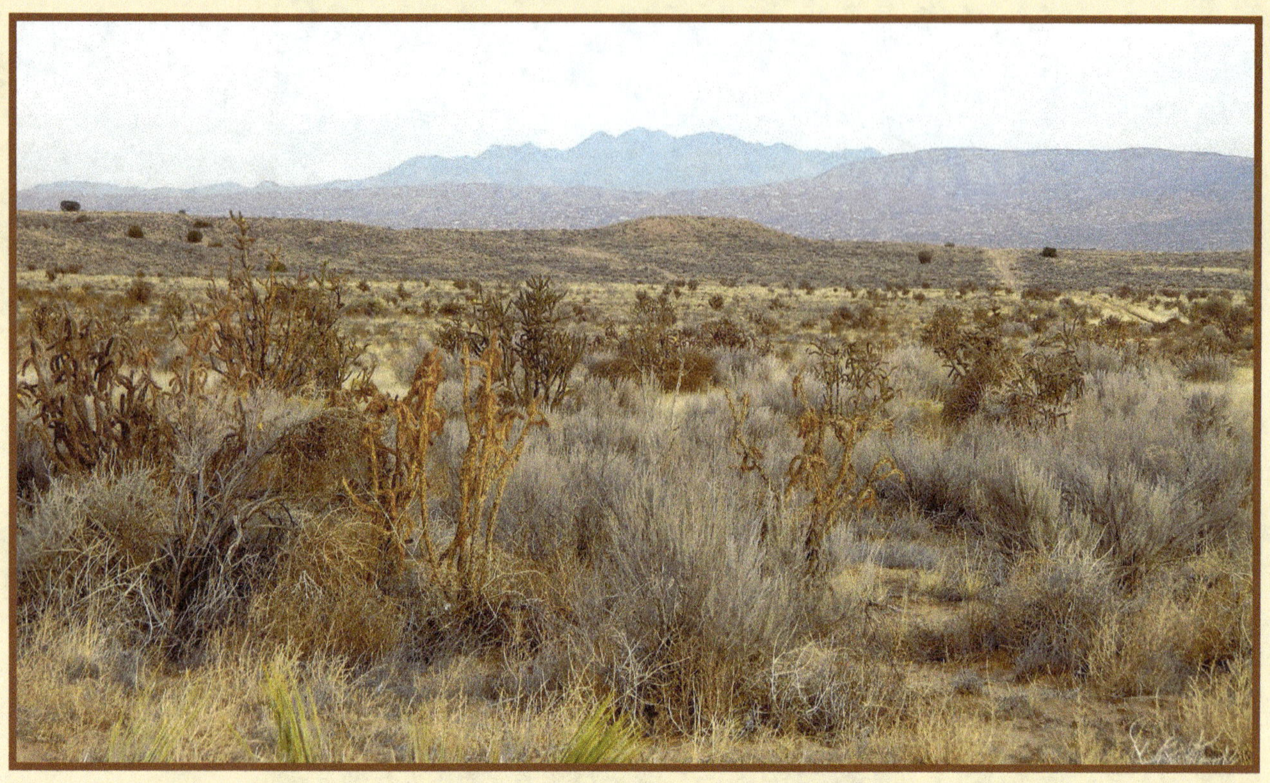

A dirt road (upper right) in the distance crosses through these desolate hills.

Chapter 4: The Bosque

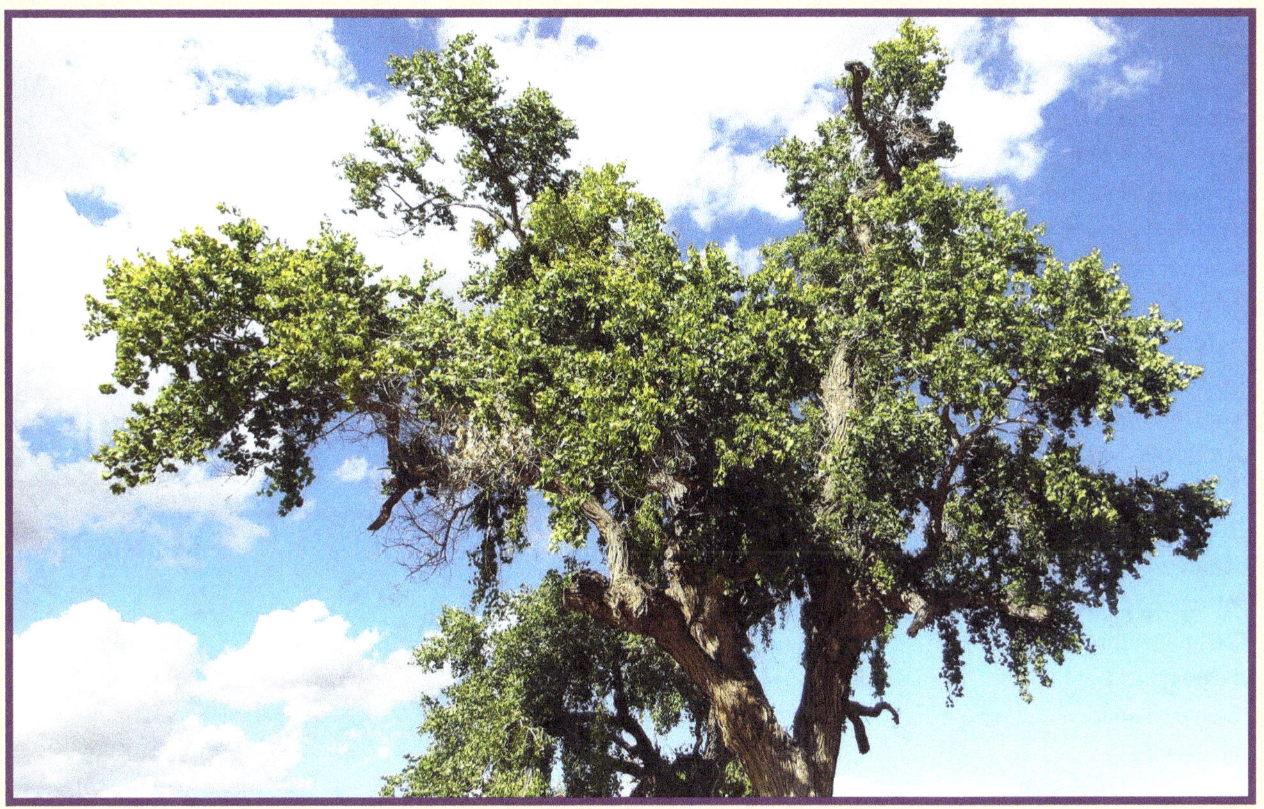

The Bosque (meaning "forest" in Spanish) is home to numerous cottonwood trees that line both sides of the Rio Grande, creating a wide swath of lush summer greenery in central New Mexico.

The Bosque extends 200 miles from Santa Fe (the state capital and oldest capital city in the United States) to the outskirts of Socorro at the Bosque del Apache National Wildlife Refuge. The Bosque is densely populated with cottonwood trees. It is described as the largest cottonwood forest in the world. This is due to the fact that the water table around the Rio Grande is only a few feet below the ground's surface.

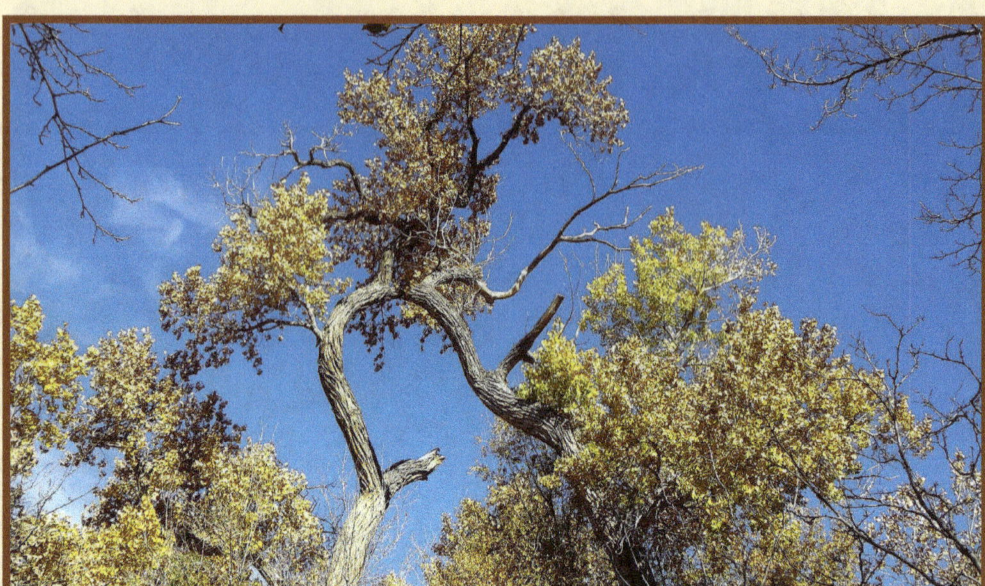

A cottonwood tree with a break in its branches. New Mexico is prone to intense summer lightning and thunderstorms. Many cottonwood trees are struck by lightning and have missing branches or charred bark.

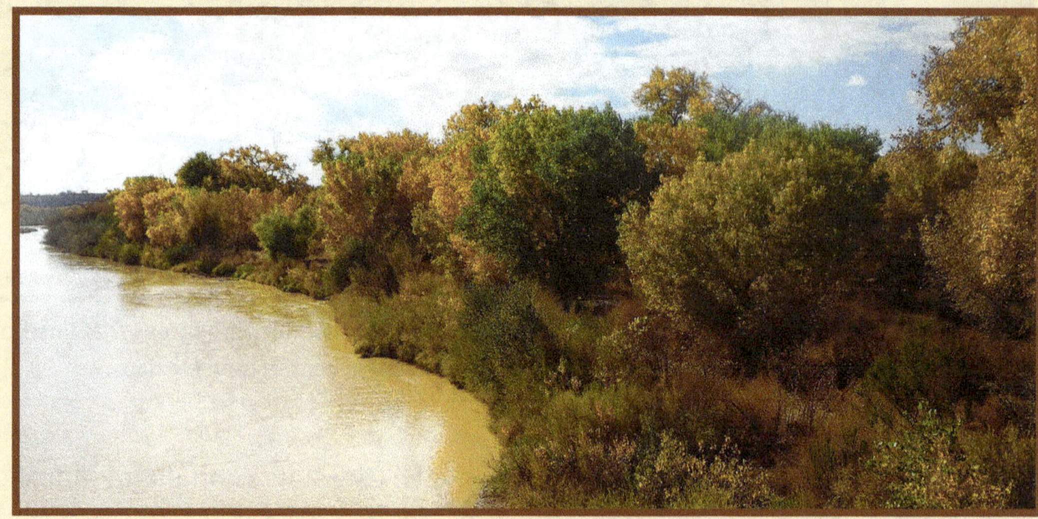

The crowns of numerous cottonwood trees rise high within the Bosque at the river's edge. Rio Grande cottonwood trees have an average crown width of 40 feet. In the fall, their leaves turn brilliant shades of gold.

As a youngster, I recall walking among giant cottonwoods to and from school along the irrigation ditches near the river. It was impossible to ride our bicycles to school on the ditches because tires would sink into the thick moist dirt and become stuck.

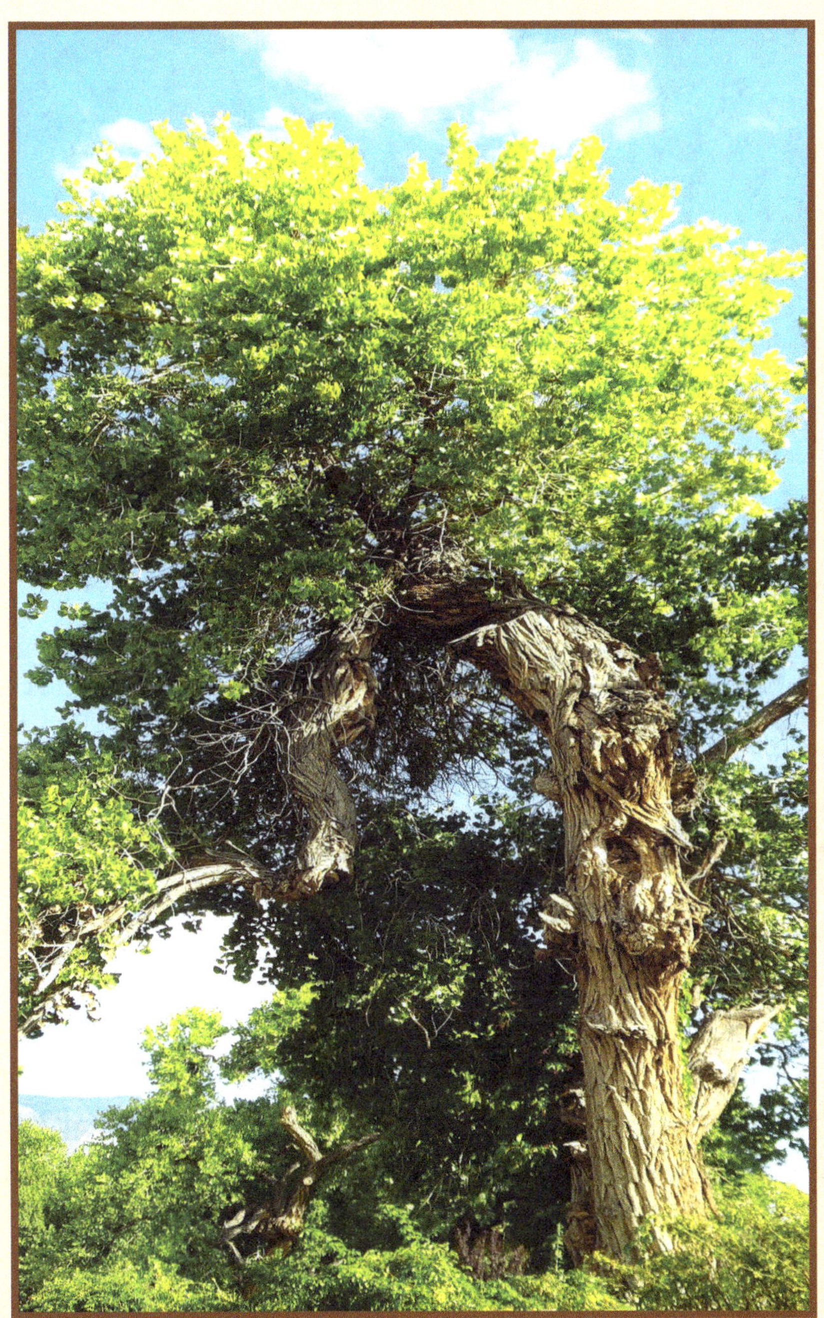

In the spring, cottonwood trees produce pea-like pods filled with a tight cotton ball that become visible if the pods are cut open.

Boys used to gather these pods, called tatones, and throw them at us girls. We would run away down the ditches screaming since tatones hurt if they hit your skin at a close distance.

Cottonwood trees in the Bosque have dramatic shapes that tower over the ground below.

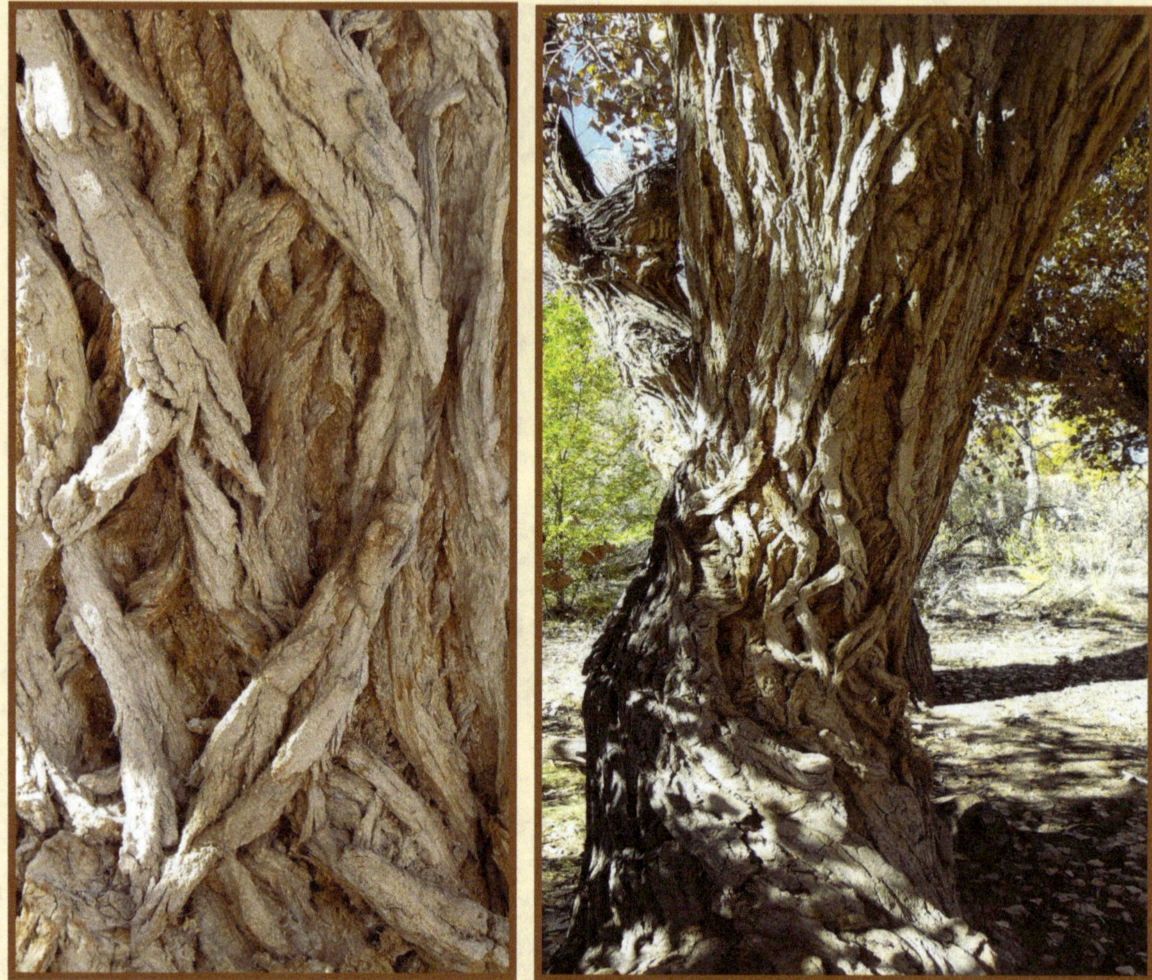

The bark of the cottonwood tree twists thickly up from its roots.

The craggy bark, along with tree cavities and hollows, provides an ideal habit for owls and brown bats. Deep furrows in the thick bark provide good footholds for tree climbing. Horses, porcupines, and beavers eat the inner bark. Cottonwood trunks can reach 3 feet in diameter. Native Americans in New Mexico have used hollowed cottonwood trees and skins from animals such as elk and deer to make log drums, which are important in their traditions and ceremonial dances.

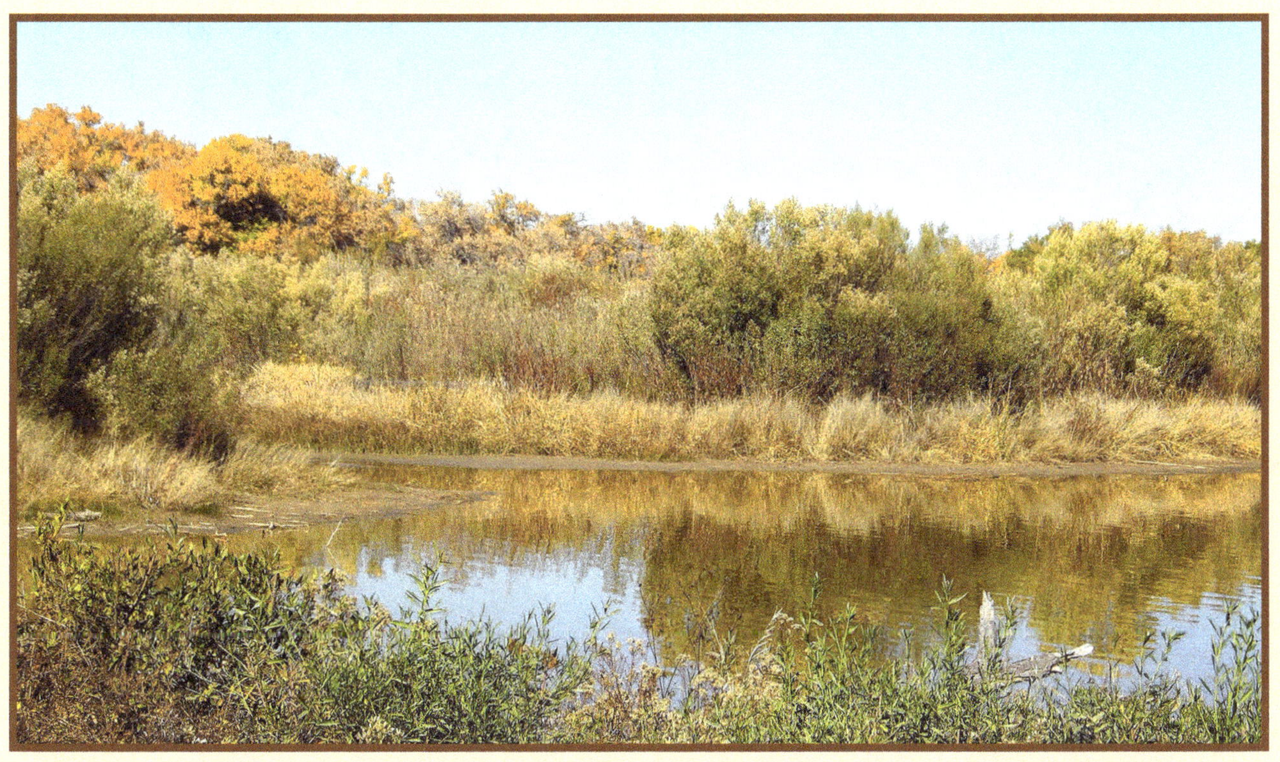

A marsh lies in the Candelaria Wetland Birdwatching Preserve, part of the Rio Grande Nature Center State Park.

The Rio Grande Nature Center State Park consists of 270 acres in the Bosque in Albuquerque where native plants and animals flourish among wetlands. This is part of an effort to restore lost habitat along the river's floodplain.

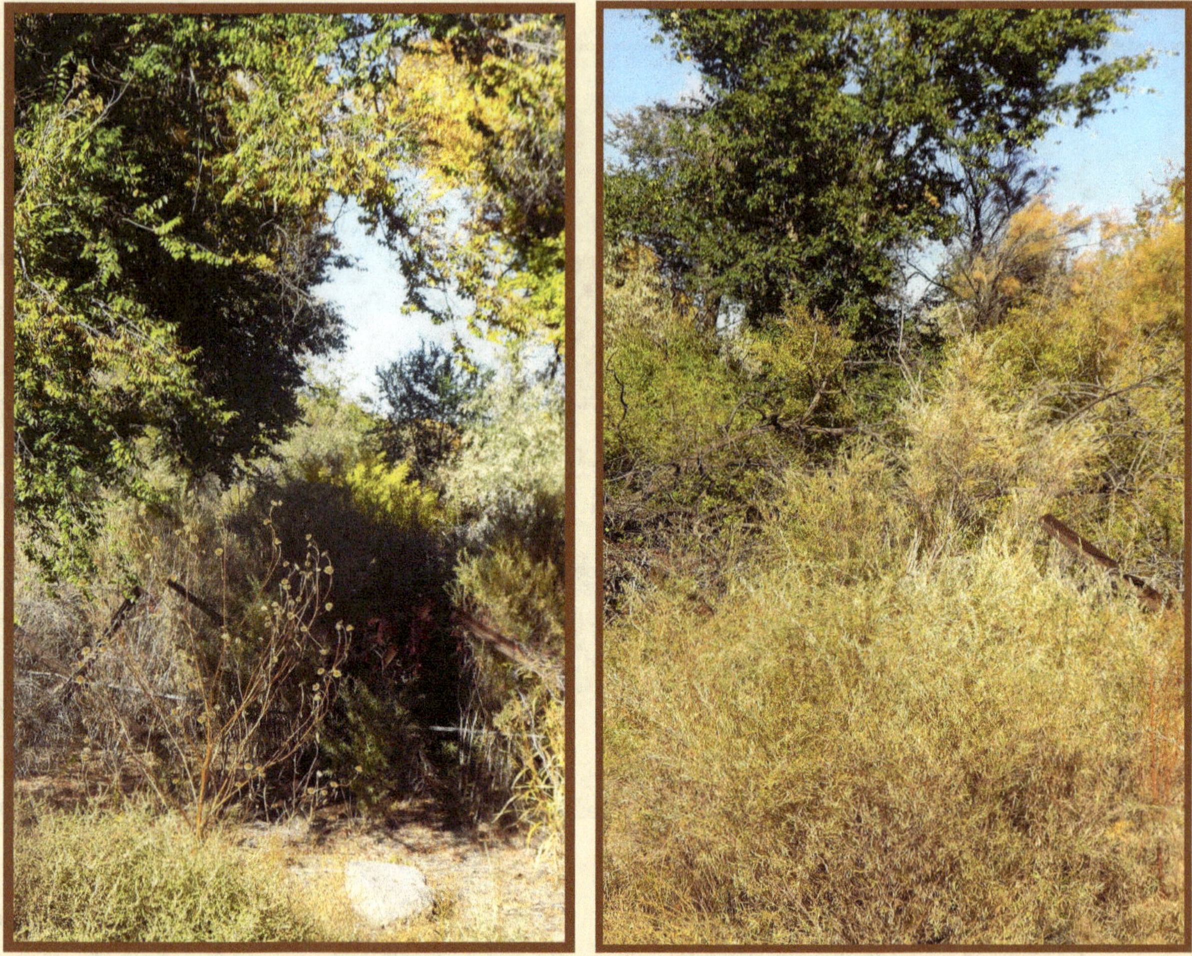

Dense brush also is found along the river.

Both photos show vegetation that has grown around rusty metal jetty jacks installed during the late 1940s/early 1950s for flood control along the Rio Grande. Although the jetty jacks slowed the river's speed and caused sediment to build up along the banks, today they are viewed as unnecessary eyesores. In recent years, government officials have removed over 100 jetty jacks. During droughts, there have been fires in the Bosque. Dried brush that accumulates around the jetty jacks are viewed as fire hazards, which also prompts calls for their removal.

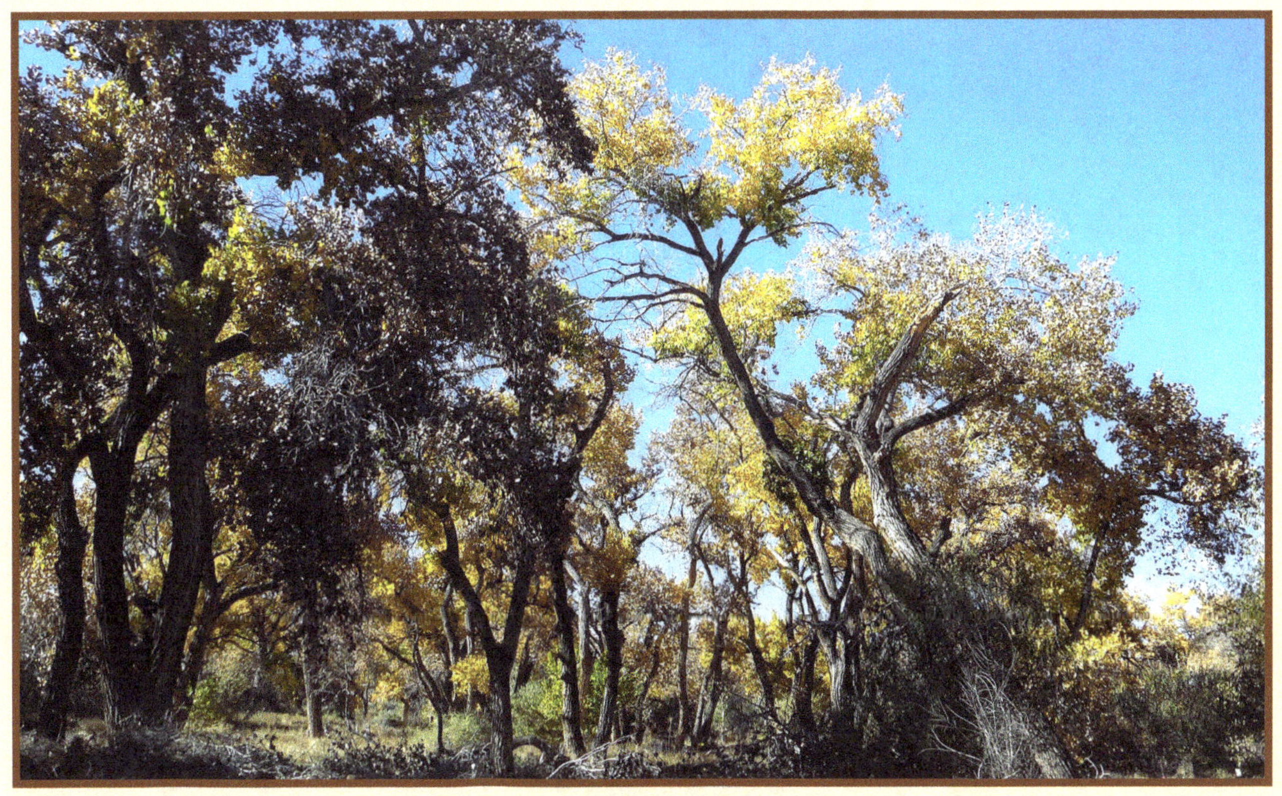

Cottonwood trees are dense in the Bosque.

My grandfather used to relate vivid descriptions in Spanish of his experiences riding horses through the Bosque. He warned us to avoid passing under tree branches because of a certain type of local whipsnake. He said this snake would hide in the branches as it hunted for small animals among the cottonwoods. This snake can lunge out to strike people passing below.

In New Mexico, most encounters with snakes occur on the ground. However, some rattlesnakes forage for birds in small trees and can be found hanging inside tree branches.

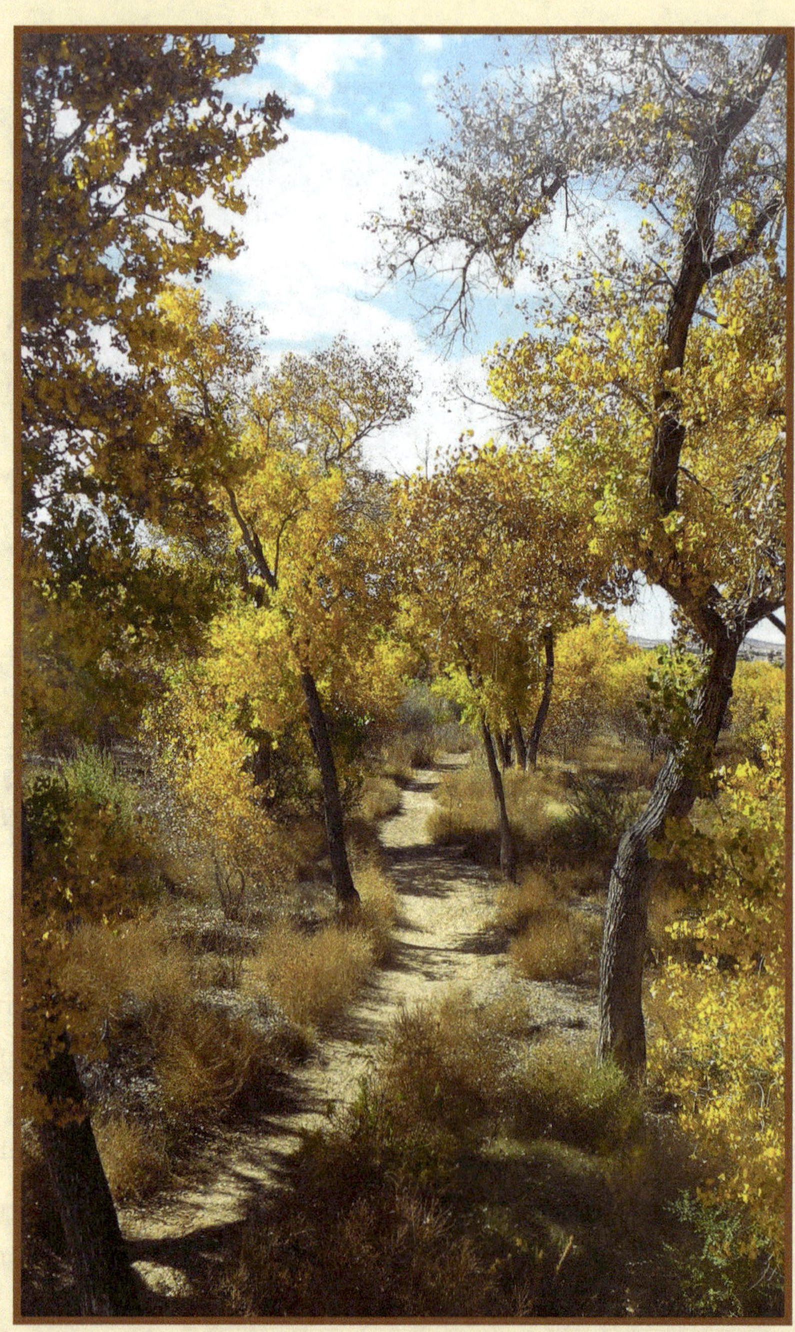

During autumn, the changing leaves of the cottonwood trees create a brilliant array of colors, including unique blends of green, gold, and bronze.

A trail winds its way through the Bosque.

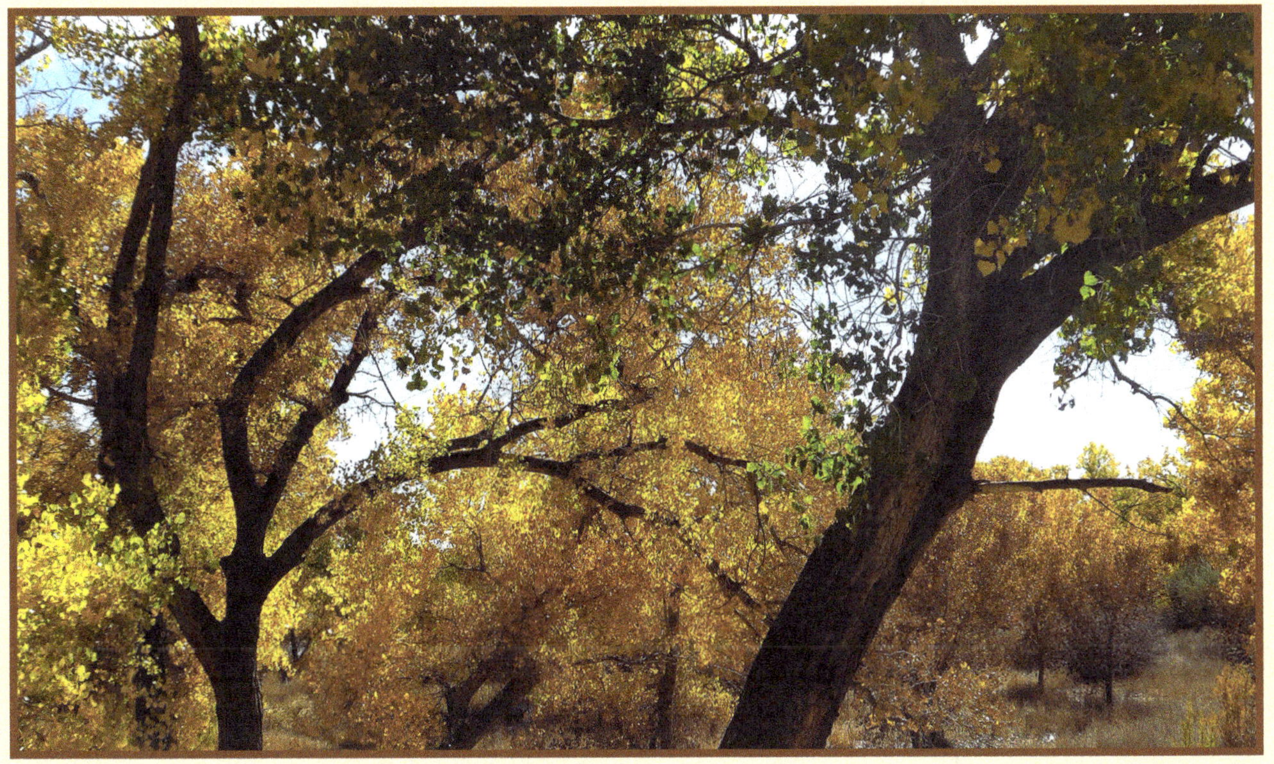

Cottonwood trees, whose leaves change in autumn, rise beside a bridge crossing the Rio Grande.

A 16-mile-long paved bicycle trail called the Paseo del Bosque Bike Trail runs alongside the Rio Grande in Albuquerque. *Sunset* magazine ranked this trail in the 11th spot among the "20 Best Bike Paths in the West." Some people also rollerblade along the trail.

My family members ride bikes on the trail in the Bosque. They have seen coyotes, snakes, Canadian geese, and cottontail rabbits. Three types of cottontails and two species of jackrabbits are found in New Mexico. These are considered non-game animals and unprotected. Unfortunately, some people take their dogs out on mesas (flat-topped hills named after the Spanish word for table) and let the dogs run loose to hunt rabbits for sport.

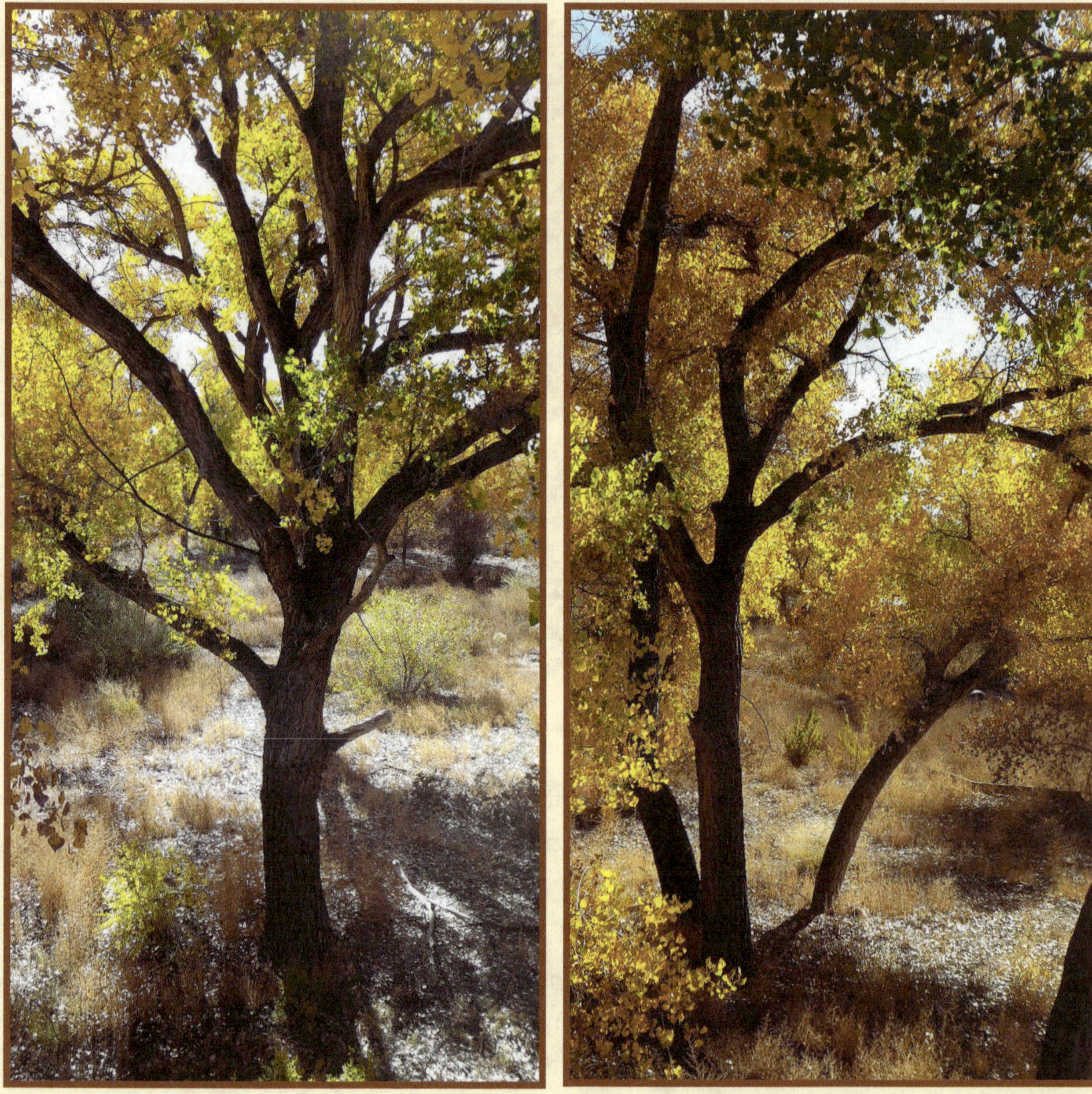

Numerous trails can be found among the cottonwood trees in the Bosque.

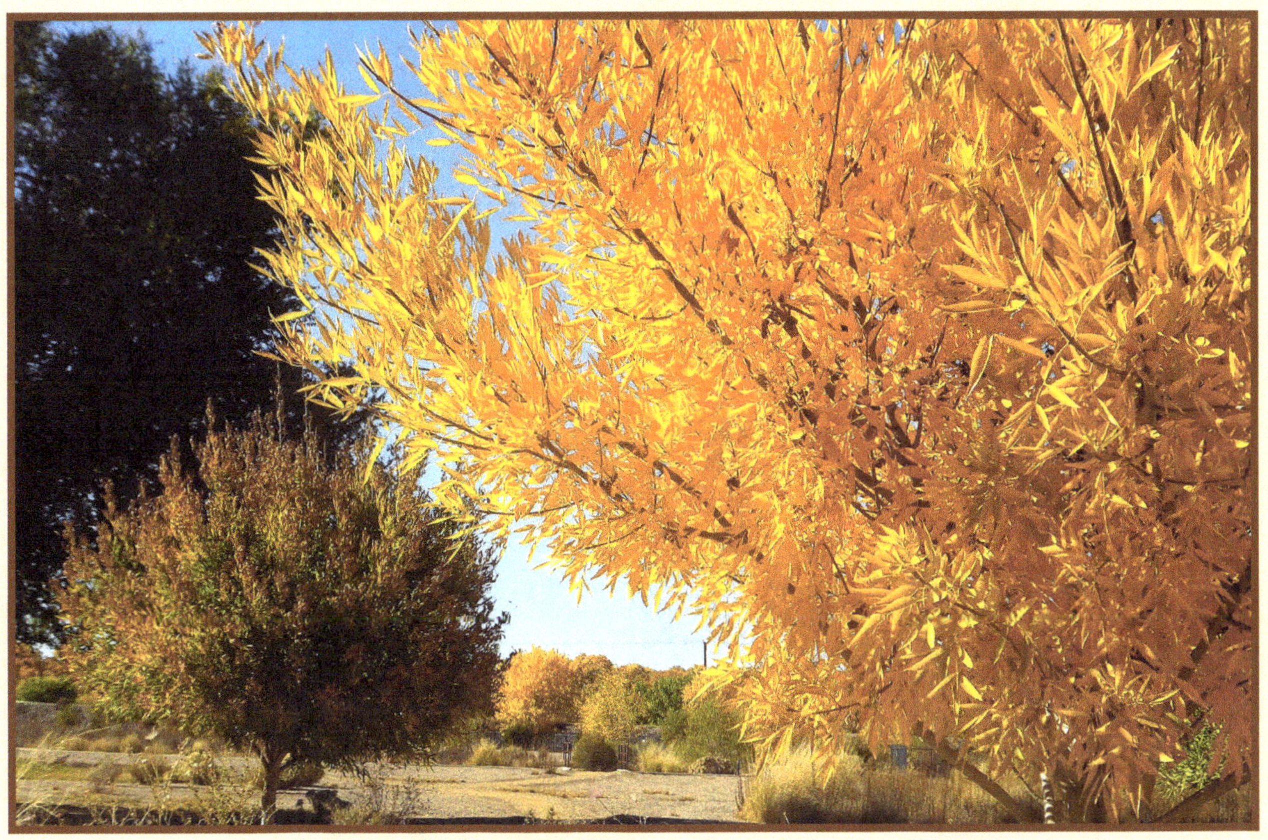

A willow (right), turned golden by the changing seasons, is flanked by other trees in the Bosque nature trail.

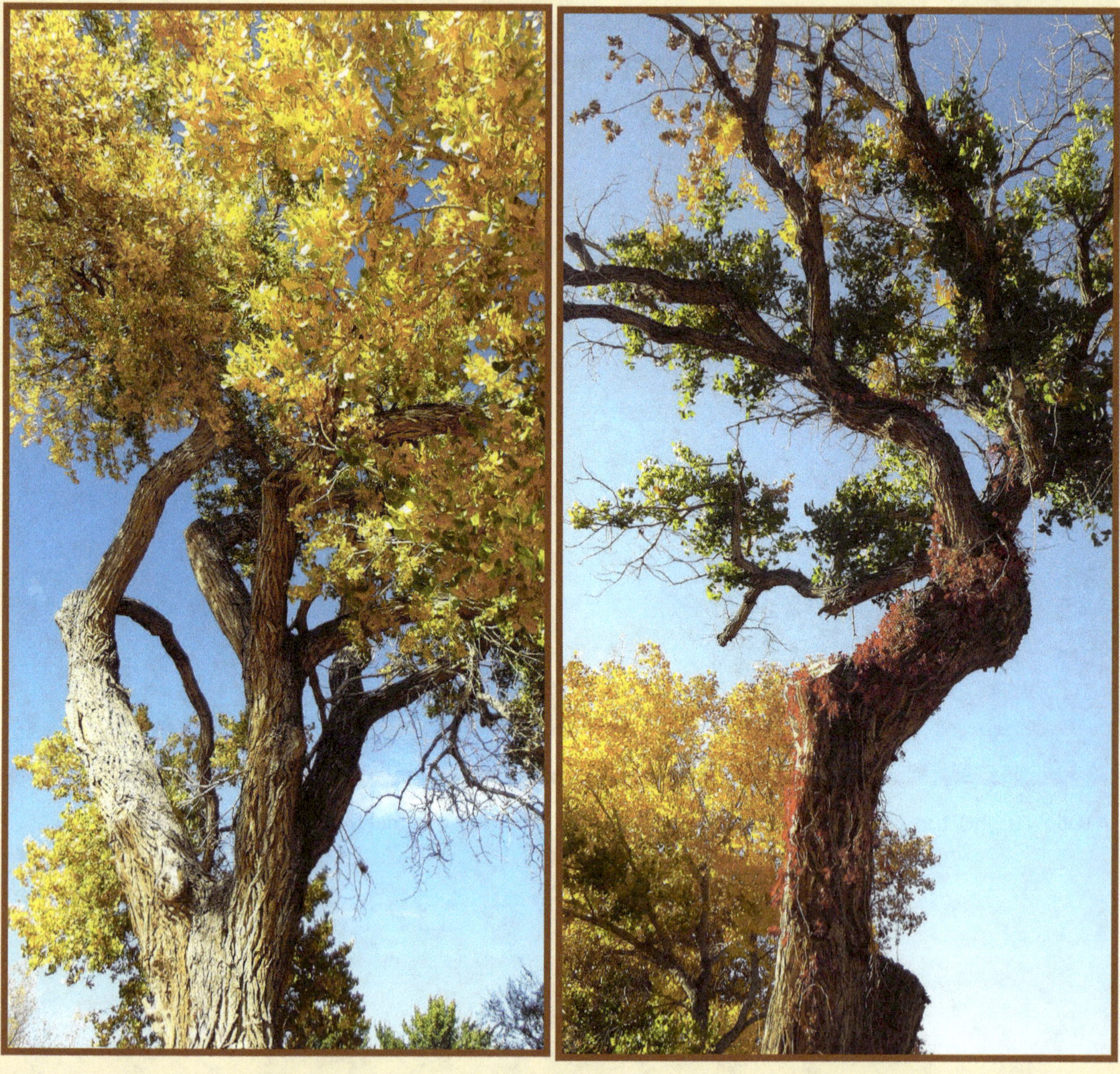

Cottonwood trees in the Bosque form different patterns with their twisting branches. The trunk of the tree on the right is masked by scarlet Virginia creeper.

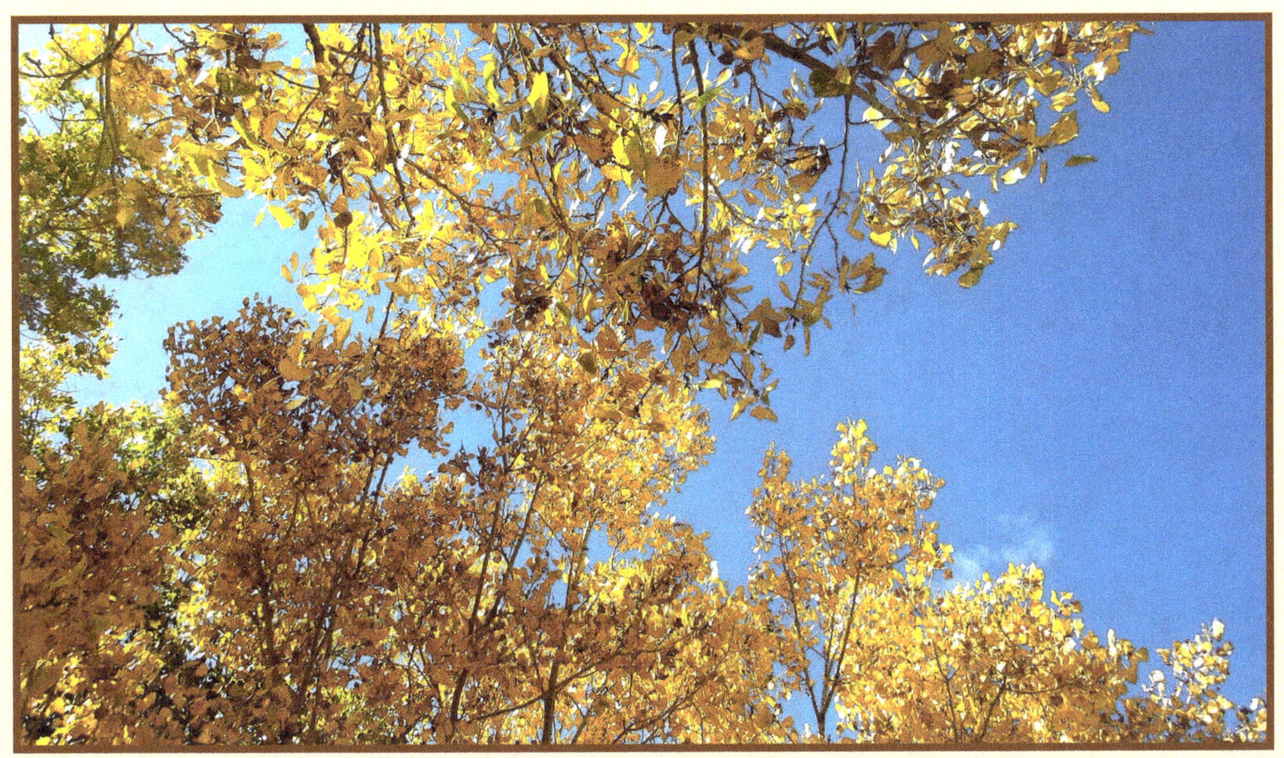

Golden cottonwood leaves shine brightly against the blue desert sky.

New Mexico is known for its beautiful clear blue skies, which are often the color of turquoise—the state gemstone that is popular in local Native American jewelry.

CHAPTER 5: TRIBUTARIES & LAS ACEQUIAS

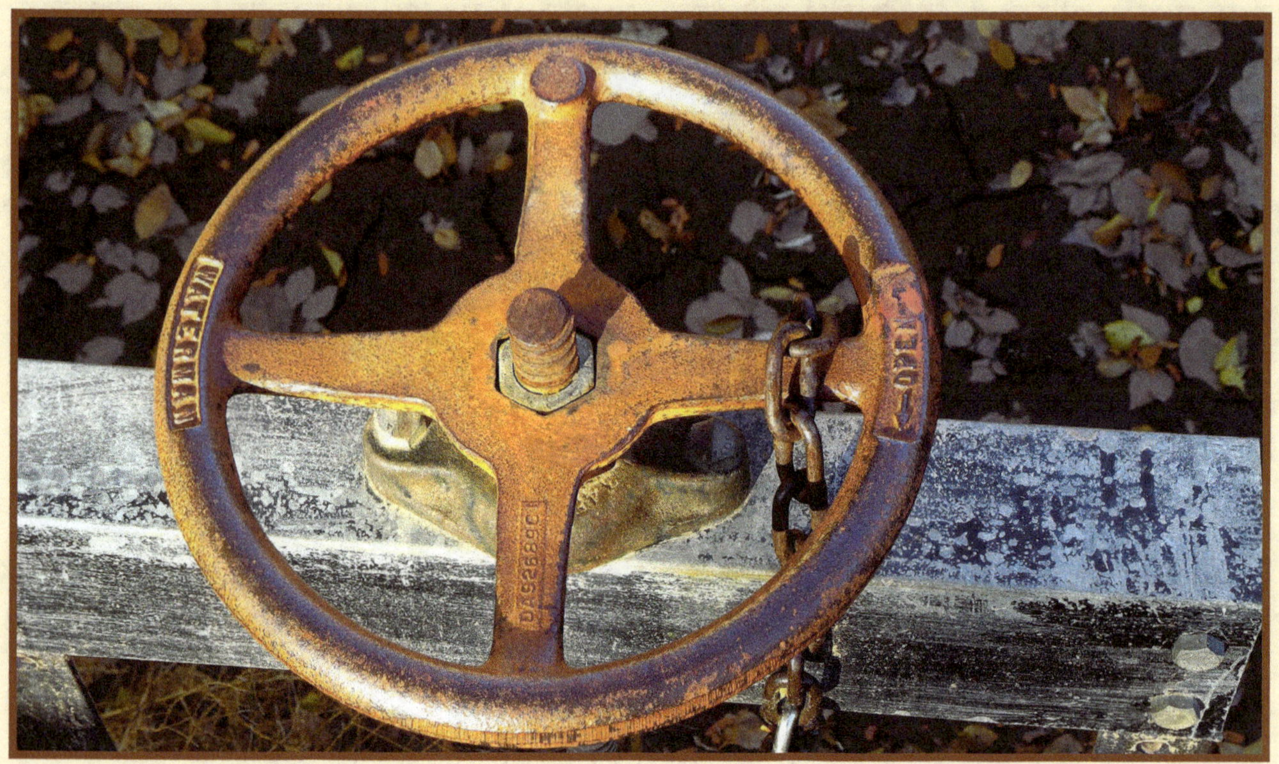

A rusted irrigation wheel awaits use in a ditch connected to the Rio Grande.

The Camino Real, linking the Spanish colonial capital of Mexico City to Santa Fe, brought vital transformation to the Rio Grande. This 1,600-mile-long wilderness highway was called El Camino Real de Tierra Adentro (Royal Road of the Interior). It took 6 months to travel one way and was the earliest Euro-American trade route in the United States. Along this road, which largely followed the Rio Grande, the Spaniards brought not only material goods, but also their advanced expertise in irrigation systems. Ditches (called *acequias* in Spanish) are at the heart of these water systems and are as relevant today to the Rio Grande and its communities as 400 years ago.

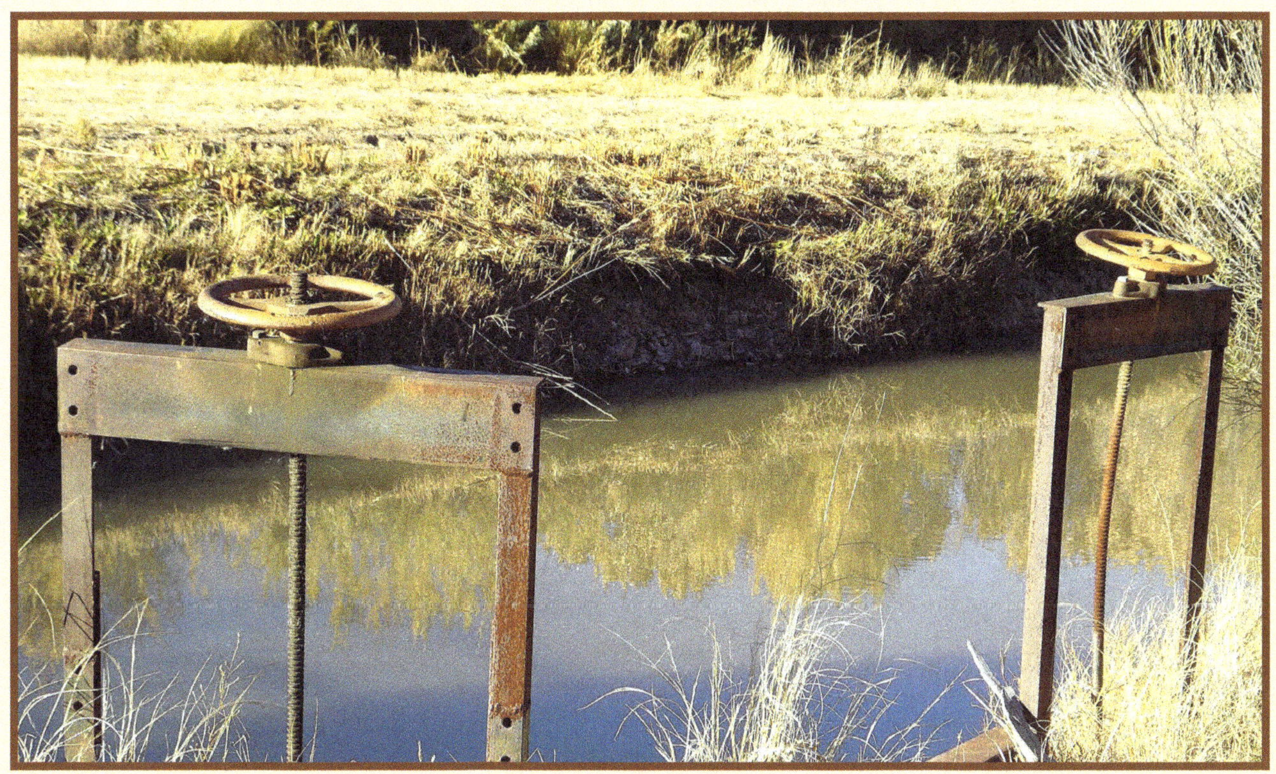

Irrigation gates stand beside a large ditch in the Bosque.

The wheels at the top of the gates open and close irrigation panels below, controlling water flow. New Mexico's irrigation system was a well-established and vibrant part of the region before it even became a U.S. territory in 1850. As early as the 1840s, while New Mexico was still under the jurisdiction of Mexico, many American explorers were impressed by the well-managed irrigation systems developed by Spanish colonialists along the central Rio Grande. These irrigation systems played a vital role in the cultivation and trade of agriculture and livestock.

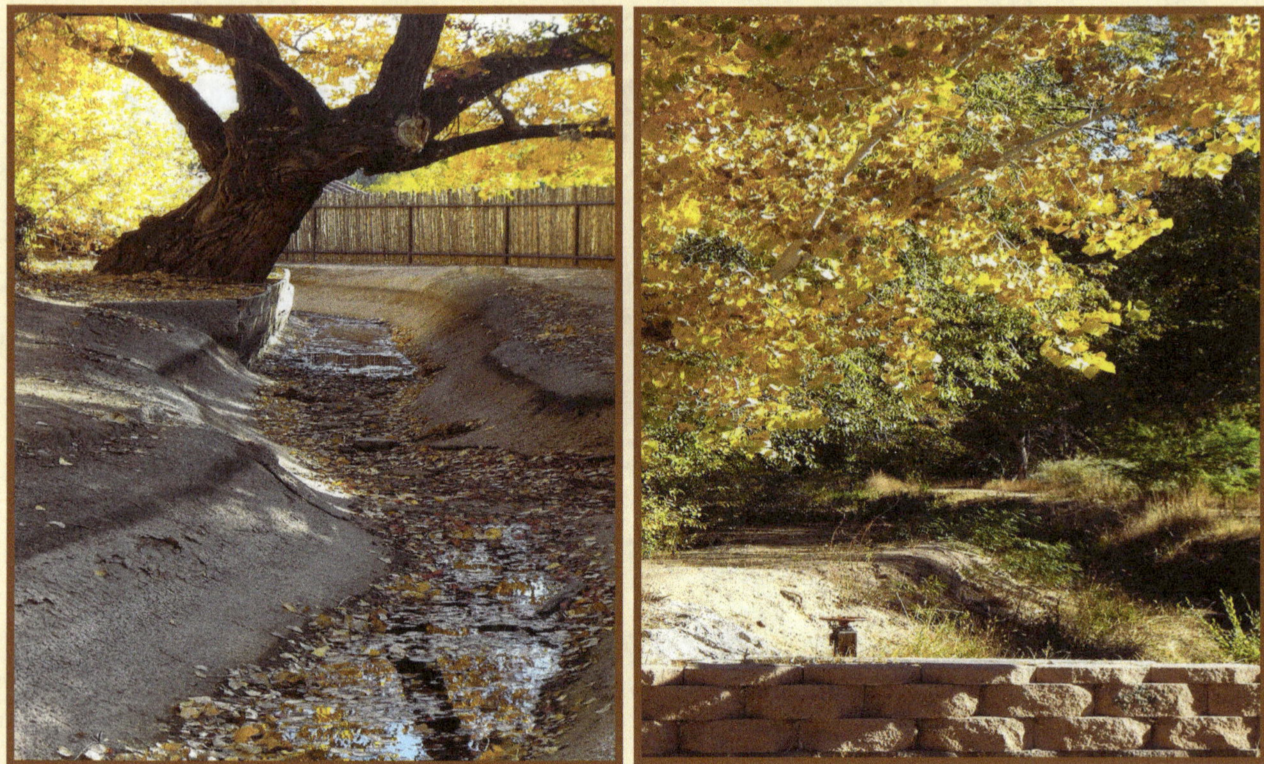

Two different *acequias* create water paths near the Rio Grande.

New Mexico has over 1,000 community irrigation-ditch systems that water 160,000 acres. According to the U.S. Army Corps of Engineers, many of today's *acequias* date back to the 1700s. It is said that the Spaniards learned irrigation techniques from the Moors during the Moorish occupation of Spain. In fact, the word *acequia* is of Arabic origin. A U.S. progress report in 1891 on irrigation relates: "The Spanish law of water, which was passed in 1366, and which is probably the most comprehensive act of its kind in existence, is little more than a codification of previous existing laws and a legalization of established customs. Generally speaking, every irrigation work in Spain has a code for its management, and the administration of these rules is in the hands of the irrigators." The report also notes that the Spanish law had 300 articles/clauses, of which 271 concerned rights to rivers, rainwater, streams, and lakes.

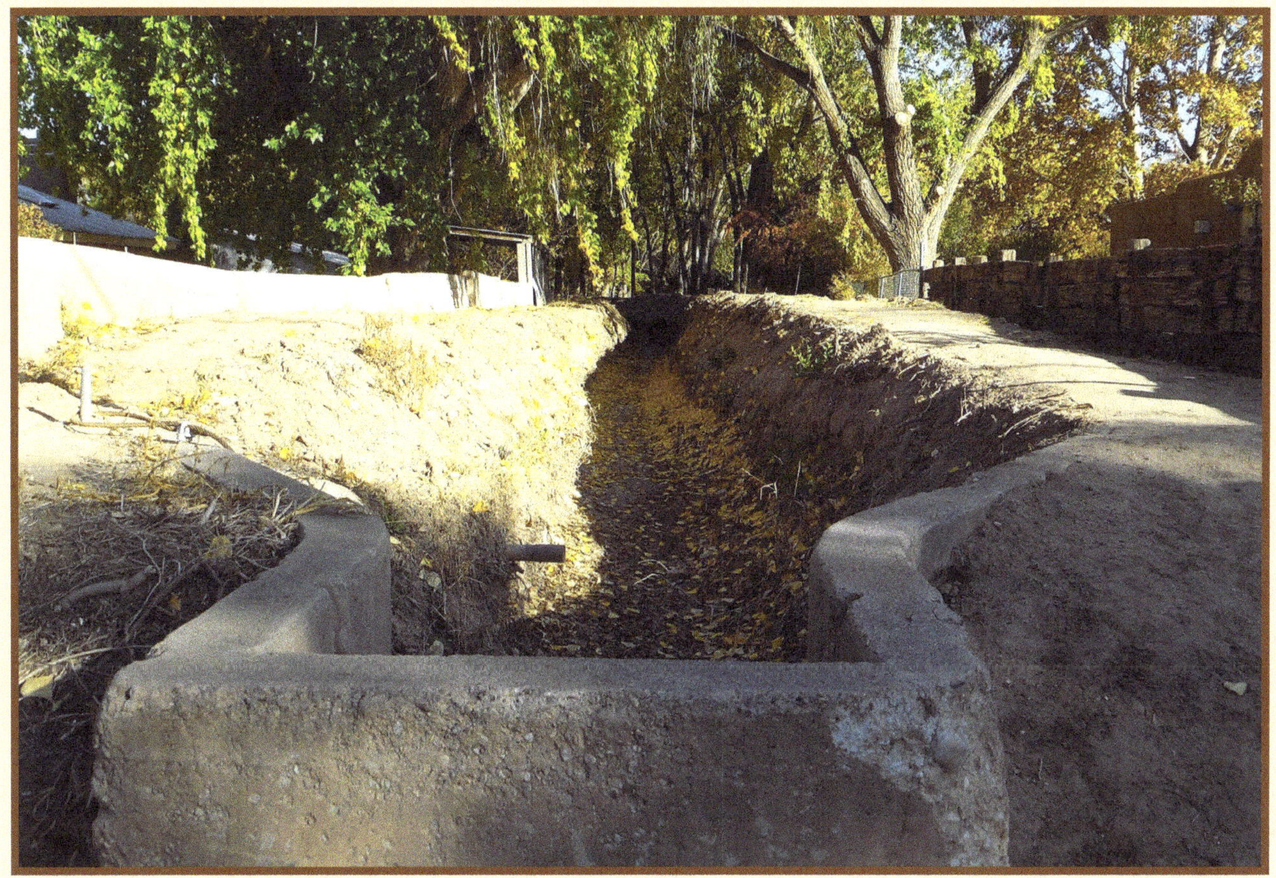

An *acequia* crosses through Los Ranchos de Albuquerque, a historic farming community on the east side of the Rio Grande.

Not all ditches are the same. Some are high, low, narrow or wide. Some have cement culverts, like the one above, for water to pass under roads and streets. The highly developed water management and irrigation systems developed by the Spaniards was brought to New Mexico and adapted to the Rio Grande for the benefit of many.

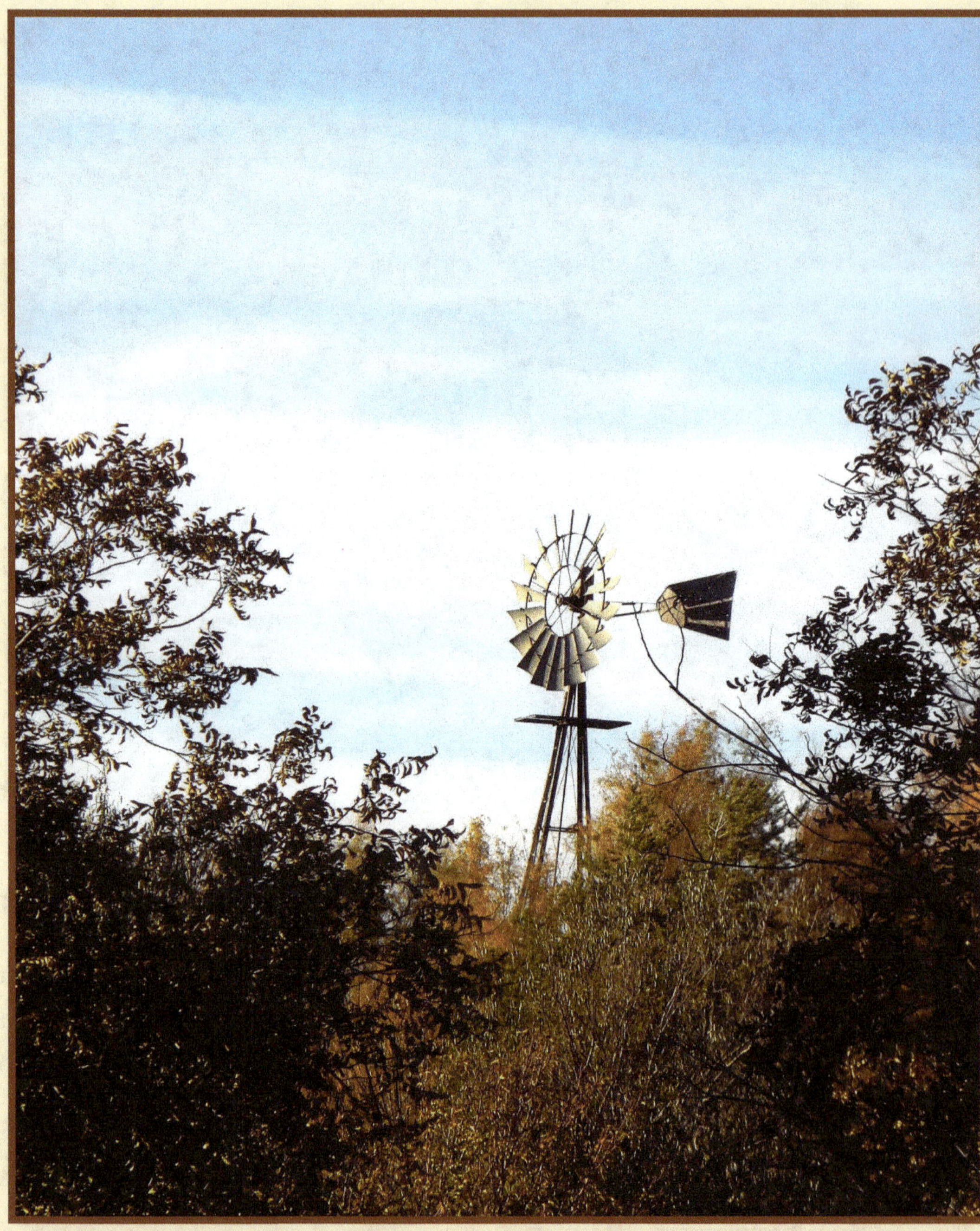

An old windpump for pumping water is visible on a ranch near the Rio Grande.

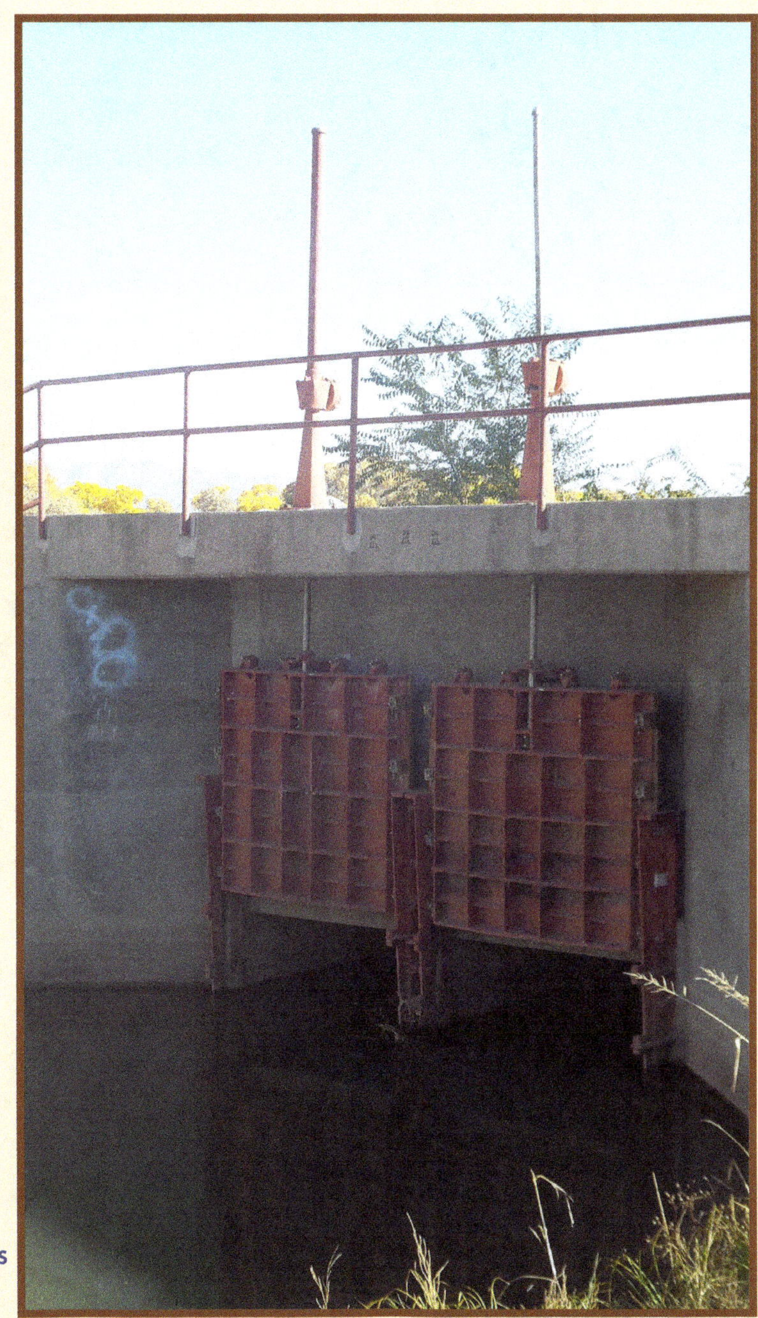

The larger ditches are called *acequia madre* (mother) ditches and have smaller ones as tributaries to transport water. This forms an intricate system of ditches surrounding and intersecting both urban communities and agricultural areas near the Rio Grande.

A large irrigation gate on the Rio Grande helps control water flows into Corrales.

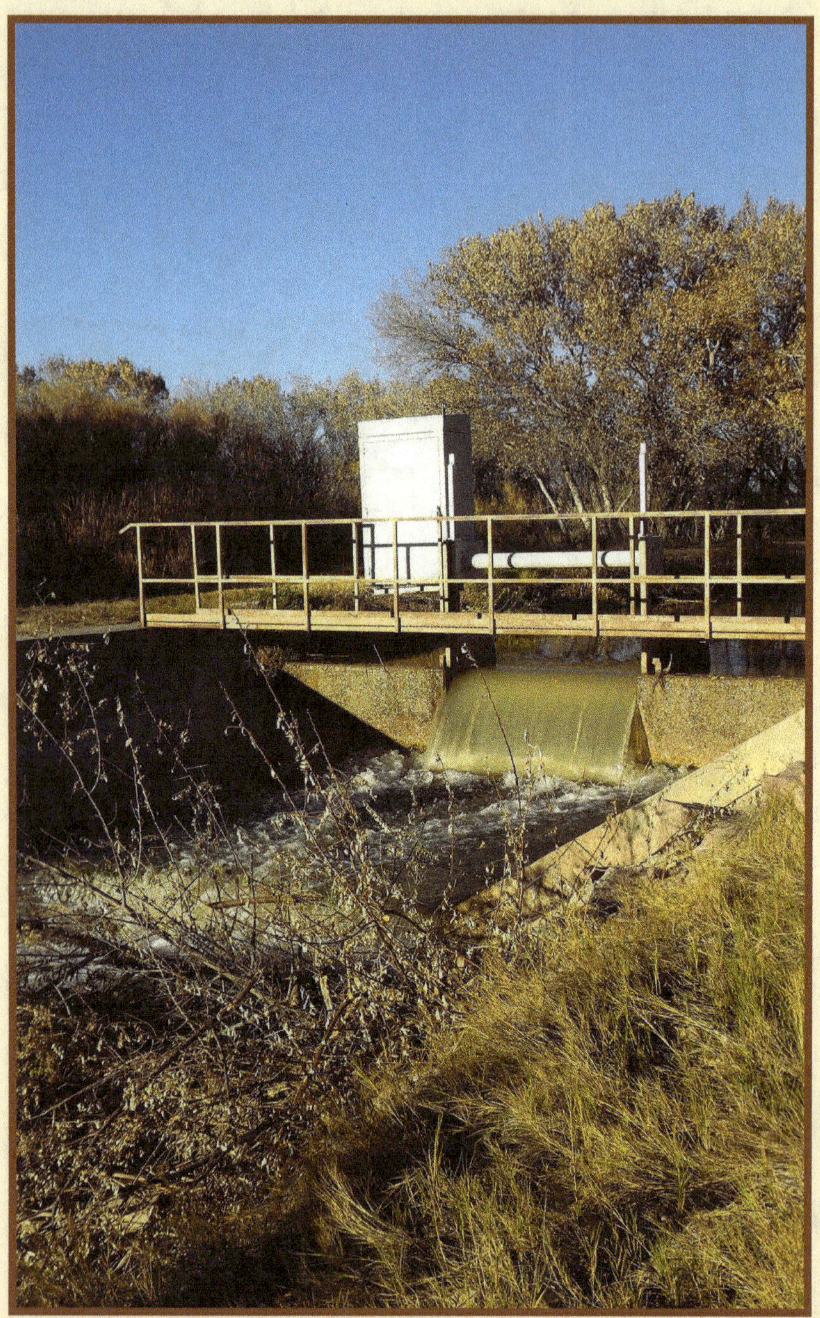

As with ditches, there are many different types of irrigation gates. When a gate is opened wide, it enables maximum water flow.

A mid-sized irrigation gate stands near Socorro County in the Rio Grande valley.

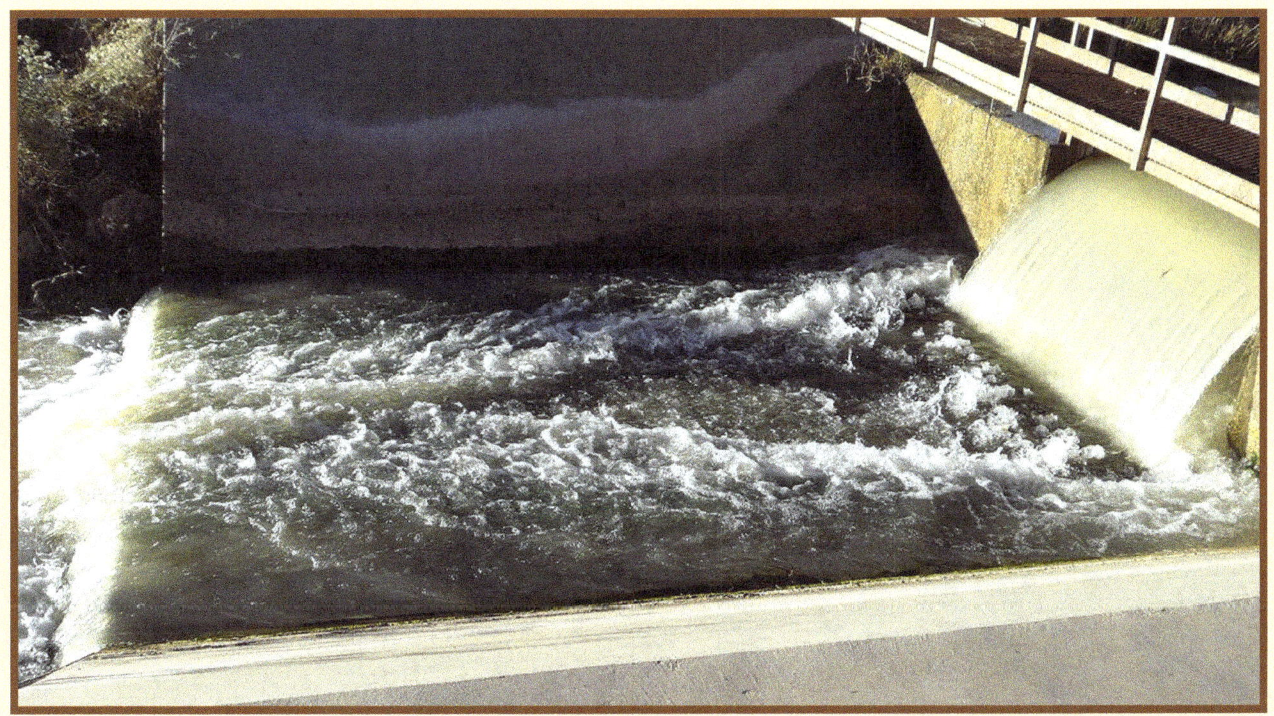

Water pours rapidly through an irrigation gate.

Since New Mexico's climate is so hot and dry, diverting water from the Rio Grande into canals and ditches is critical to the ecosystem.

Average annual precipitation ranges from about 7 inches in the northwest to about 20 inches in the mountains. In the summer months, temperatures can soar past 100 degrees Fahrenheit for many weeks, with occasional afternoon thunderstorms bringing much-needed moisture. Otherwise, the climate is very dry.

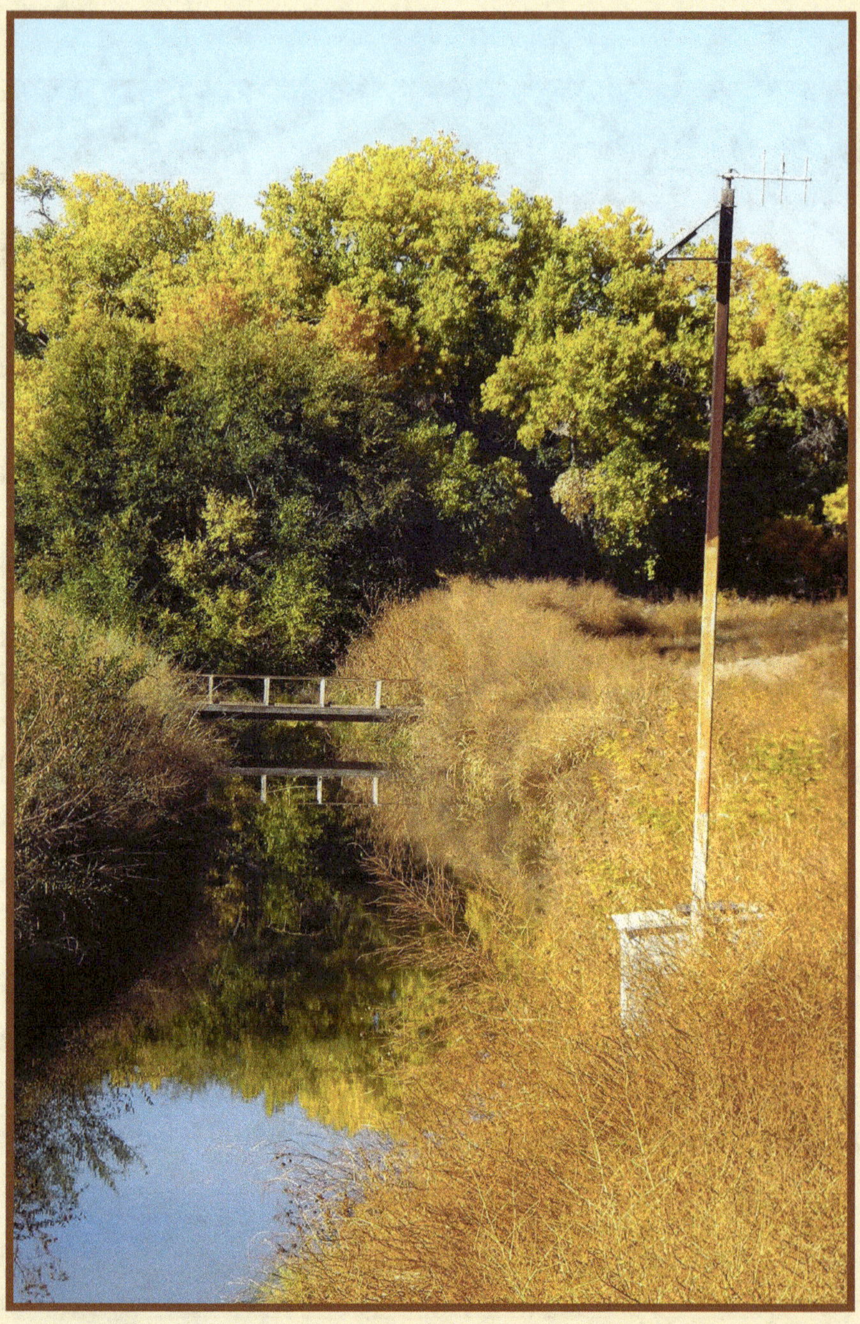

The *mayordomo*, or ditch boss, of an *acequia* plays an important role in the management of local irrigation systems.

My great-grandfather Abenicio was a *mayordomo* in charge of the irrigation ditch system in Corrales. A *mayordomo's* responsibilities include settling water disputes, managing water flows from the river, monitoring for possible obstructions in the *acequias,* checking for potential flooding, and overseeing the general maintenance of irrigation ditches.

A bridge spans an irrigation ditch in Corrales beside the Rio Grande.

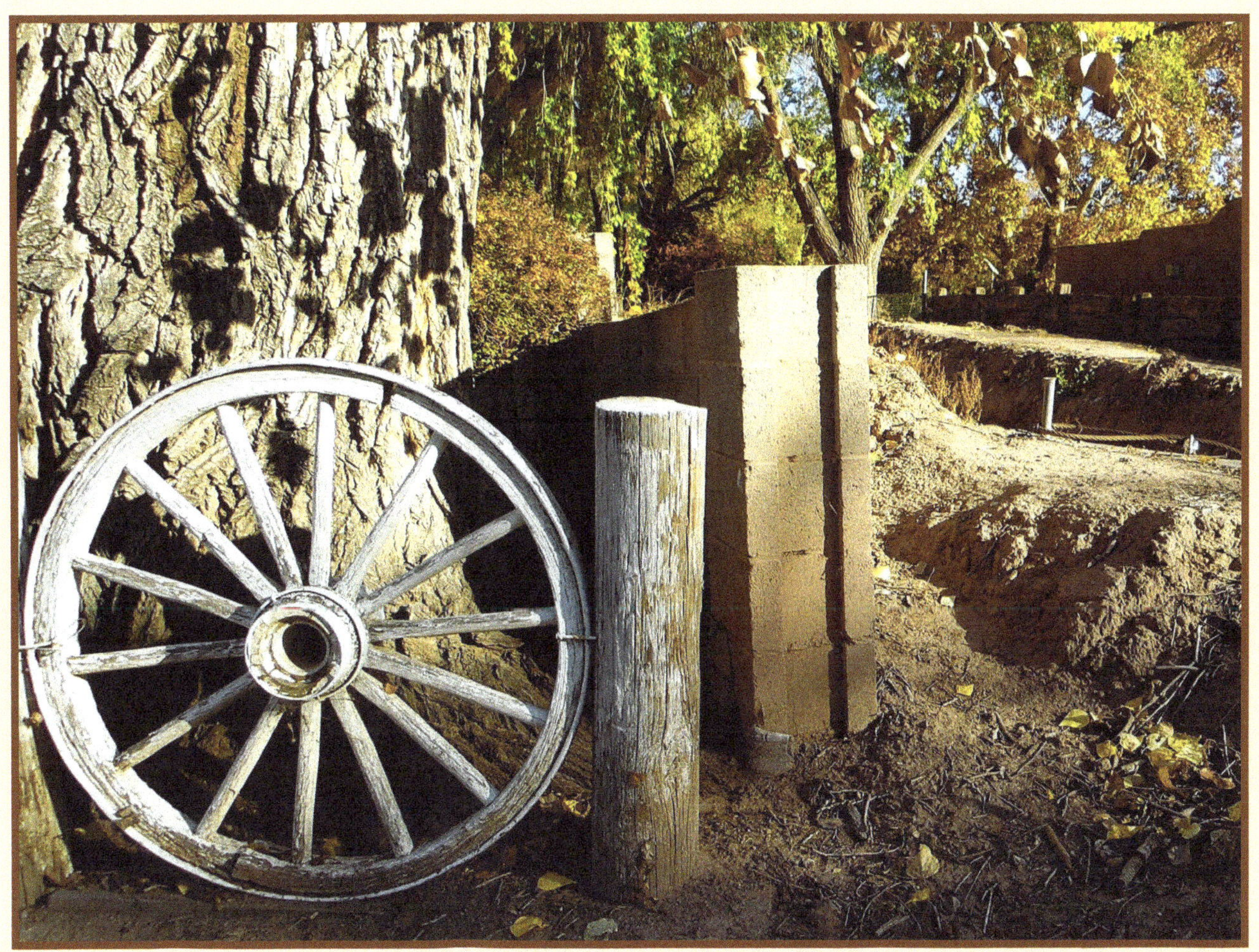

An old wagon wheel sits at the base of a cottonwood tree beside a rural irrigation ditch.

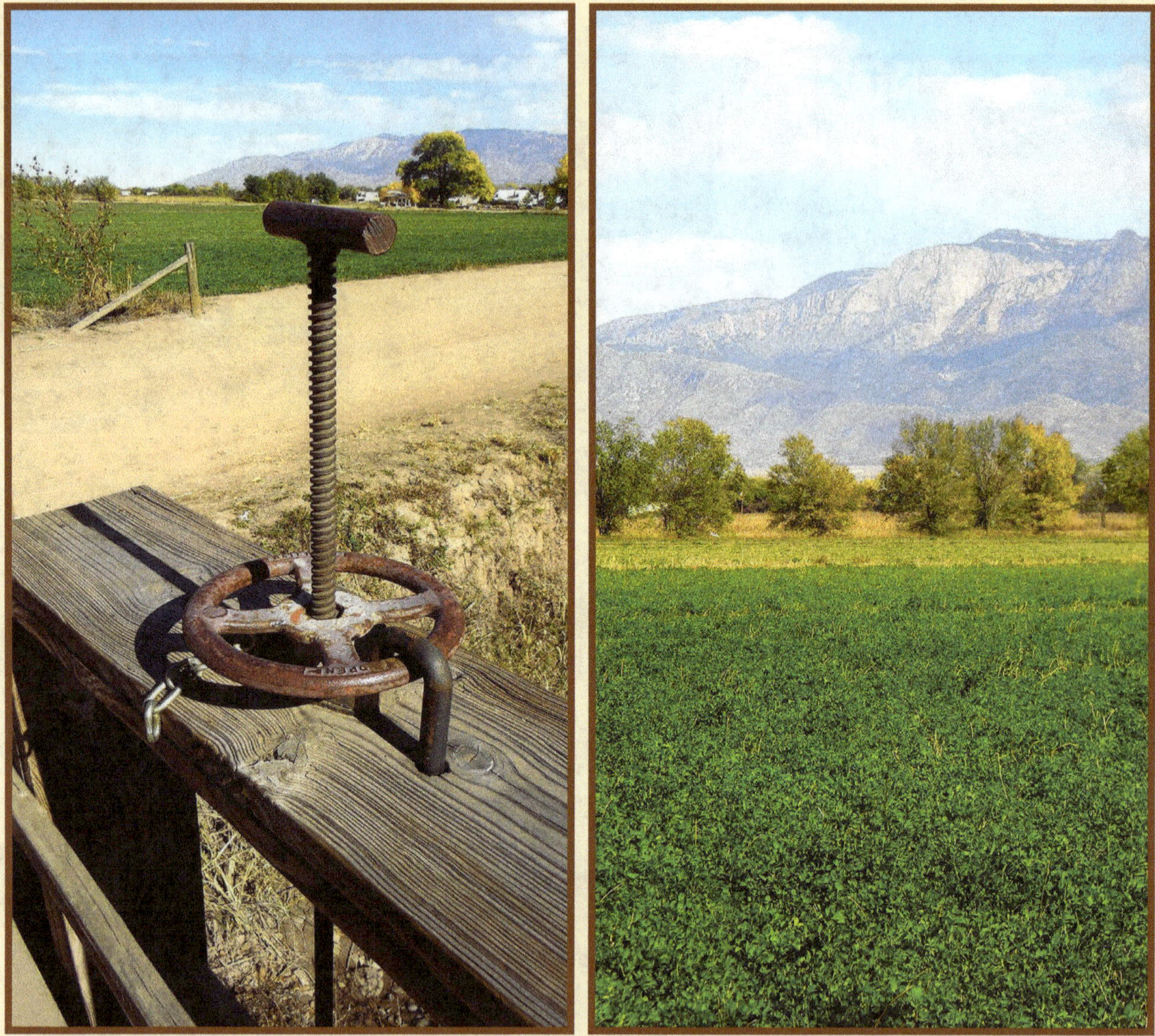

An irrigation gate (left) regulates water to alfalfa fields in the distance. A closeup of the alfalfa field (right) provides a view of another ditch between the trees. The Sandia Mountains rise in the distance.

Notice that this irrigation wheel is locked to prevent theft. Irrigation wheels are precious—they are the only means of controlling water flow from ditches and are frequently stolen.

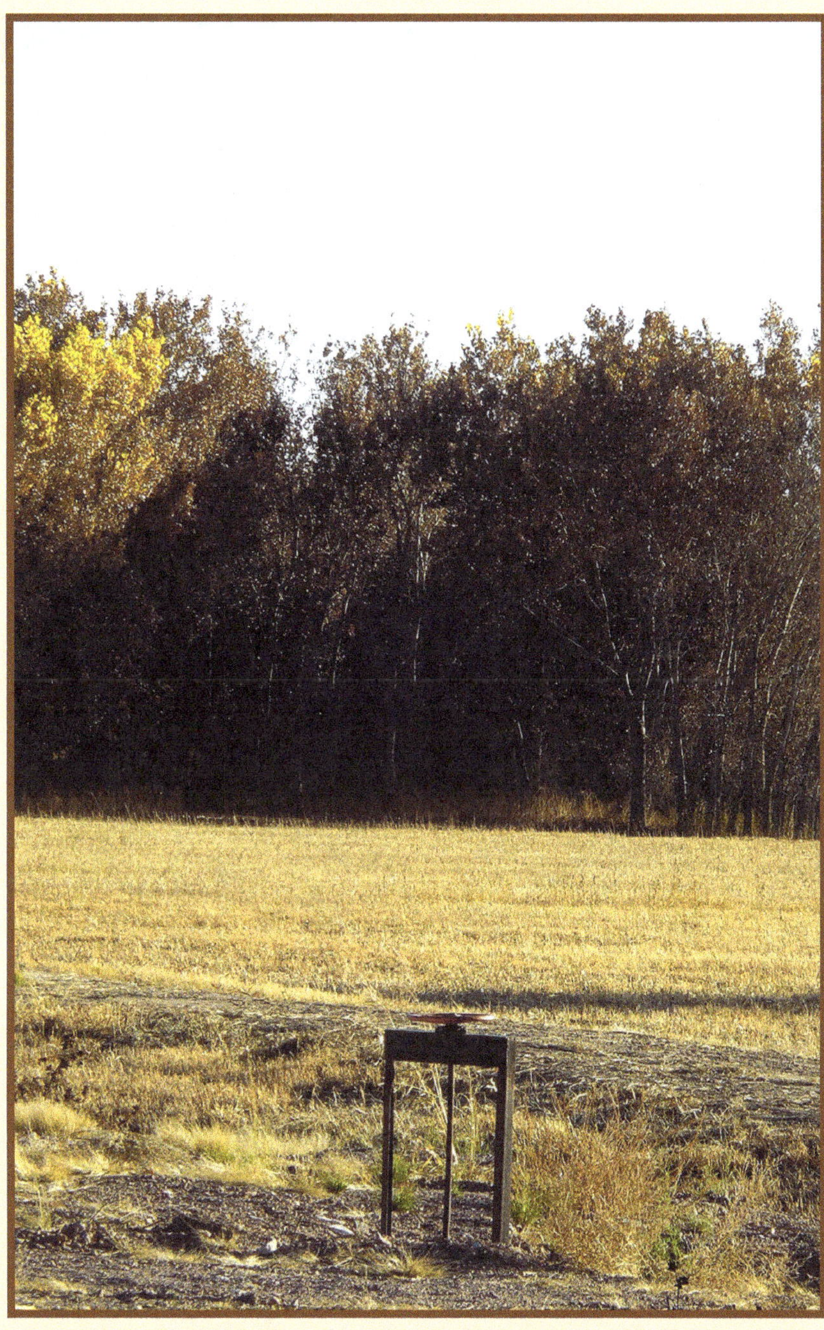

An irrigation gate (center) sits next to a shallow ditch in the Bosque.

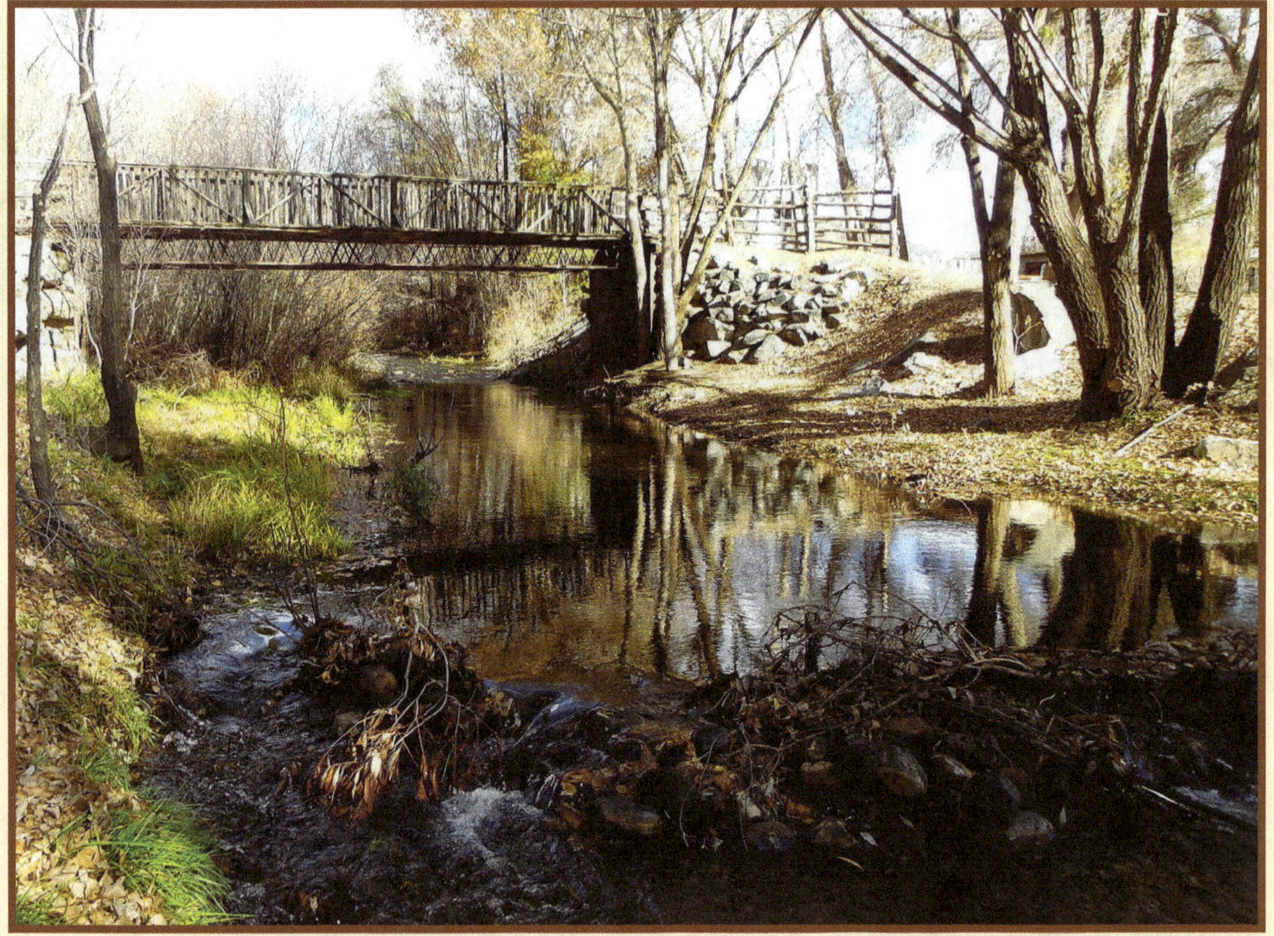

A wooden bridge near Taos crosses an *acequia* connected to a tributary of the Rio Grande.

Water runs high in ditches on designated irrigation days. Once as a child, I fell into a ditch and nearly drowned while trying to catch tadpoles with an empty coffee can.

While a youngster, my daughter also enjoyed frolicking through the muddy waters with the family cattle dogs. The irrigation water covers the ground like a cool wet blanket. Rich silt underneath feels like brown slush under bare feet.

Irrigation days also attract numerous toads, which chirp loudly on warm summer nights.

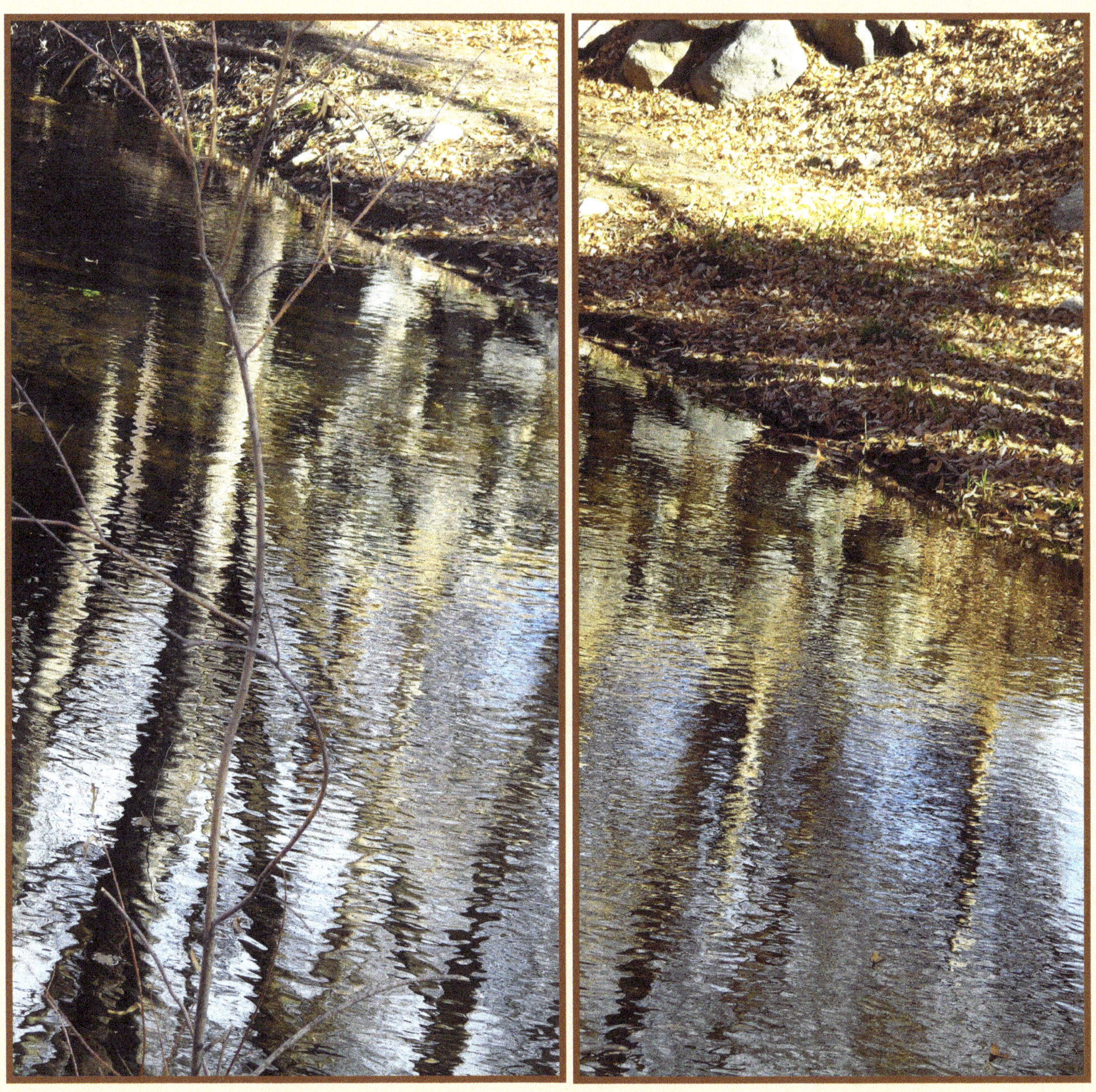

The reflections of trees shimmer in the quiet waters of an *acequia.*

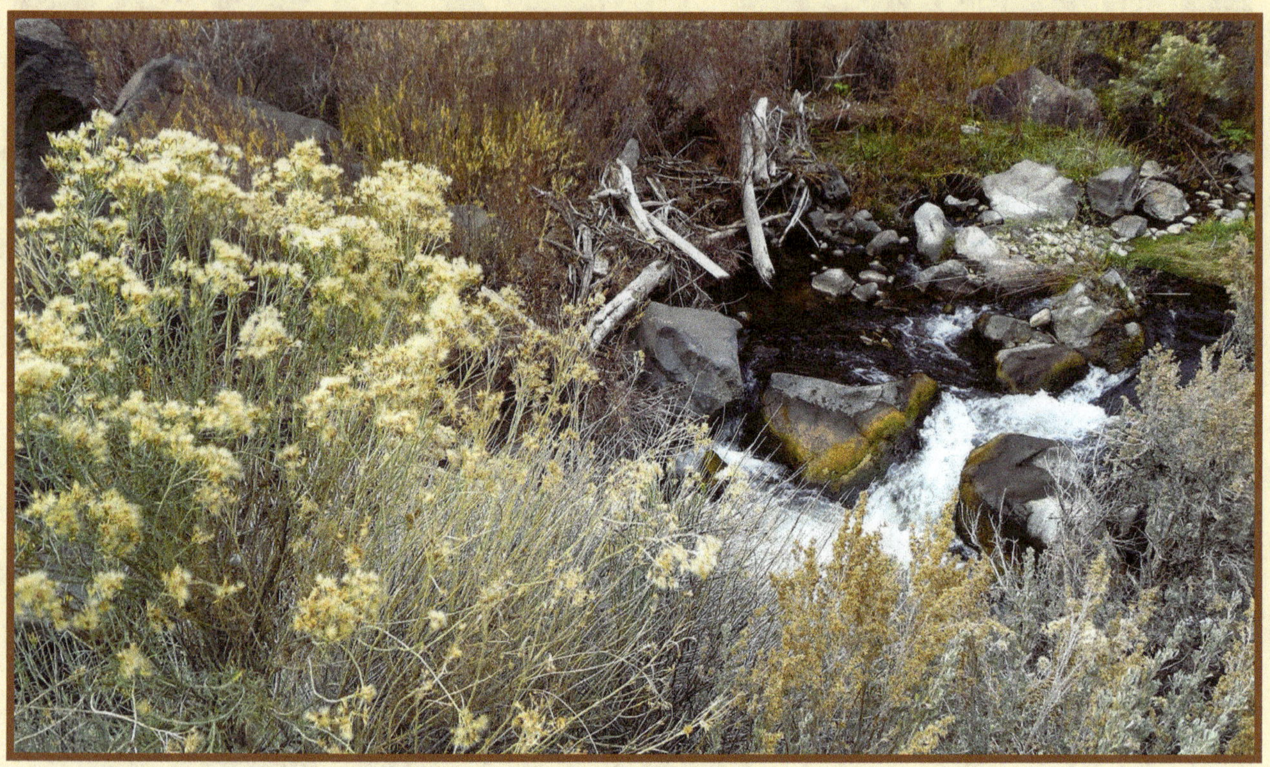

In the high plains near Taos, a stream from the Rio Grande Gorge flows into an irrigation ditch, sustaining farms and cattle.

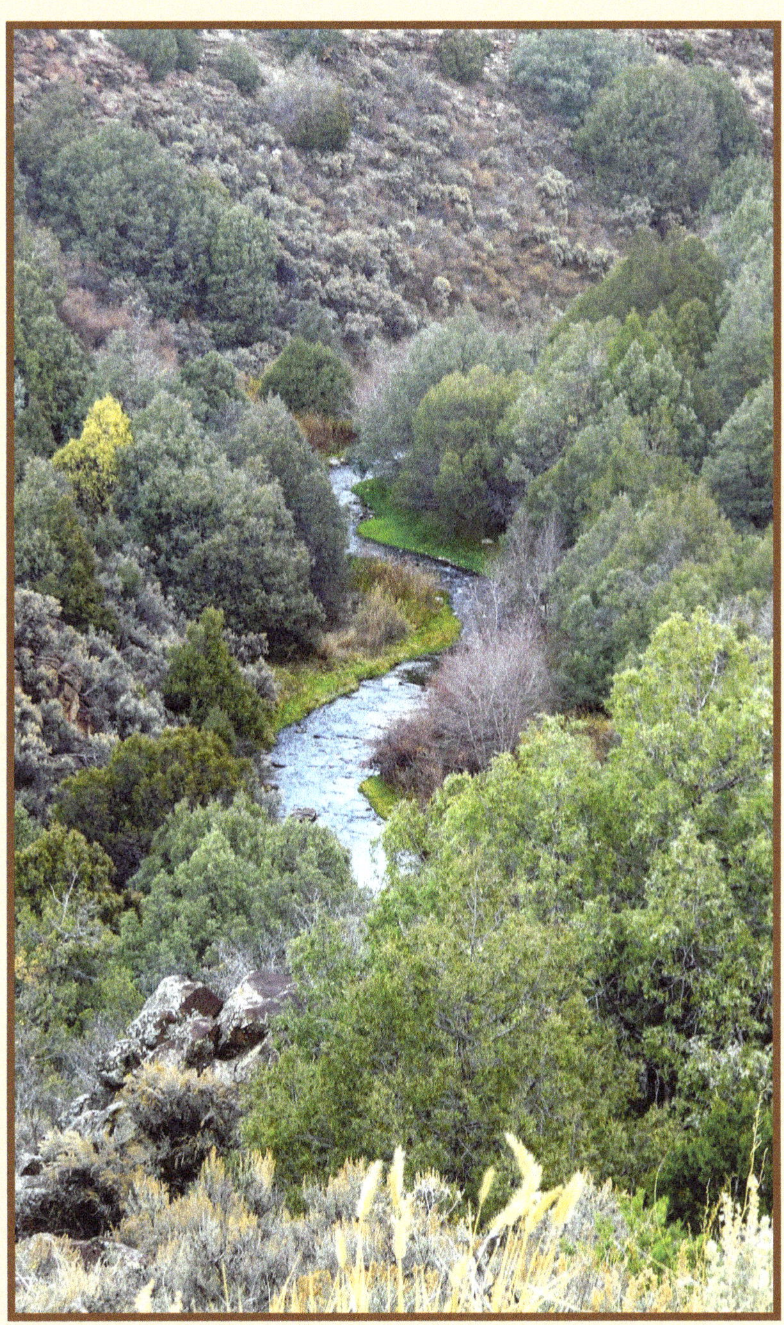

A tributary from the Rio Grande Gorge winds through canyons as it descends to farmland below, where its waters will be used for irrigation.

CHAPTER 6: WILDLIFE

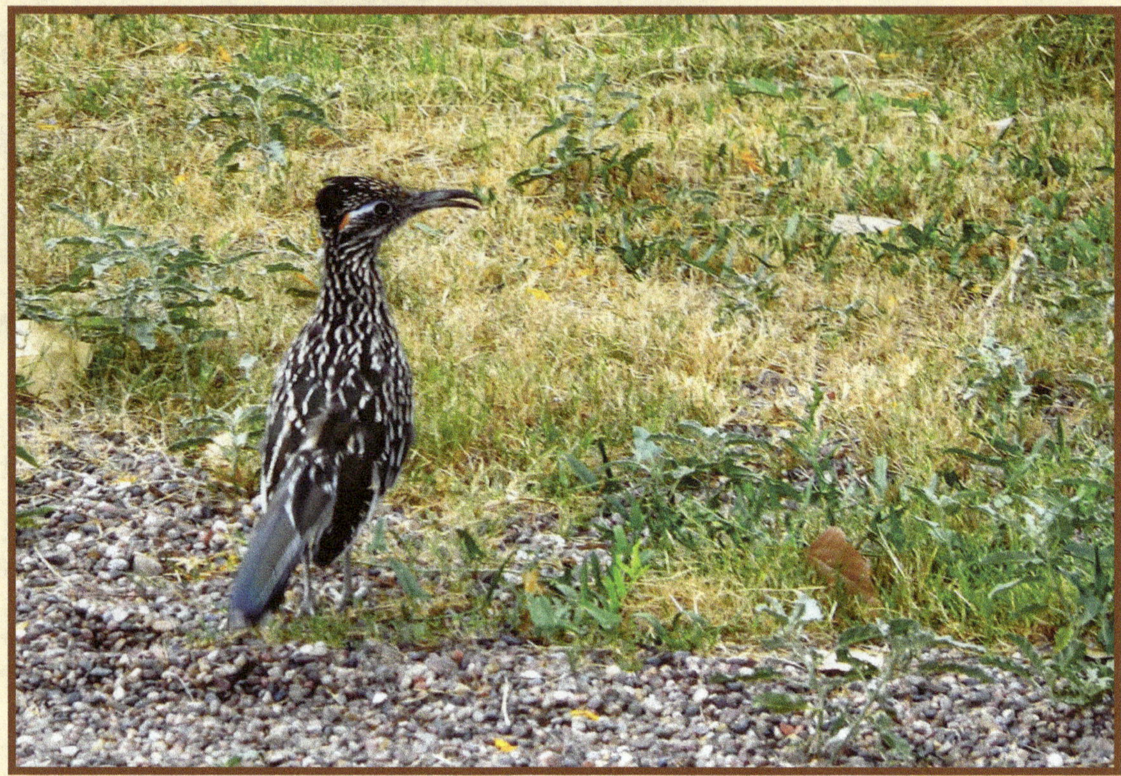

A young roadrunner stands upright in a neighborhood near the Rio Grande.

The waters of the Rio Grande and its tributaries help sustain the many species of abundant wildlife found in New Mexico, such as the roadrunner. The roadrunner is New Mexico's state bird. It can fly, but prefers to scurry on the ground and can run up to 20 mph. "It is called roadrunner," noted a description in 1869, "from its frequenting the highways along which it runs faster than the fleetest horse; as the outer hind toe is reversible and very flexible, it can be equally well adapted for perching or climbing and for running; when it is directed backward, the bird proceeds by the irregular but vigorous hops and when forward by a smooth running pace." In 1901, the Territory of New Mexico enacted a law preventing killing roadrunners and other birds "regarded as harmless in their habits, and whose flesh is unfit for food; except such as are destructive to orchards, gardens and fields, or crops of fruit, berries or grain."

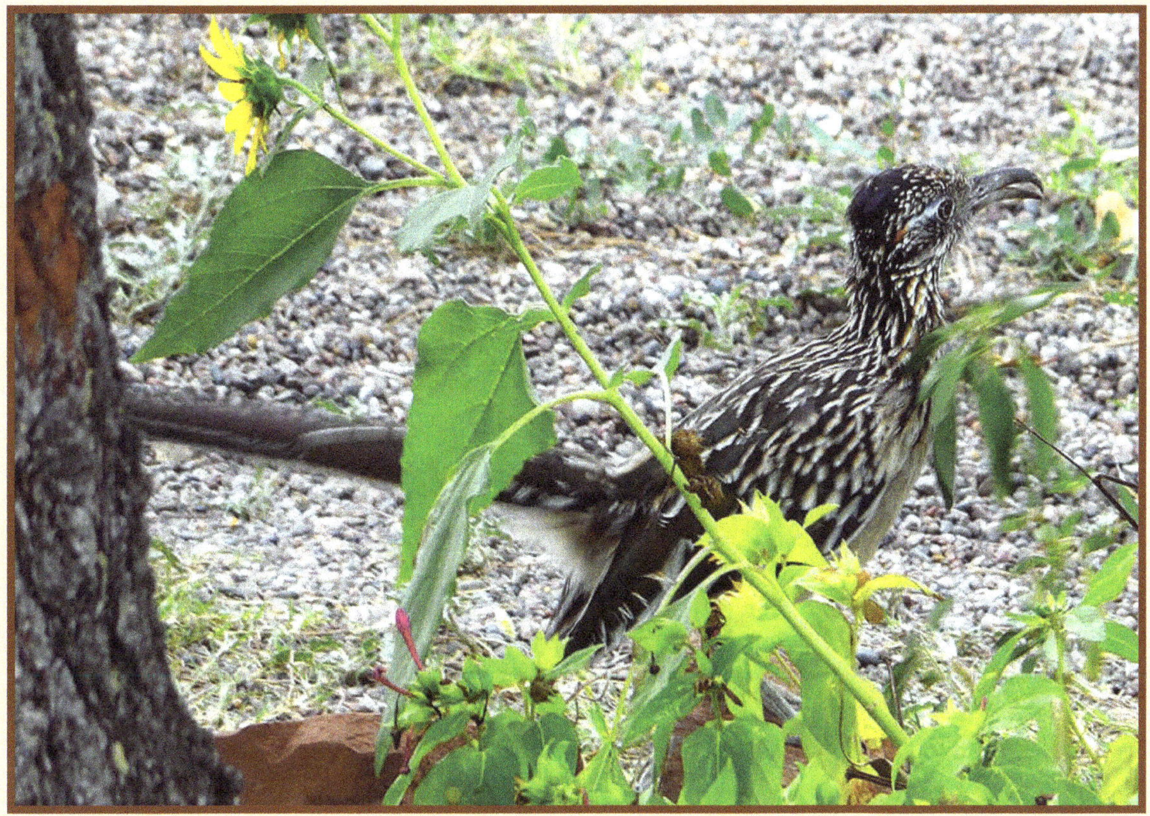

The roadrunner hides near wild sunflowers and raises his tail in alarm while preparing to depart.

This roadrunner, shown here and on the previous page, is known in a local neighborhood as "Junior." He likes to chase birds in people's yards. He also likes to chase cats. The nickname "Junior" was given to him since he was the youngest (and boldest) of a roadrunner family living near the Rio Grande who frequented this neighborhood. Roadrunners were always a common sight each summer when I was growing up. As a child, I could always tell when a roadrunner was nearby because its presence caused the songbirds to shriek in the trees. Roadrunners are carnivorous; they eat rattlesnakes and also hunt for baby birds in their nests. When surprised, roadrunners can jump up to 8 feet and seek shelter in shrubs and trees. Some roadrunners are more social than others. Junior has no fear of people; he will get very close to humans. One day, I parked my car beside Junior and stood near him to take these photos. He didn't mind at all!

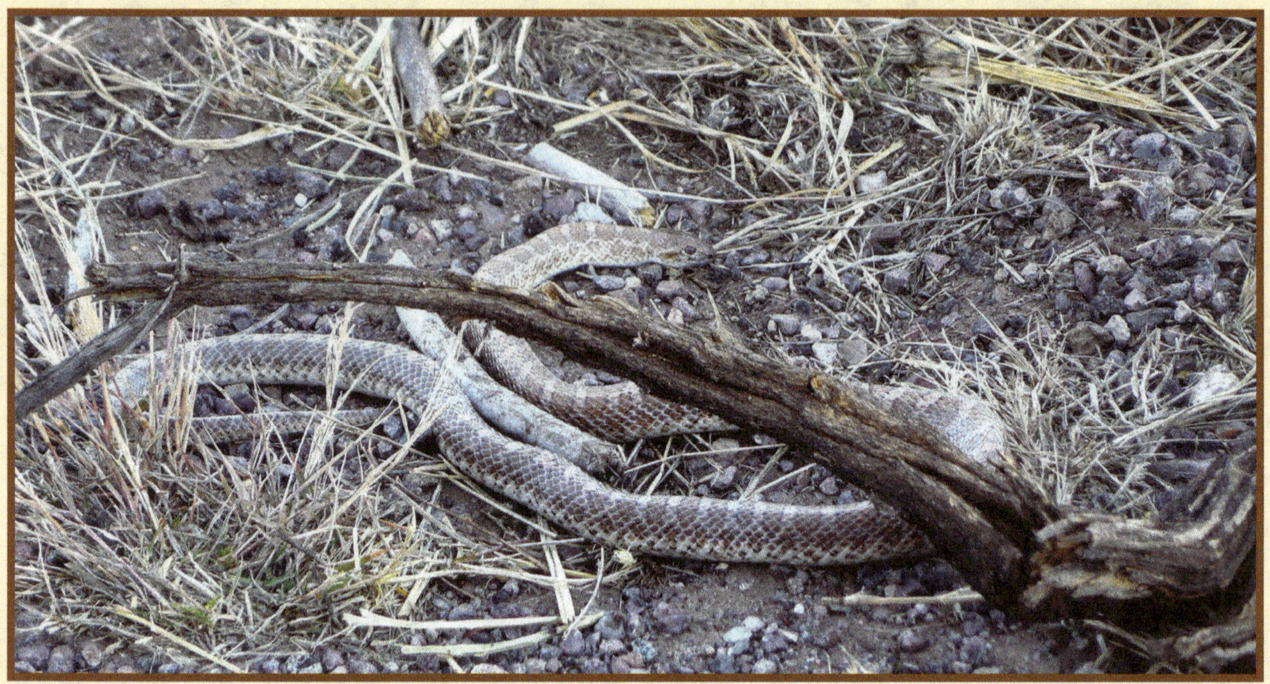

A painted desert glossy snake coils beside a road near Socorro. It is non-venomous. Photo by Zita.

When my daughter and I were traveling through New Mexico, we almost did not see this snake. We would have stepped on it while alighting from the car, had my daughter not spotted it on the ground outside her passenger door.

This photo was taken from the safe vantage point of the car window. Although the diamond-like pattern on this snake's scales might cause it to be mistaken for a rattler, its other features reveal that it was not. In addition to the rattles on their tails, rattlesnakes can be identified by the distinctive triangular shape of their heads.

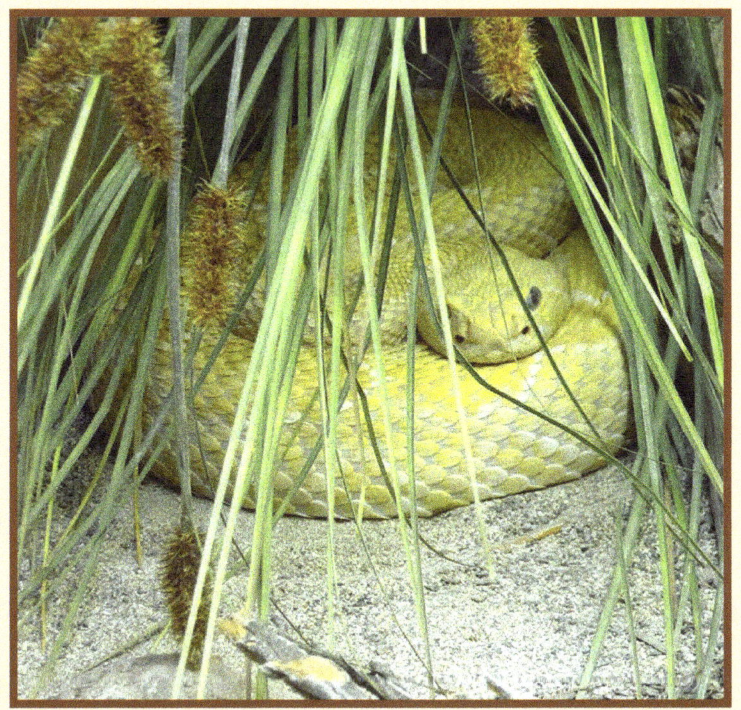

An albino western diamondback rattlesnake coils beneath leaves.

[Note: all photos of rattlesnakes in this book were taken at the Rio Grande Zoo since I have no desire to find rattlers in the wild—and thankfully did not encounter any while working on this book. Moreover, I believe it is equally important to show rattlers in captivity as examples of wildlife found along the Rio Grande.]

Growing up in New Mexico brings with it an awareness of rattlesnakes. My family relied on oral history to share knowledge. The harsh life in the Southwest was much more difficult in the past when people were more isolated, medical assistance was harder to come by, and perils were greater. Knowledge about the desert terrain—and the dangerous snakes that live in it—has been handed down in my family from previous generations. For example, we were warned against going into wilderness areas in the spring when the weather warms up. At this time, rattlers come out of winter hibernation and mating season begins—they will be more agitated and likely to bite. Elders also provided instructions on places where rattlesnakes are likely to sun themselves, have dens, or seek shade. When hiking in mountains during the summer, we benefitted from their shared knowledge. It enabled us to know how to climb without provoking a rattlesnake—to step on the tops of rocks and avoid seeking toeholds at the bases of rocks or crevices where snakes are likely to live. Instruction about desert snakes is even available for dogs. There are snake aversion classes offered for dogs in New Mexico to teach them to avoid being curious about snakes, especially rattlesnakes.

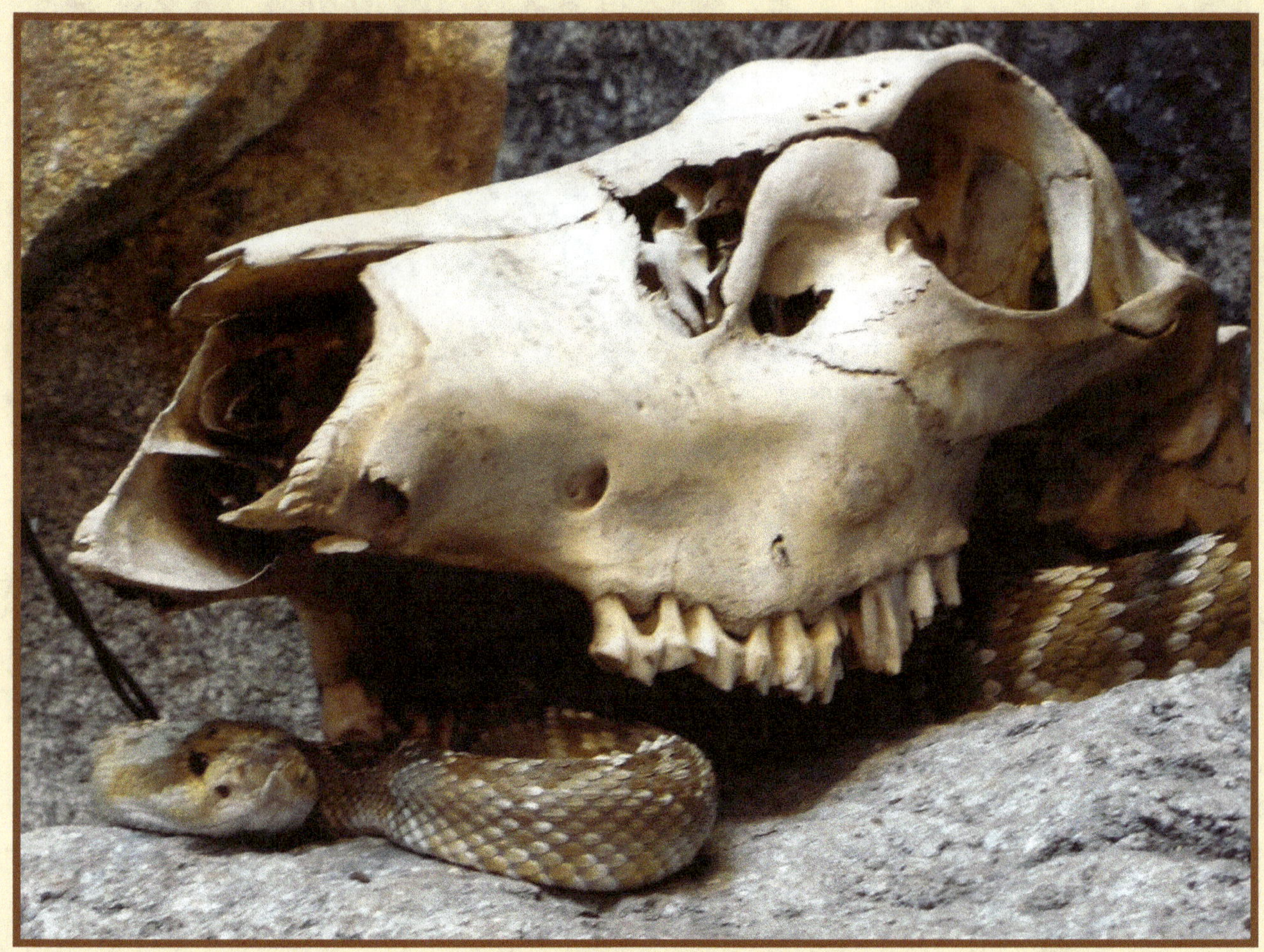

A rattlesnake crouches under a cow skull.

Of 46 snake species found in the state, New Mexico has 7 types of rattlesnakes. These are the desert massasauga rattler, the northern black-tailed rattlesnake, the Mojave rattler, prairie rattlesnake, ridged-nosed rattlesnake, rock rattlesnake, and the western diamondback. Different rattlers have different colored scales (brown, gray, green, pink, red or yellow), which vary depending on their particular habitat.

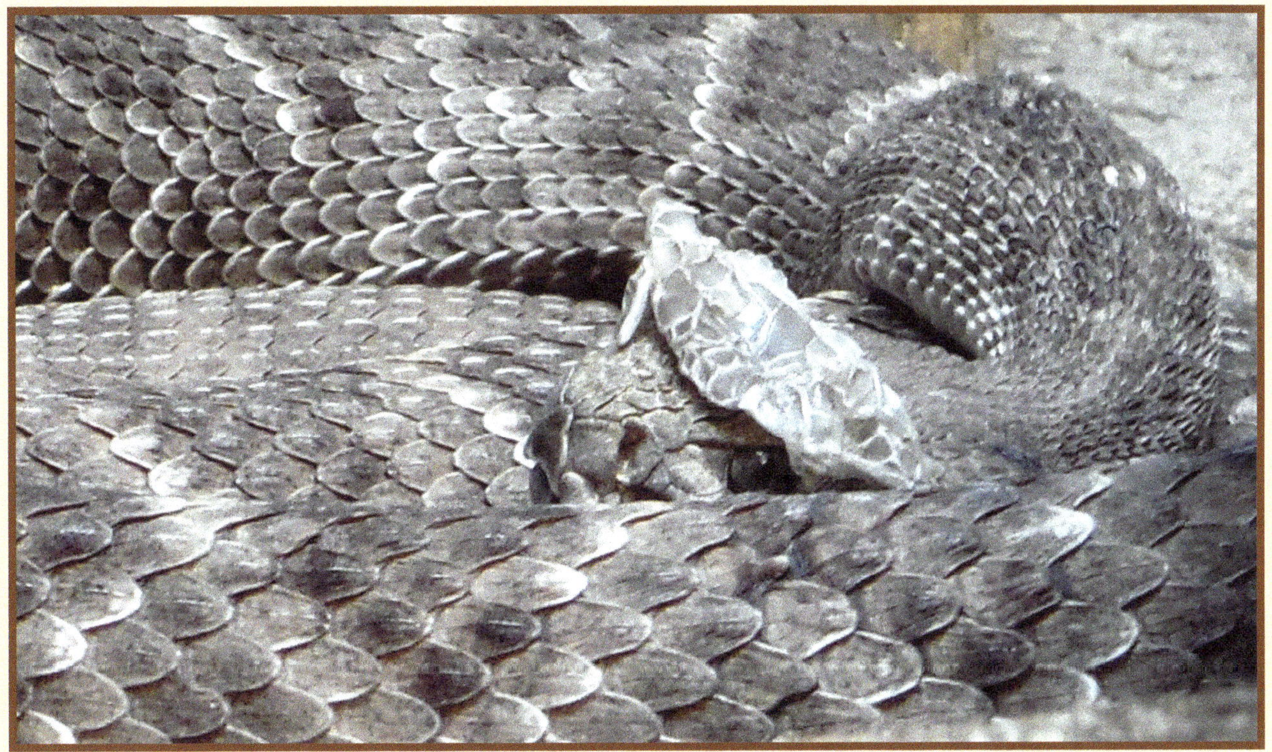

This series of four photos shows a diamondback shedding its skin.

Rattlers shed their skin several times a year, each time adding a new segment to their tails. Among the largest of all rattlers is the western diamondback, which is common throughout New Mexico. It is also the type of rattler that most people are likely to encounter in the state.

The Pereas often came across deadly rattlesnakes on their ranch in Corrales. I remember visiting my great-grandmother, Doña Adelaida. She was a petite slender woman, always dressed in black, who wound her long white braid into a bun at the nape of her neck. Living on the frontier her whole life, she was used to killing snakes and kept a shovel by her front door. She said that a shovel was the best weapon for killing snakes because of its weight and sharp edges. Shortly before her death at age 86, she found a rattler outside her adobe home and chopped its head off with the shovel.

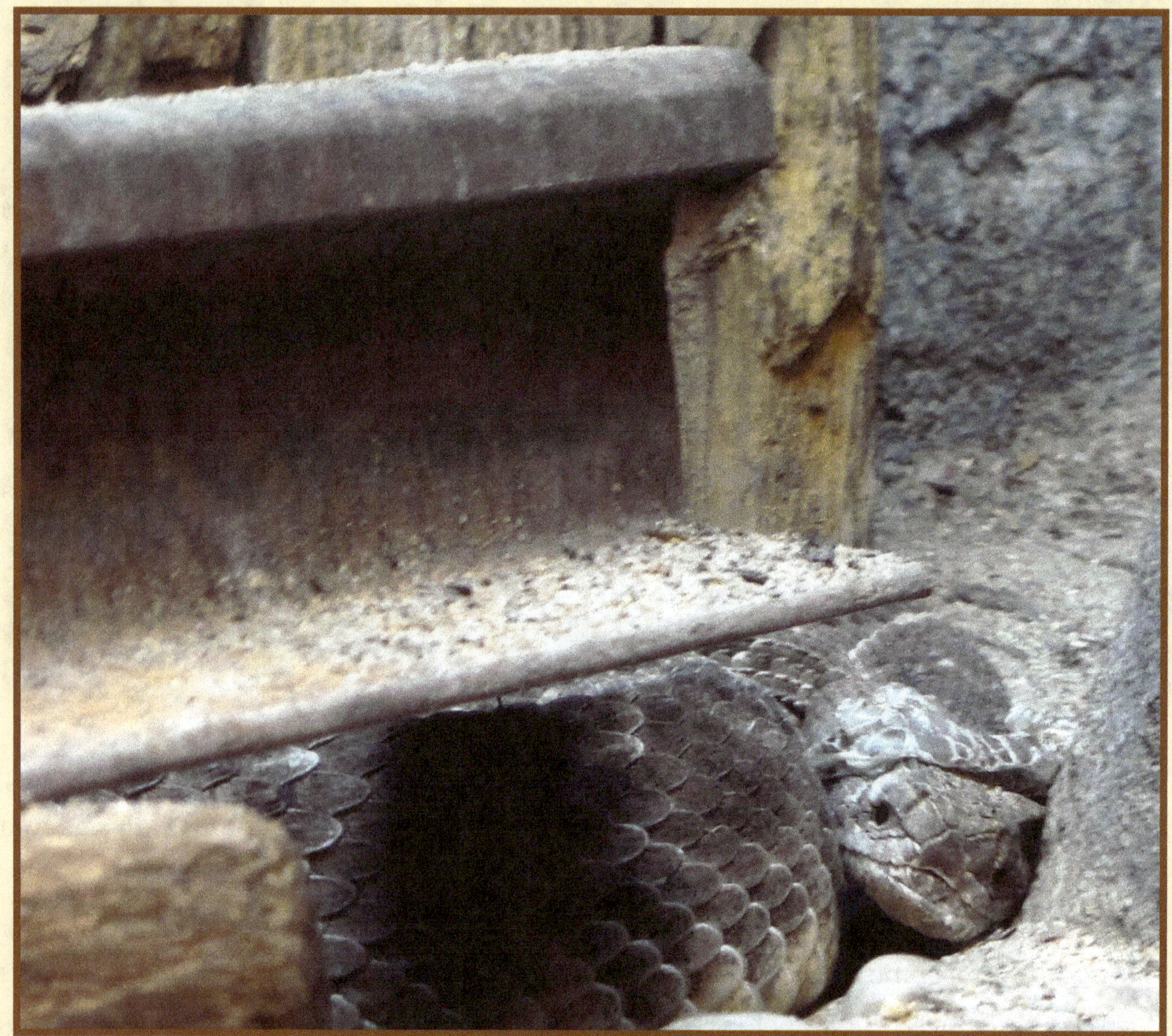

The rattler tries to remove the dried skin by rubbing its head against a wall inside its cage.

According to the New Mexico Dept. of Game and Fish, rattlesnakes can detect the heat of a candle from as far as 30 feet away. They are deaf, but feel ground vibrations. Also, young rattlesnakes are born live since eggs hatch within the bodies of adult snakes.

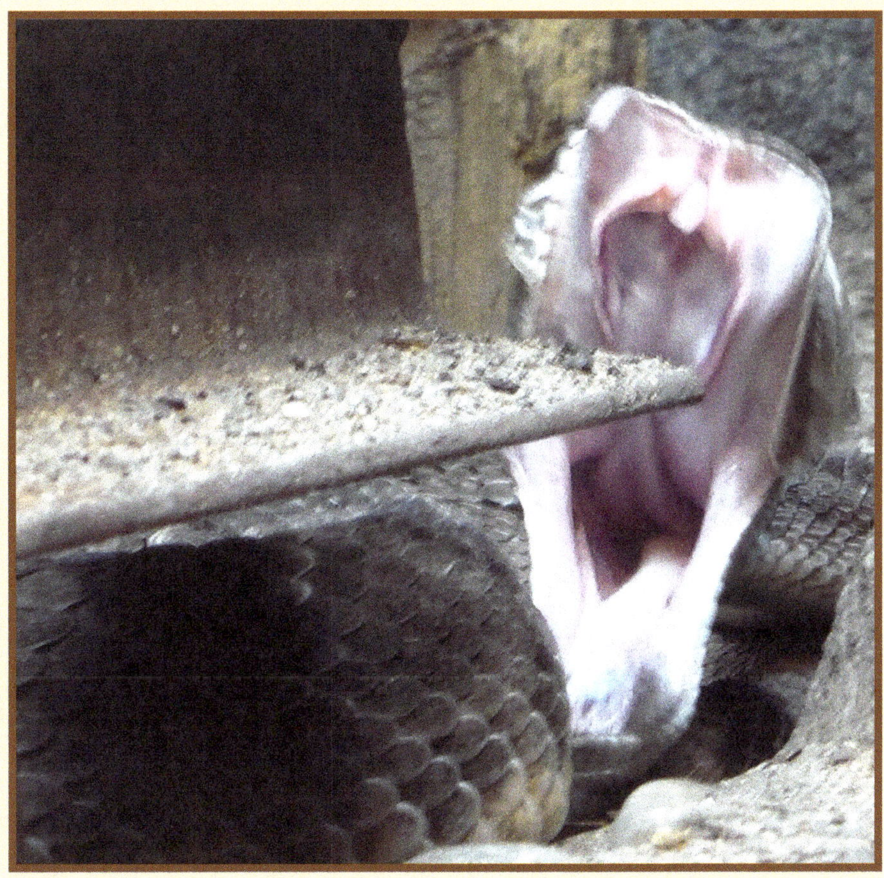

This rattler opens its mouth.
Photo by Zita.

In addition to shedding skin, rattlesnakes also shed their fangs several times a year. This snake had no fangs evident when it opened its mouth. Diamondbacks are aggressive rattlesnakes that will stand their ground and hunt by ambushing their prey. They can grow to 7 feet long—providing a greater striking distance since they may be able to strike as far away as 2/3 of their total body length. Spanish ranchers in the mountains and on the plains developed a warning system to alert passersby about nearby dangers, such as snakes. While I was a teen, I heard firsthand from my grandfather after he witnessed this custom. He was in the mountains picking piñon (pine nuts) one fall. Near a dirt road, hanging from a tree branch, was a huge rattlesnake, missing its head. Ranchers in the area left the dead snake as a warning to anyone coming into the area that such snakes could be found there.

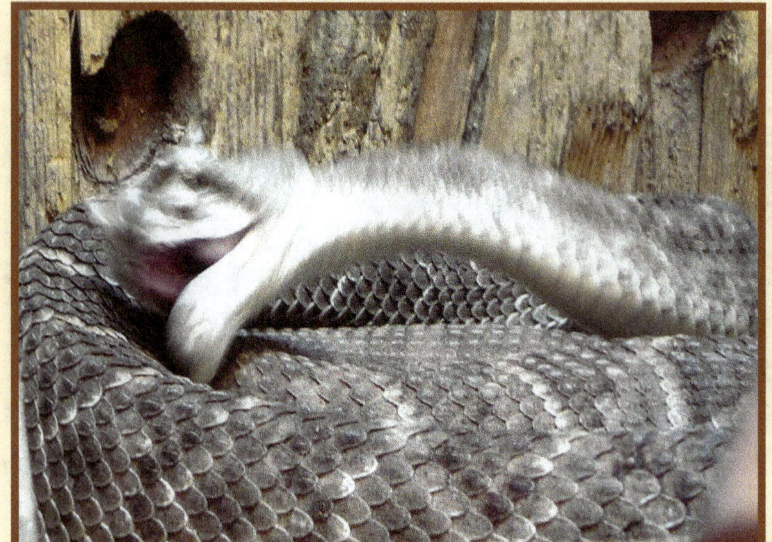

Since diamondbacks are the type of rattler most frequently found in New Mexico, they have a record of biting more people than the other local rattlesnake species.

The rattler squirms around (above) while continuing to try removing its dead skin. The diamondback (below) finally coils after removing the final skin from its head. Photos by Zita.

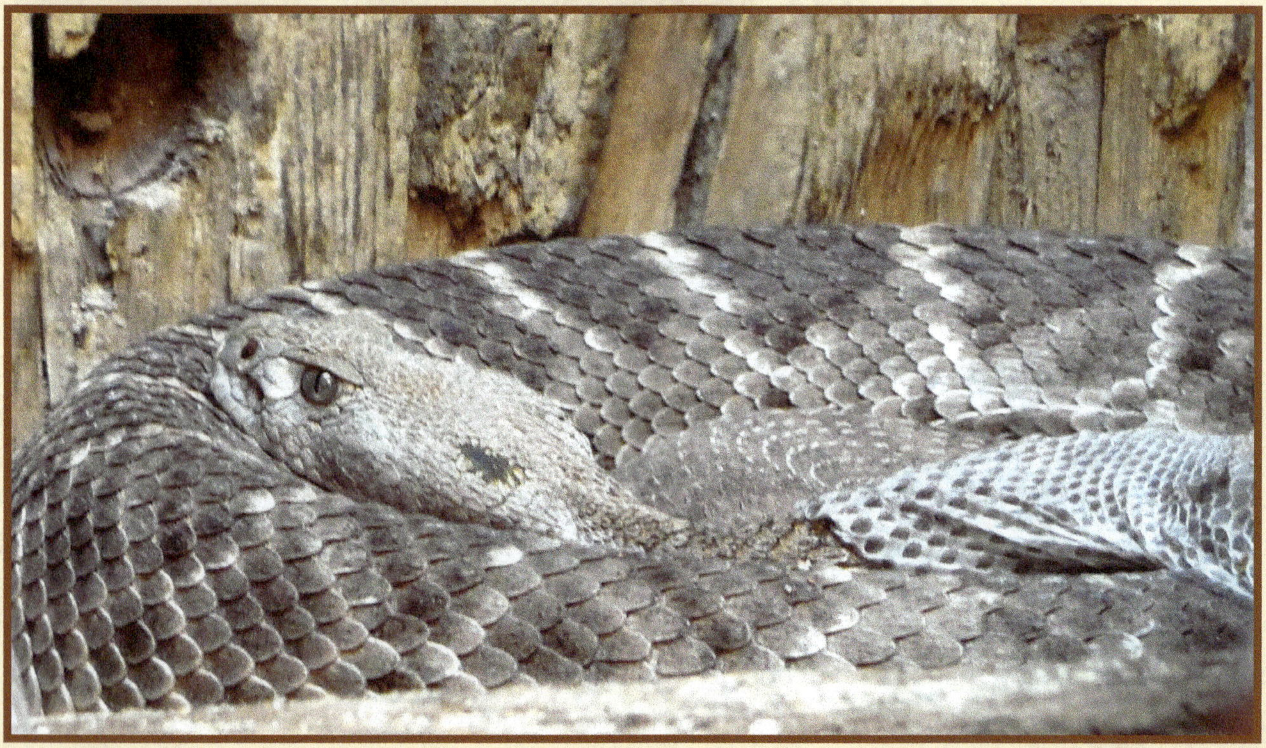

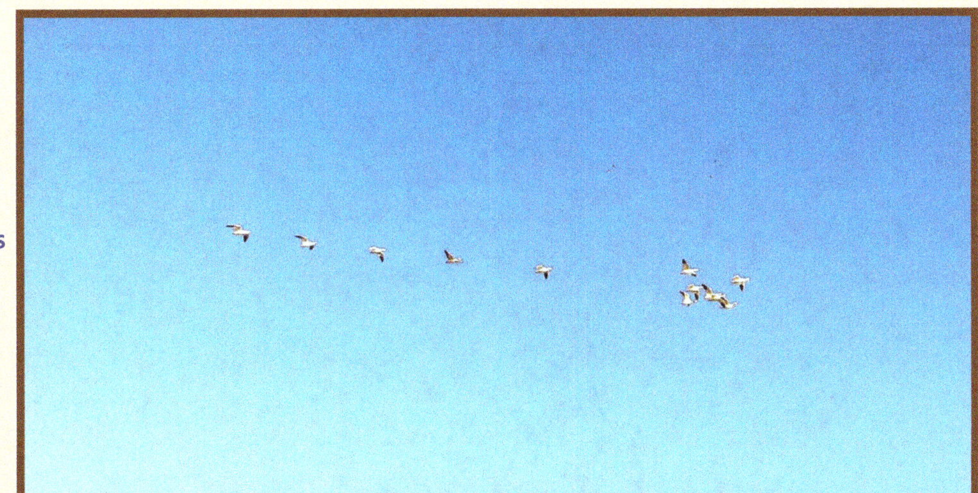

A flock of migratory birds fly over the river one sunny October day.

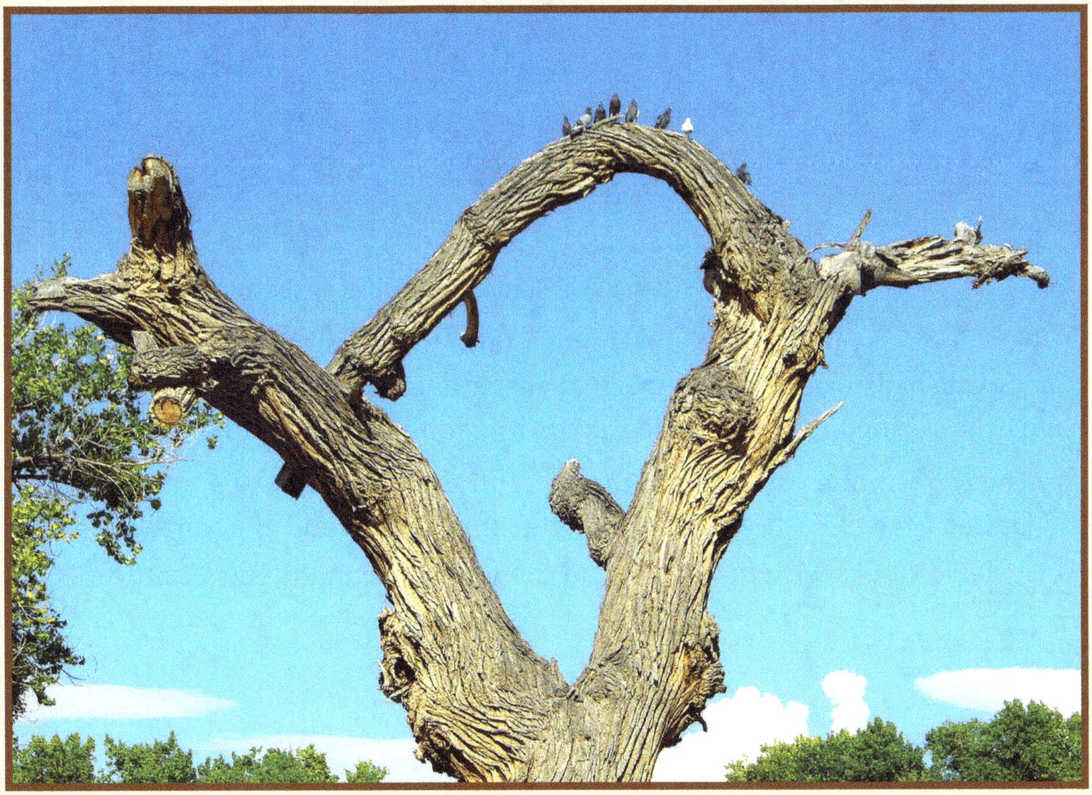

Several birds gather atop an old cottonwood tree near the Rio Grande.

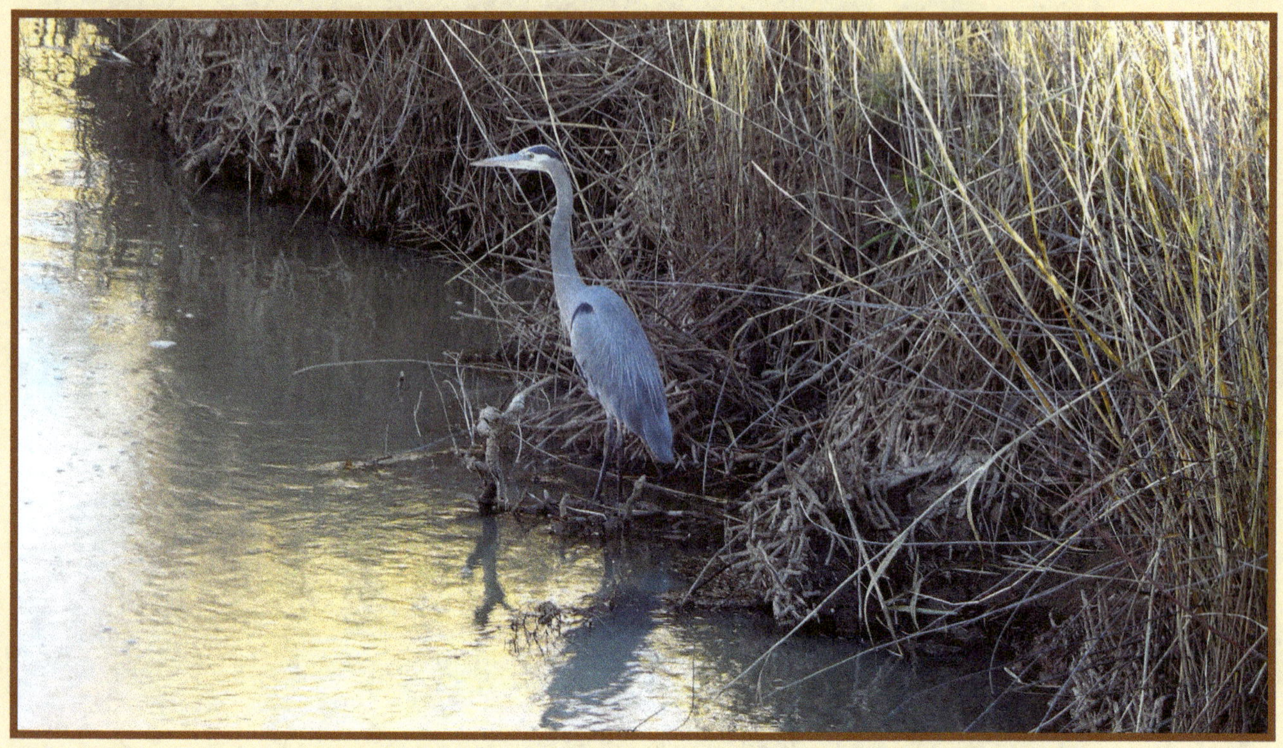

A Great Blue Heron stalks fish in the Bosque.

New Mexico ranks 2nd in the United States for the most varieties of birds. Reports dating from Spanish historical records in 1540 to as recent as 2013 show that nearly 540 species of birds have been verified in New Mexico, according to the state Ornithological Society.

The Rio Grande passes through the Central Flyway, one of 4 migratory bird pathways in the United States. Each year, waterfowl from Canada and the northern United States fly to New Mexico and seek a place to spend the winter along the Rio Grande.

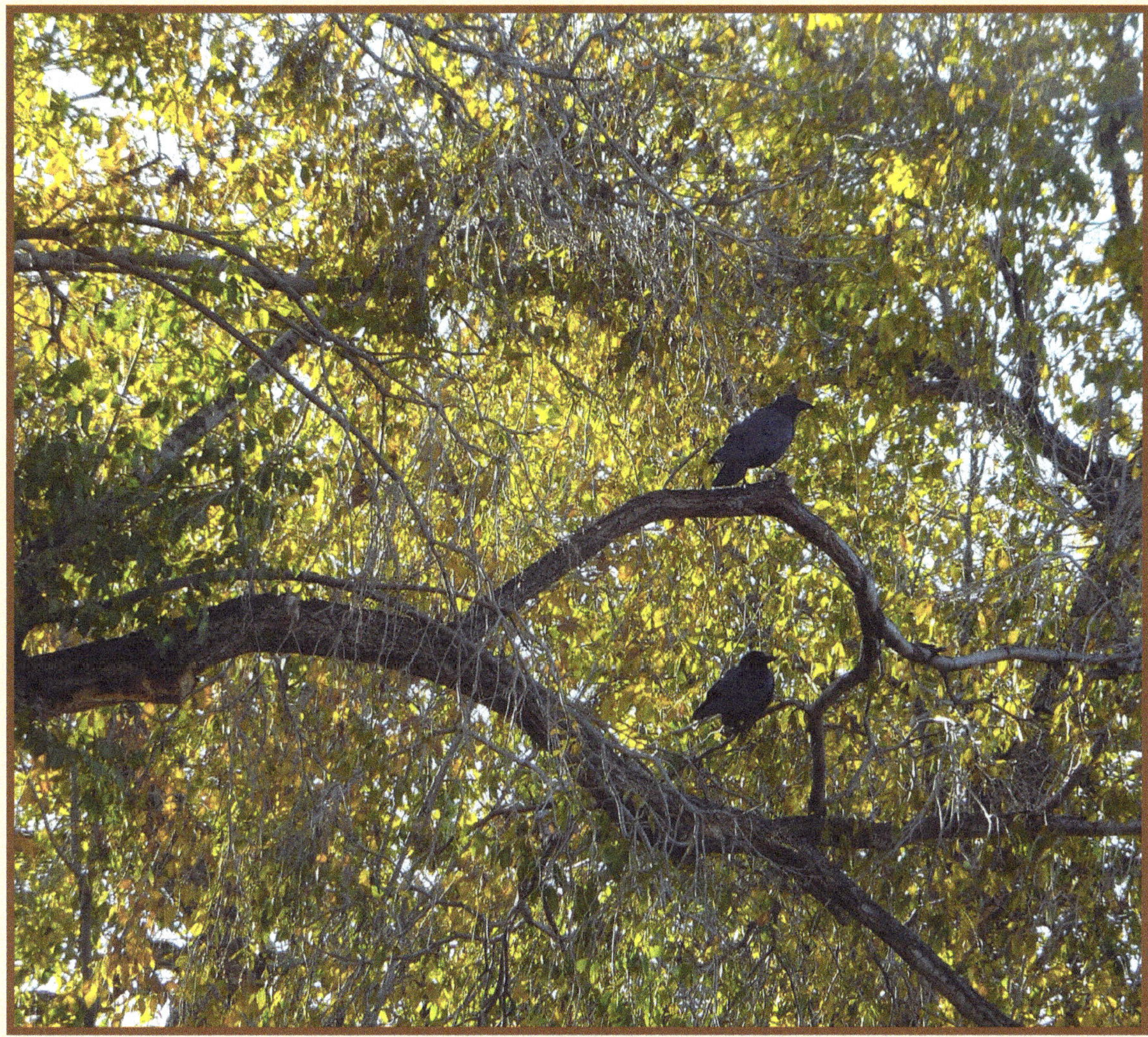

Crows perch in a tree near the Rio Grande. Photo by Zita.

In Albuquerque, a heavy presence of crows can be seen by the river. They will fly in greater numbers from the Sandia Mountains to the Bosque during the winter months. This is always a sure sign to locals that colder weather—possibly even snow—will be arriving soon in the city. Although crows are considered a protected bird, some people do shoot at them.

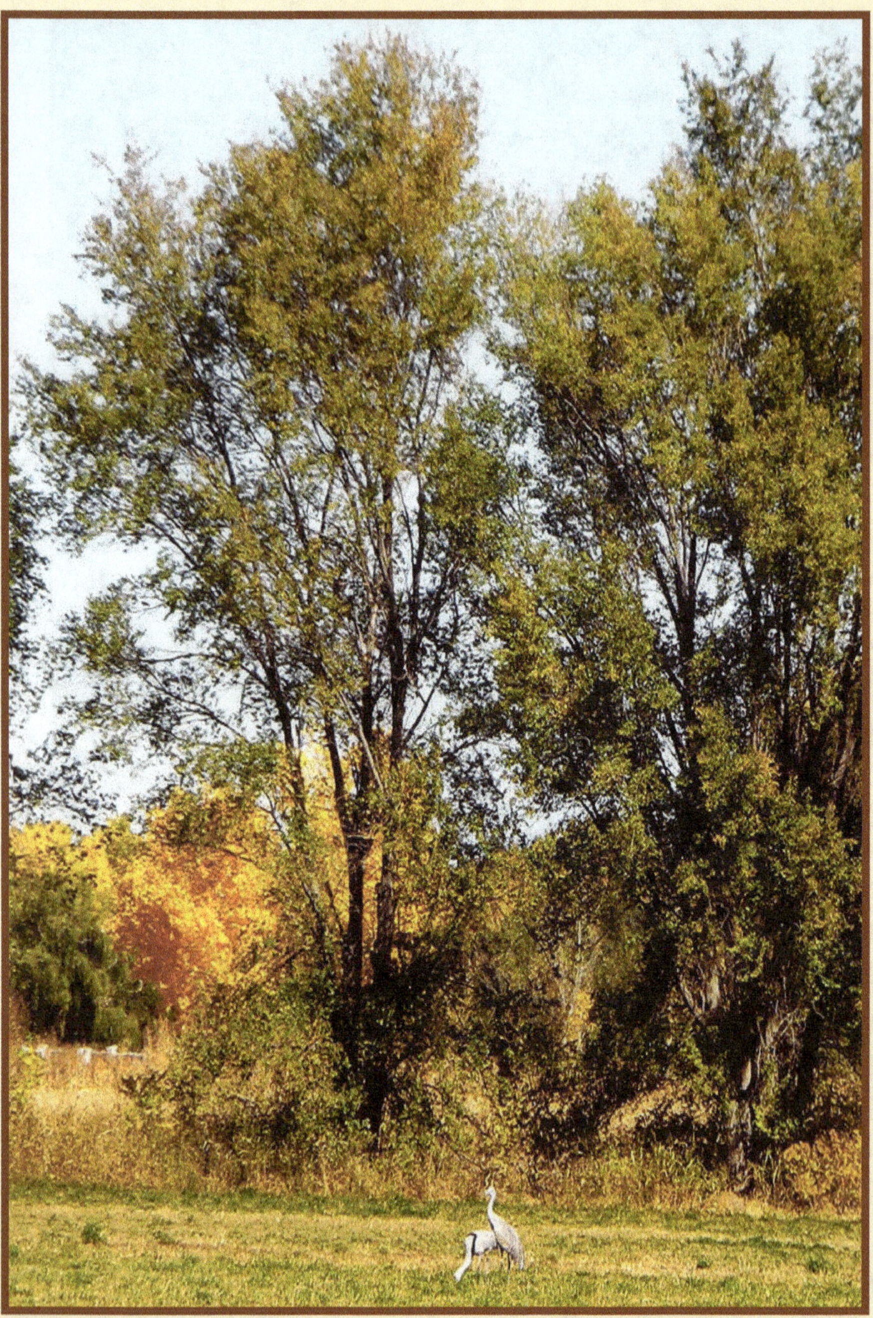

Hundreds of cranes settle around the 138-acre Los Poblanos Fields Open Space area each winter due to its proximity to the Rio Grande flyway for migratory birds.

With a wingspan of nearly 7 feet, sandhill cranes can grow as high as 4 feet tall and can live for 25 years.

Sandhill cranes are supposed to have excellent eyesight—a fact that I can attest to because they proved difficult to photograph.

Each time I spotted them in a field and tried to approach from a distance for a clear picture, they quickly found a way to move out of camera range.

A pair of sandhill cranes stands amid alfalfa in Los Poblanos Fields Open Space next to the Rio Grande.

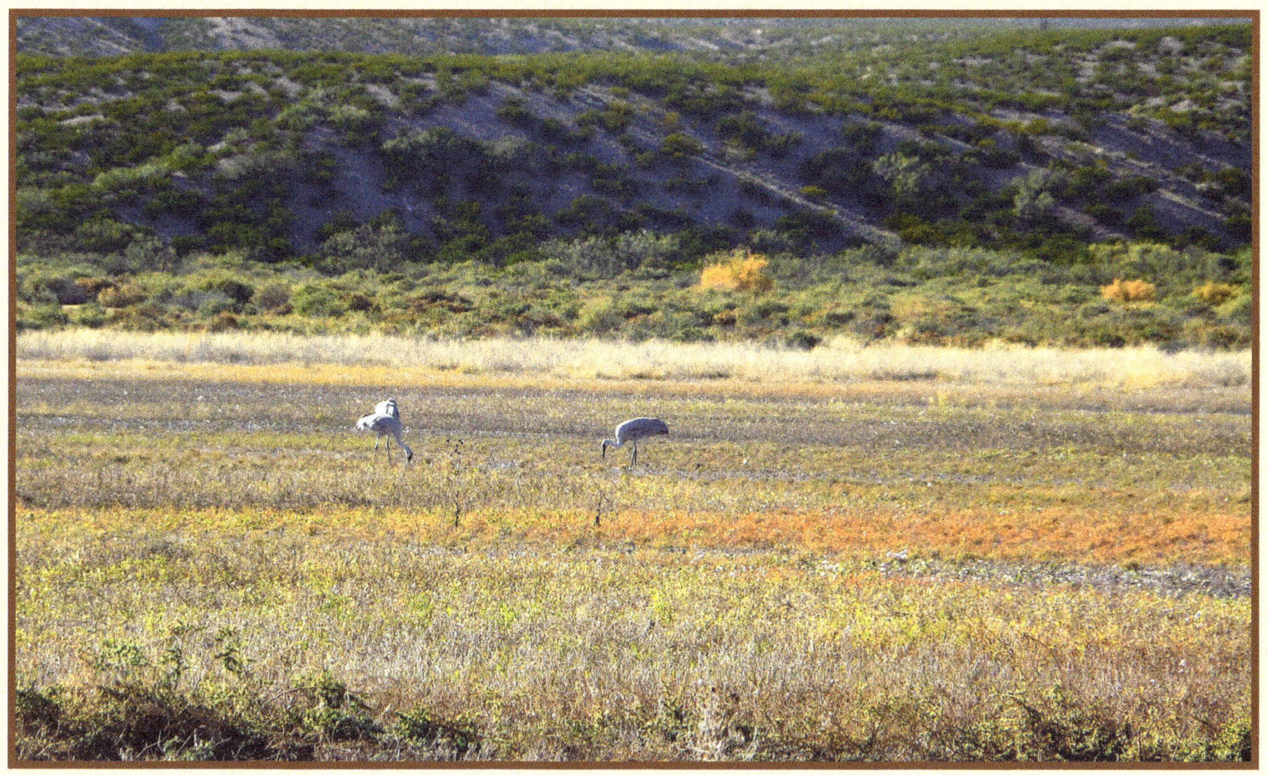

Sandhill cranes search for food in the Bosque near Socorro.

It is estimated that the world's largest concentration of sandhill cranes journey every autumn to New Mexico, where they winter along the Rio Grande Valley. State wildlife officials estimate 30,000 sandhill cranes migrate to New Mexico each year, where they find a warmer winter wetland environment to feed on seed, grain, alfalfa, and other food sources in shallow marshes. Some private landowners complain about sandhill cranes destroying agriculture on their property. In response to these complaints, the state allows hunters to obtain a permit to shoot sandhill cranes roosting and feeding sites on non-public land to encourage the birds to move elsewhere. State officials encourage hunters to use camouflage clothing and blinds because the cranes have such good eyesight. Not all private landowners object to the presence of the cranes. Some take advantage of financial assistance to promote crane conservation on their property.

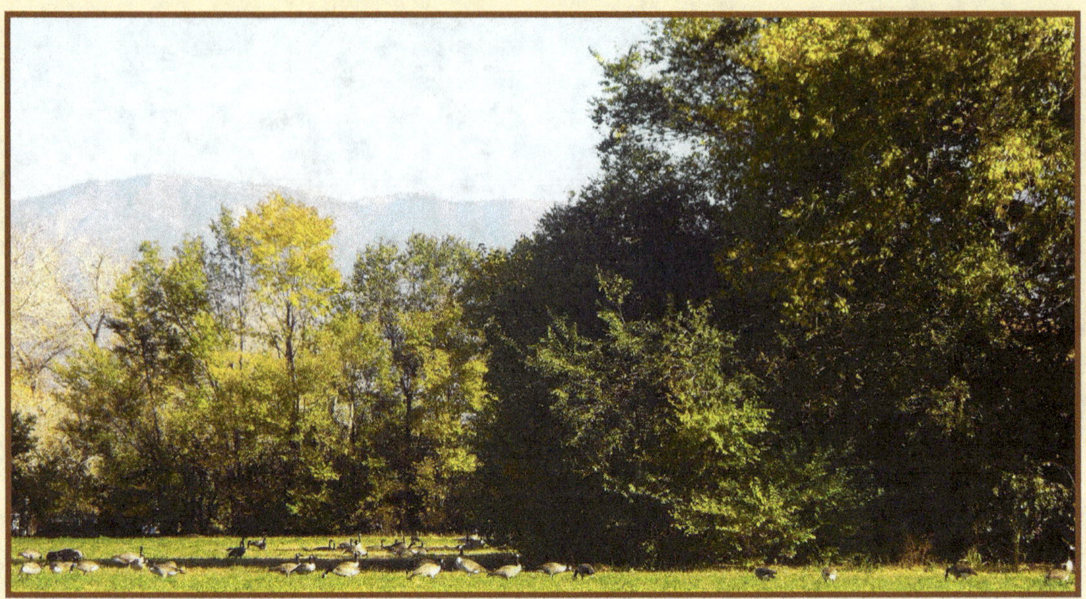

Canadian geese make themselves at home in a field near the Bosque.

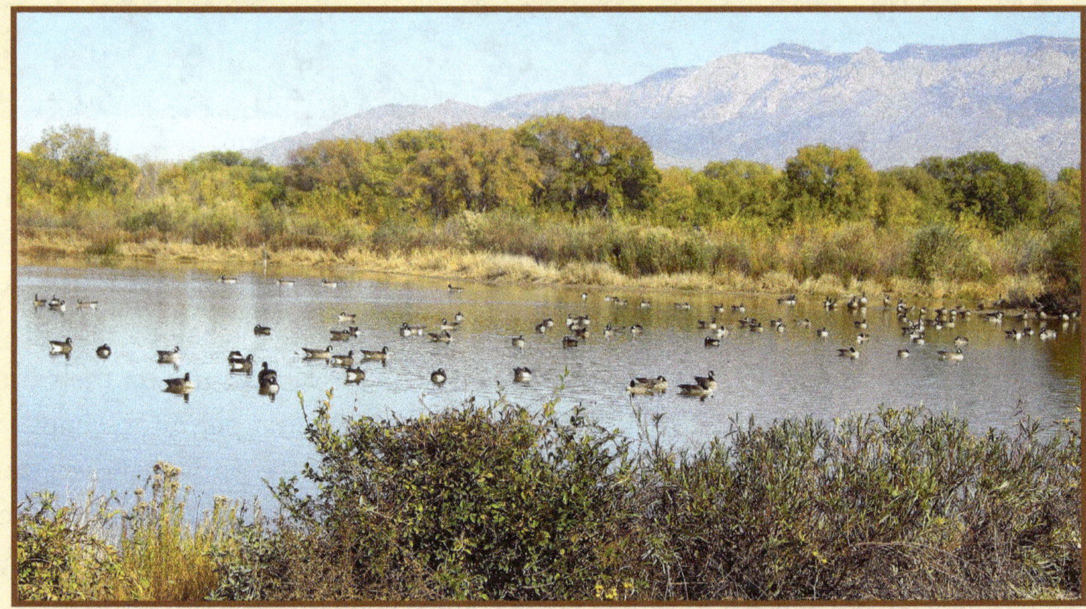

Canadian geese swim in the Rio Grande Nature Center State Park (upper and right).

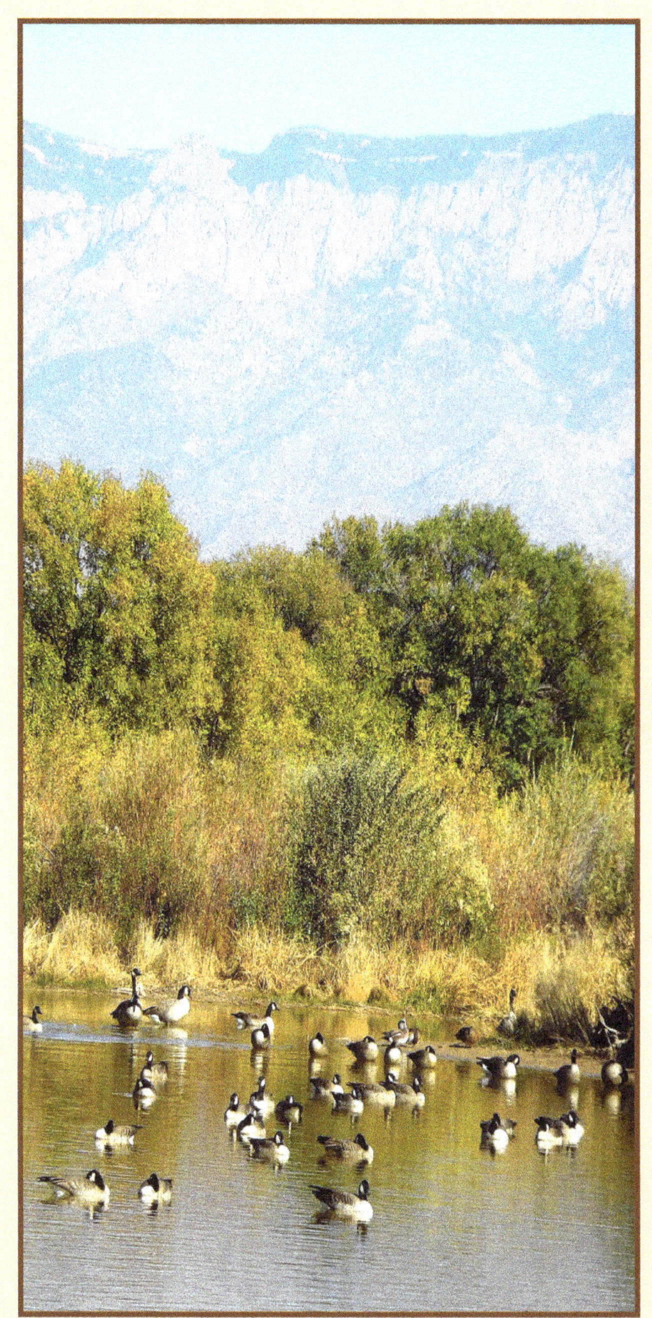

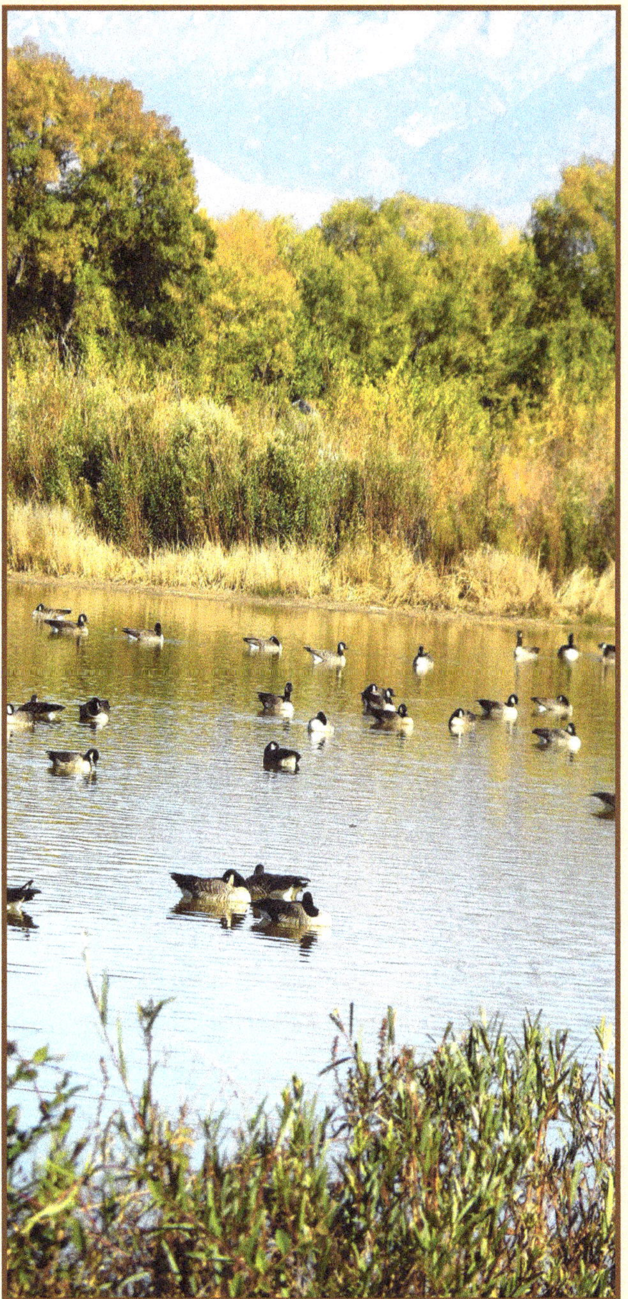

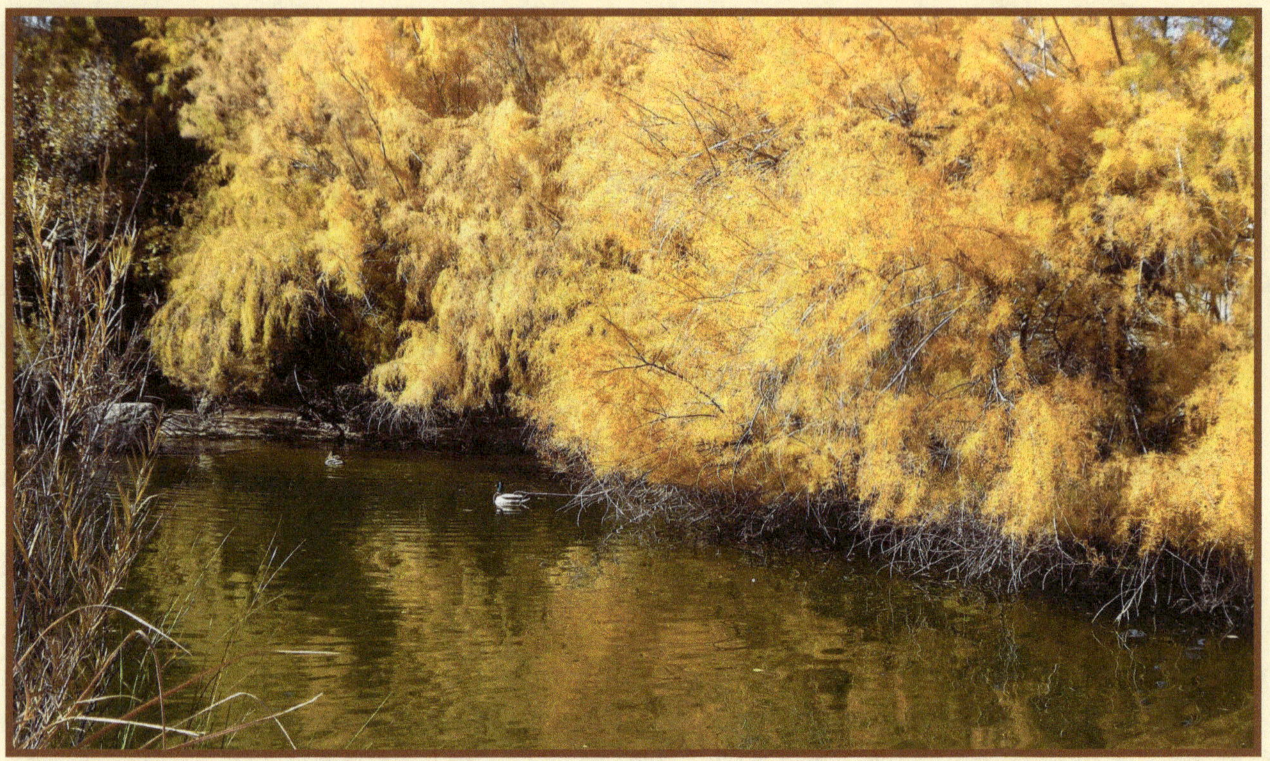

Ducks swim underneath golden salt cedar near the Rio Grande.

Federal, state, and local officials are working to eradicate salt cedar, an invasive species introduced in the 1900s along the river. Also known as tamarisk, the tree poses a fire hazard in the Bosque, especially during drought years, and has fueled several major fires recently along the Rio Grande corridor. Several studies have been conducted about using goats as a cost-effective means to remove salt cedar from river areas.

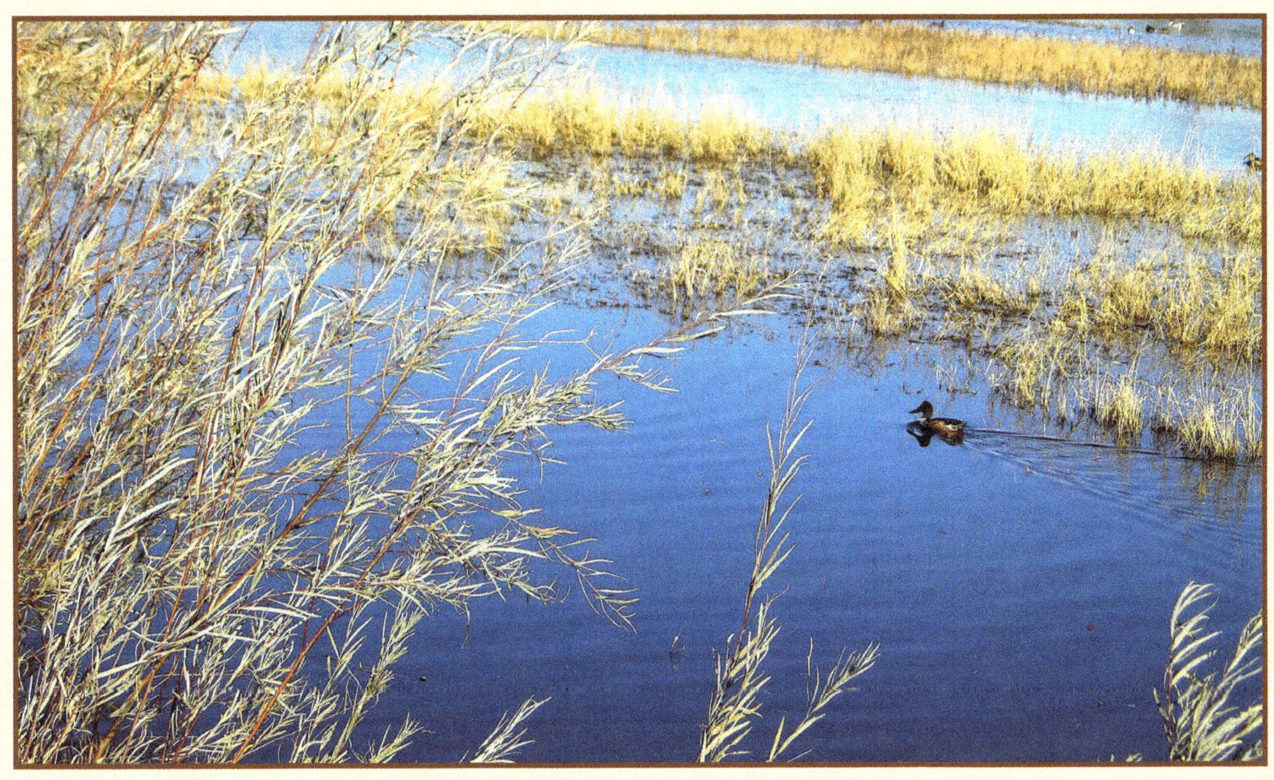

A duck swims in a marsh along the Bosque.

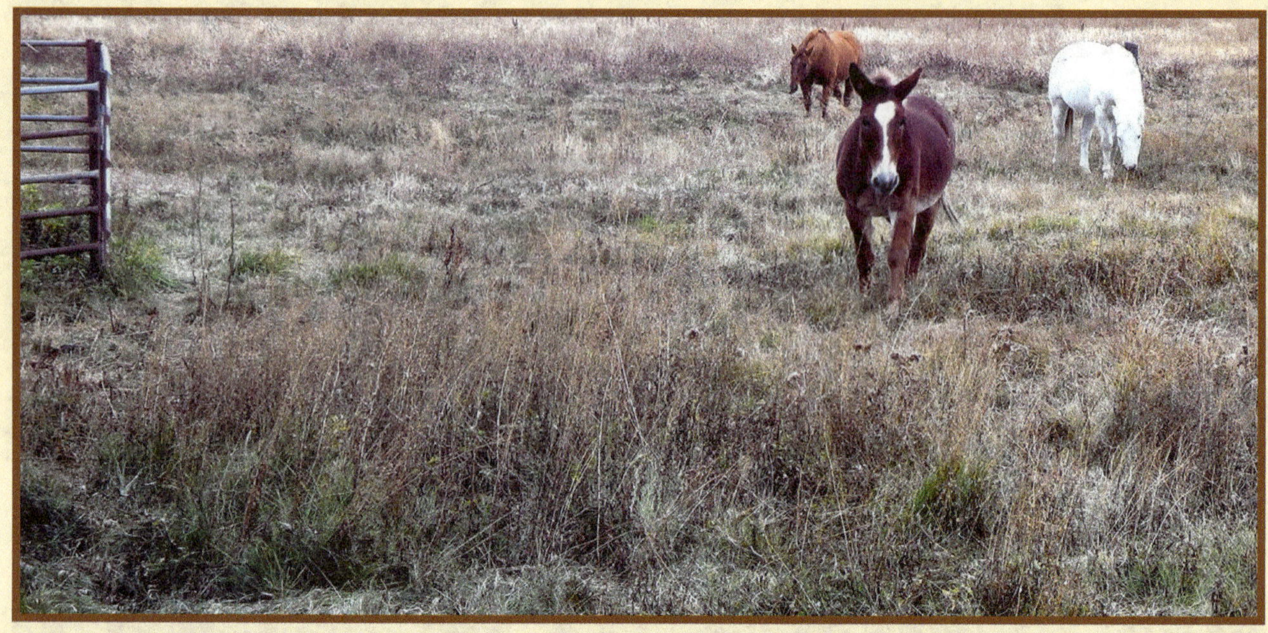

A horse trots over to have his photo taken in a pasture near the Rio Grande in Northern New Mexico. Photo by Zita.

Horses have remained an important part of life along the Rio Grande since the time when they were brought to New Mexico by Spanish conquistadors.

The first horses to arrive in New Mexico came with Cortez. Not until the 1540-42 expedition of Francisco Vázquez de Coronado did a great number of horses, estimated at over 1,000, venture up the Rio Grande during Coronado's famed quest to find the Seven Cities of Gold.

While the explorers wintered near Albuquerque, the first horse race ever recorded on American soil took place in present-day Bernalillo, N.M. in 1541.

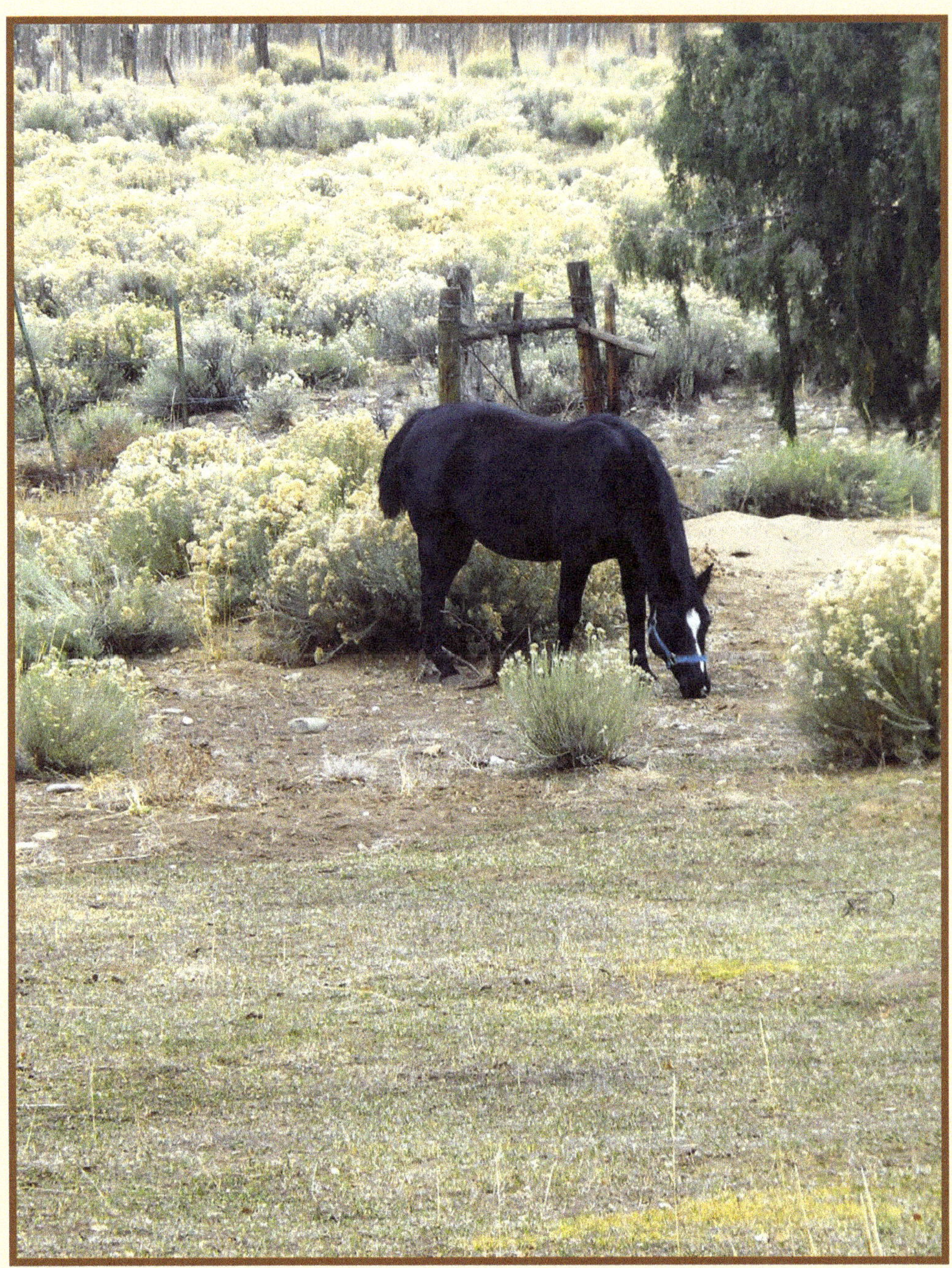

Upon departing the New Mexico area, Coronado left behind some Spanish horses, which roamed the plains and evolved into a breed of wild Spanish Mustangs.

Mustang is derived from the Spanish word *mesteño*, meaning "wild" or "stray".

A horse in northern New Mexico near the Rio Grande Gorge nibbles on wild grass. Photo by Zita.

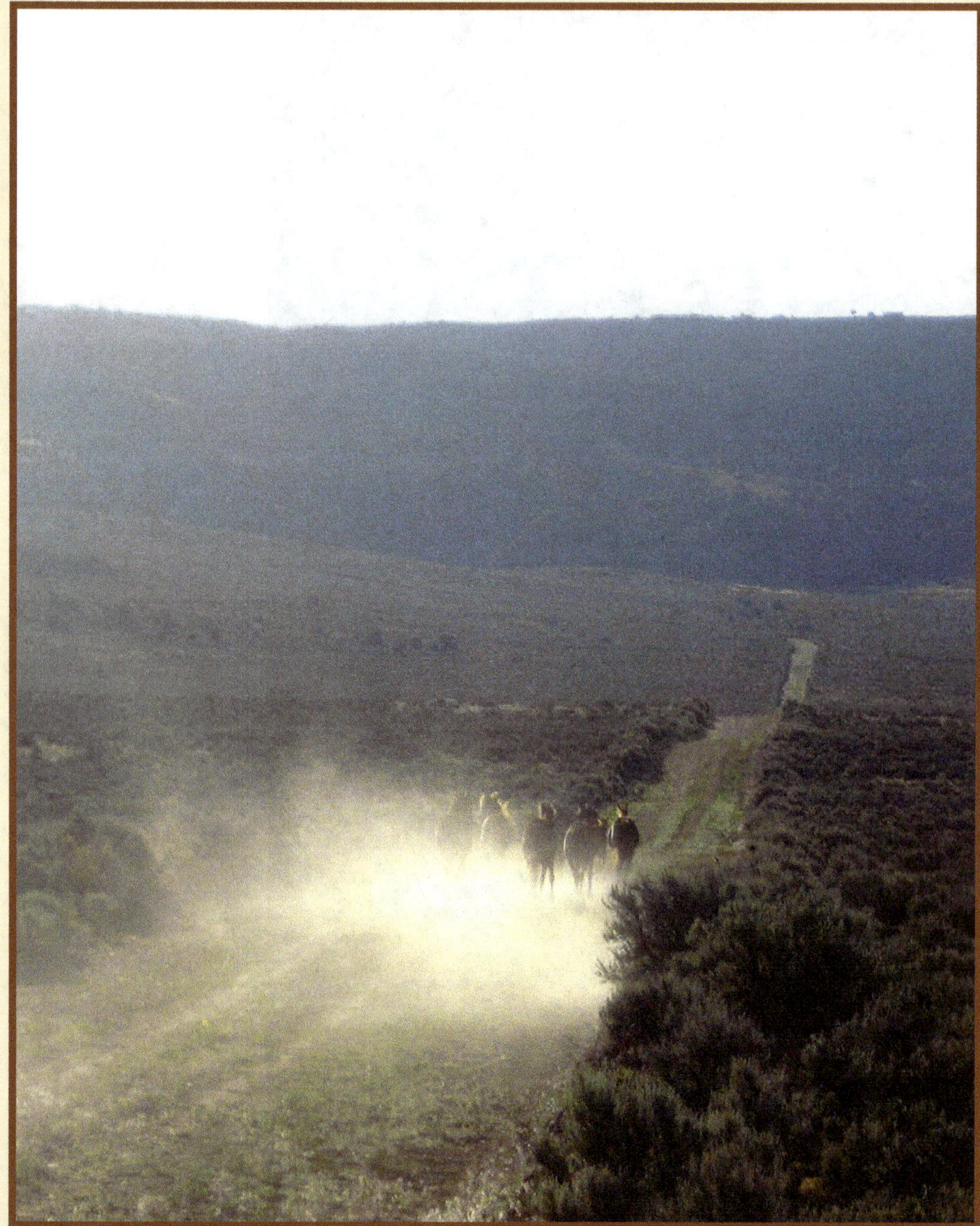

My daughter took this photo of wild horses a few years ago.

The Bureau of Land Management-New Mexico holds an annual program to adopt wild Mustangs and burros.

The horses are adults and yearlings offered for adoption. They mostly have solid colors (bay, black, brown, and sorrel). Some are paints, roans, palominos, buckskins, grays, and albinos.

Photo by Zita.

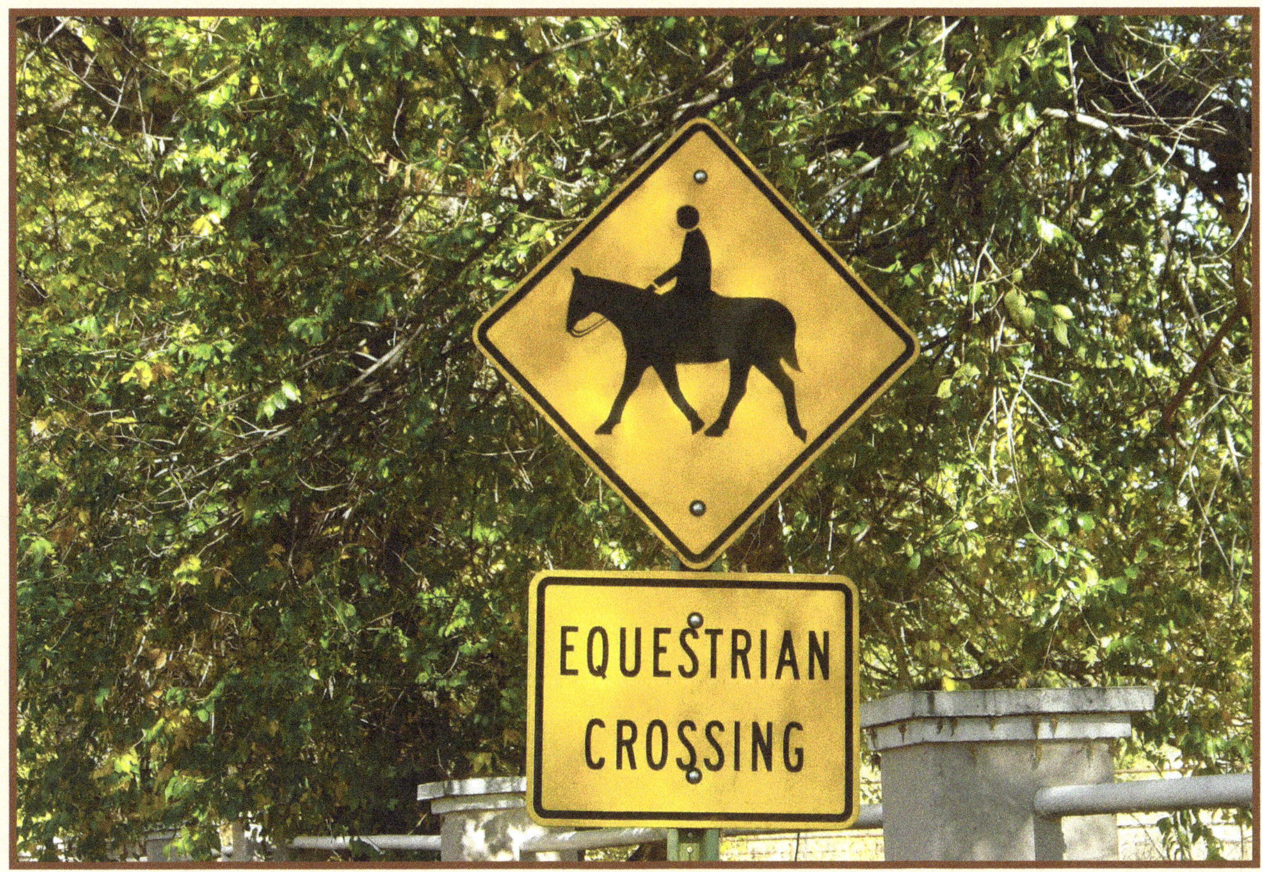

Horses are so numerous in New Mexico it is said there are 17 horses for each person in the state. There are some 100 horse associations, including groups for breeds such as pintos, palominos, Arabians, Appaloosas, Quarter horses, and paint horses. There are also numerous horse rescue groups for abused and neglected animals.

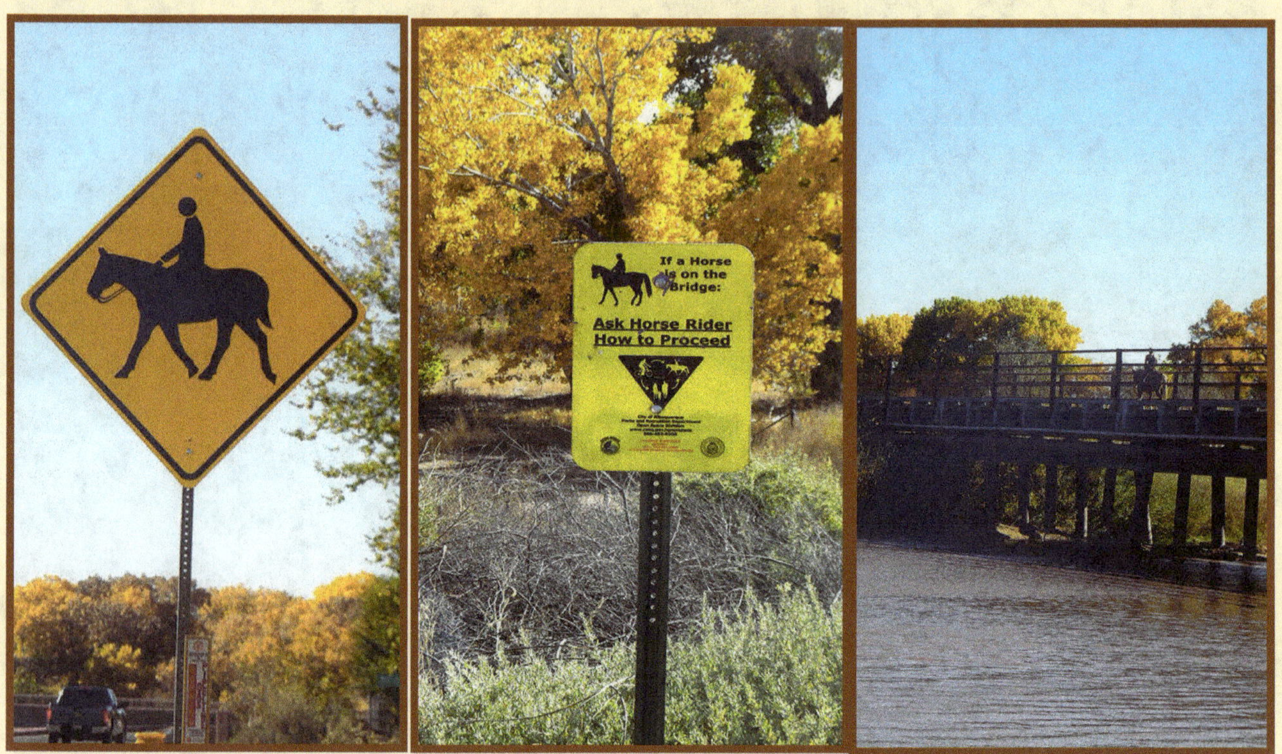

Additional horse traffic signs alert drivers, cyclists, and pedestrians over near the Rio Grande and on bridges crossing the river.

Horseback riding is common along the river, its ditches, and in surrounding areas. New Mexico continues to have an active rural life in its communities throughout the state. Most people on horses wear cowboy boots and ride Western style. Pickup trucks pulling horse trailers are common sights along city roads and on interstates.

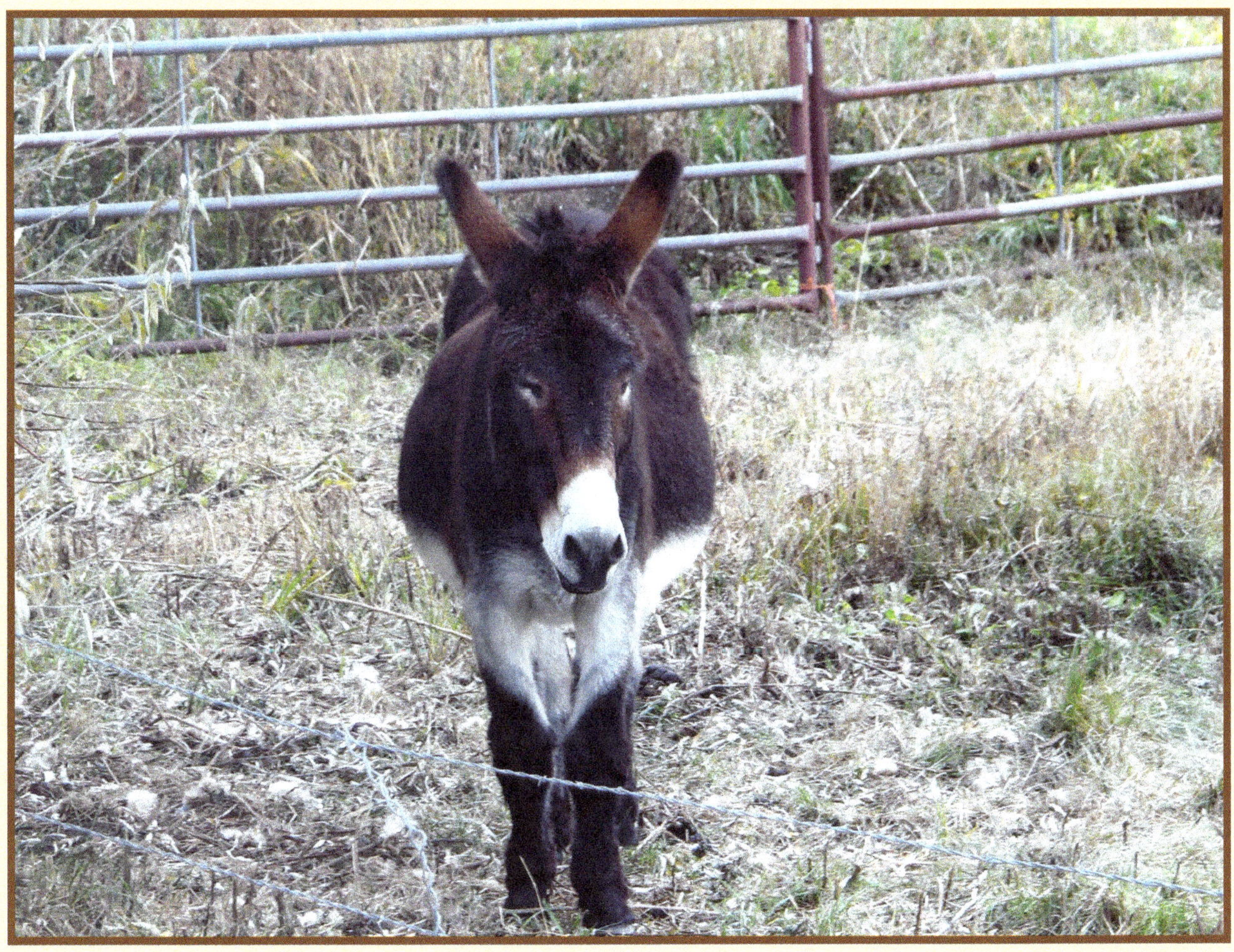

A burro stands in a pasture near the Rio Grande. Photo by Zita.

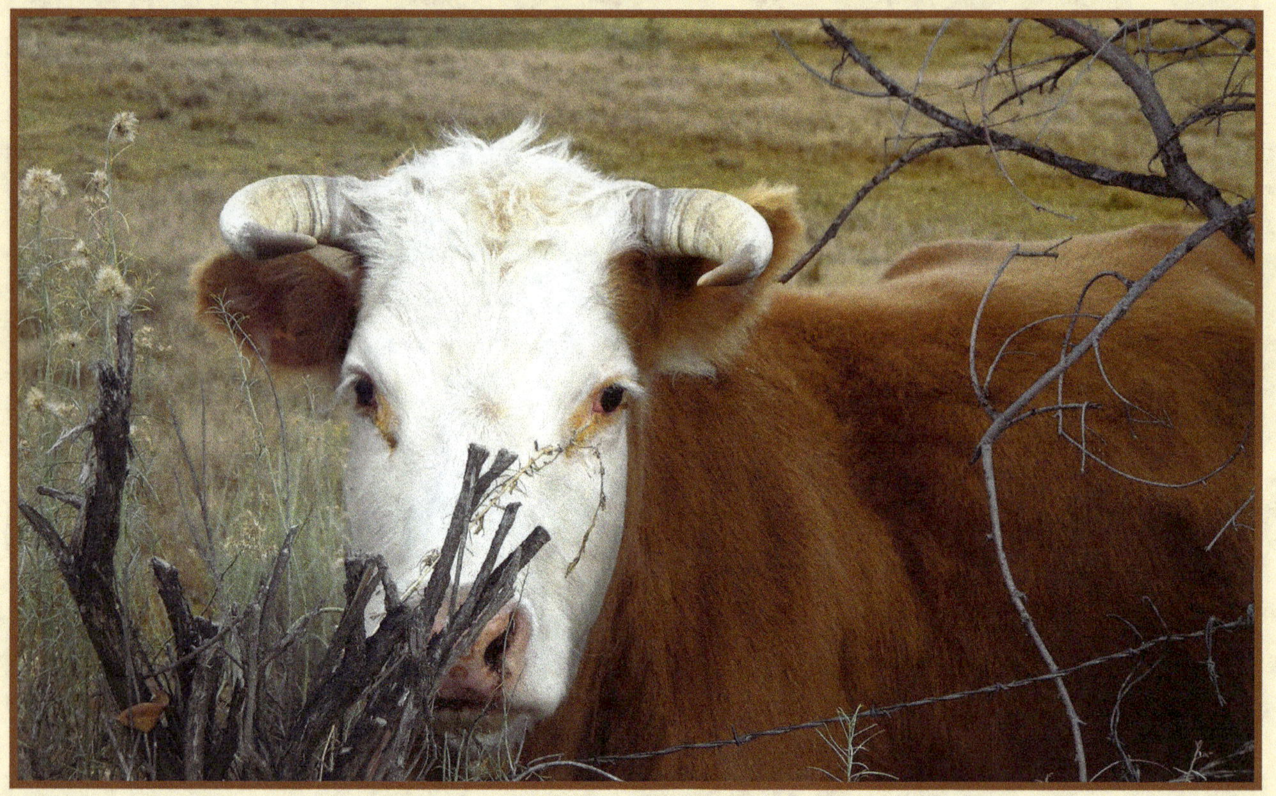

A curious cow peers through a fence near the Rio Grande Gorge.

Cattle also were introduced by Spanish conquistadors to New Mexico. In 1598, Oñate brought a caravan of 83 wagons with over 400 soldiers, 130 families, and 7,000 branded cattle from Mexico into an area near present day Santa Fe. He also is credited with introducing the first hot iron brand for cattle into New Mexico.

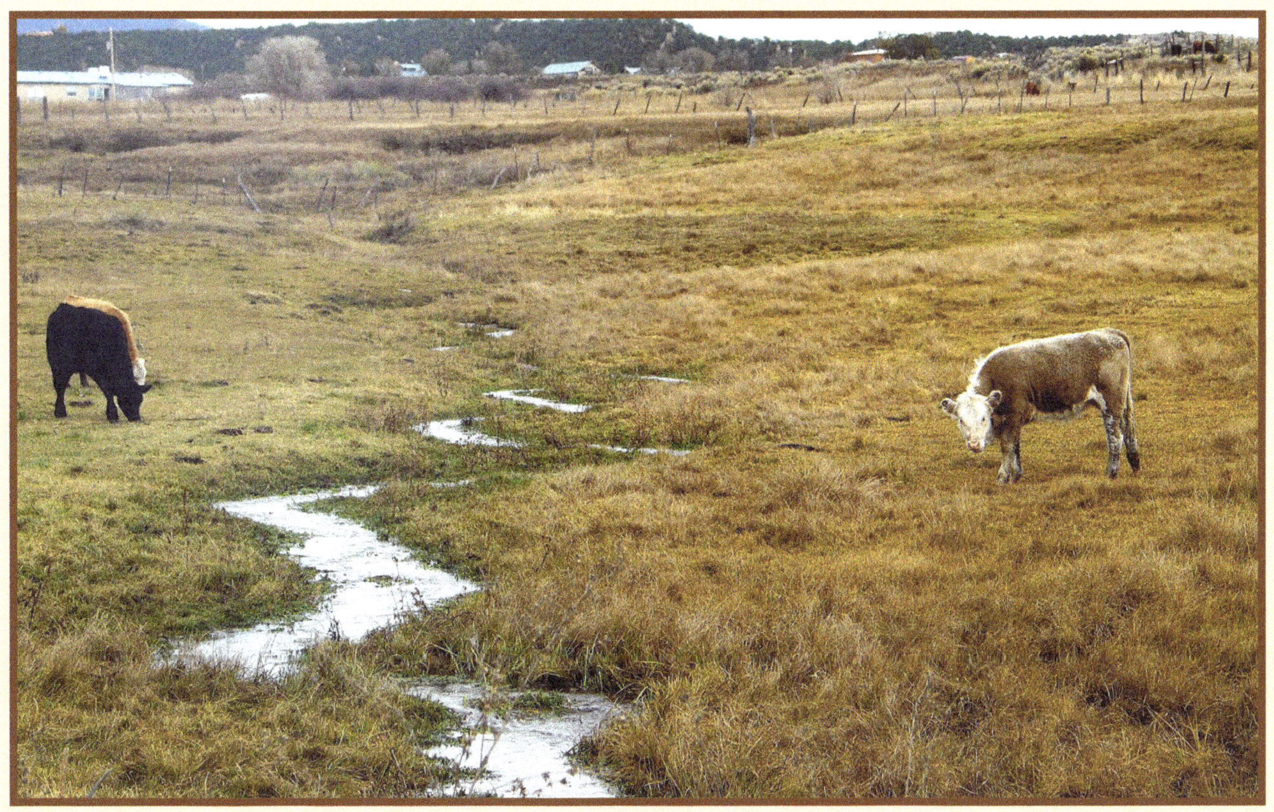

Cattle graze alongside a tributary of the Rio Grande.

The livestock industry accounts for an important part of New Mexico's economy; over 1.5 million head of cattle feed on rangeland and in feedlots.

Protecting cattle also is important. Some 25 years before New Mexico became a state, it had a Livestock Board, which is the oldest government entity. The N.M. Livestock Board has the strictest laws for brands in the United States.

Its inspectors have broad law enforcement powers (similar to the N.M. State Police) to arrest suspected cattle thieves anywhere—an important deterrent for cattle rustlers.

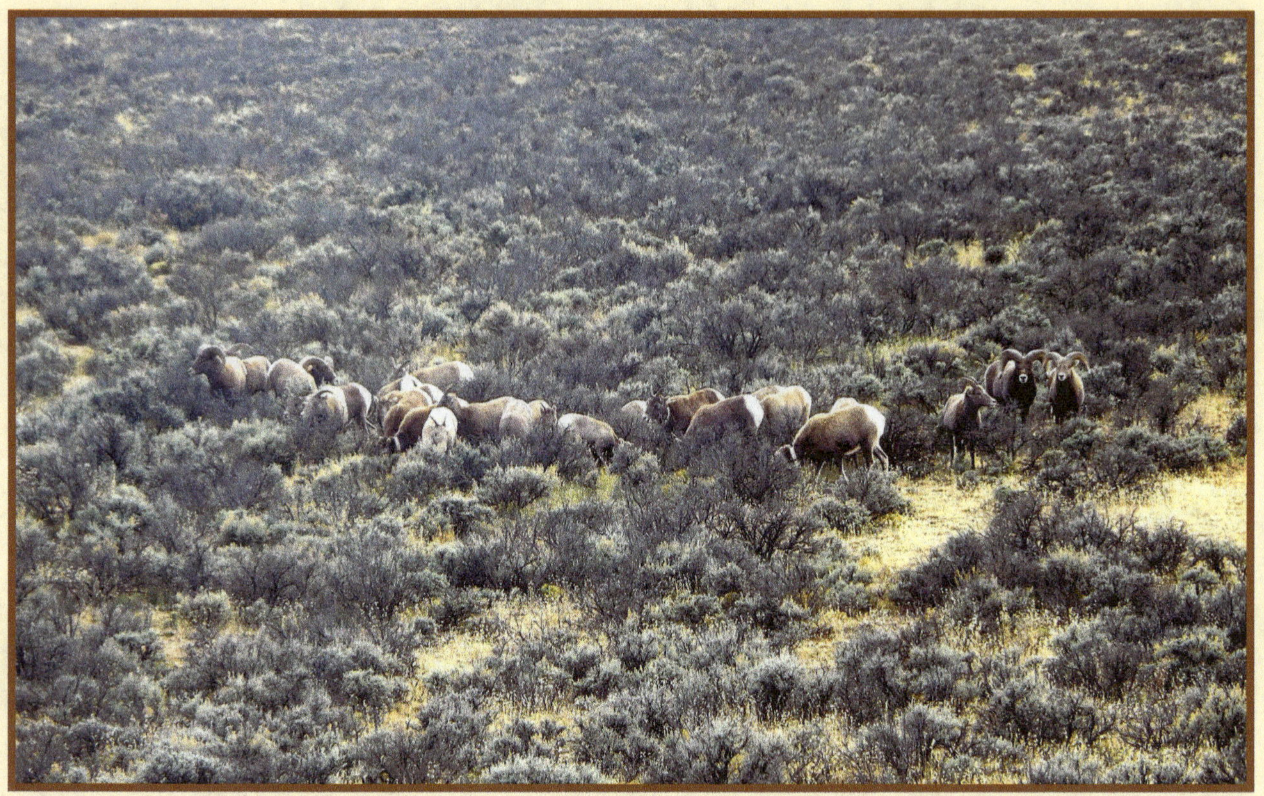

Rocky Mountain bighorn sheep forage among sagebrush near the Rio Grande Gorge outside of Taos, N.M.

Rocky Mountain bighorns live next to the Rio Grande. Bighorns are opportunistic eaters who adapt their diets. In addition to ordinary plants, bighorns eat various types of wild grasses and shrubs. They are social animals that live together and usually remain within 1 mile from a water source. This high plateau overlooking the Rio Grande is among several areas in the state where 350 Rocky Mountain bighorns have been transplanted since 1998 in state and federal programs to increase wild herds and prevent disease among the animal populations. Bighorn populations in New Mexico have dwindled since the late 1800s due to hunting, disease, and habitat loss, but bighorn programs in 20 states have increased the total bighorn population to 75,000 — 5 times more than in the early 1900s.

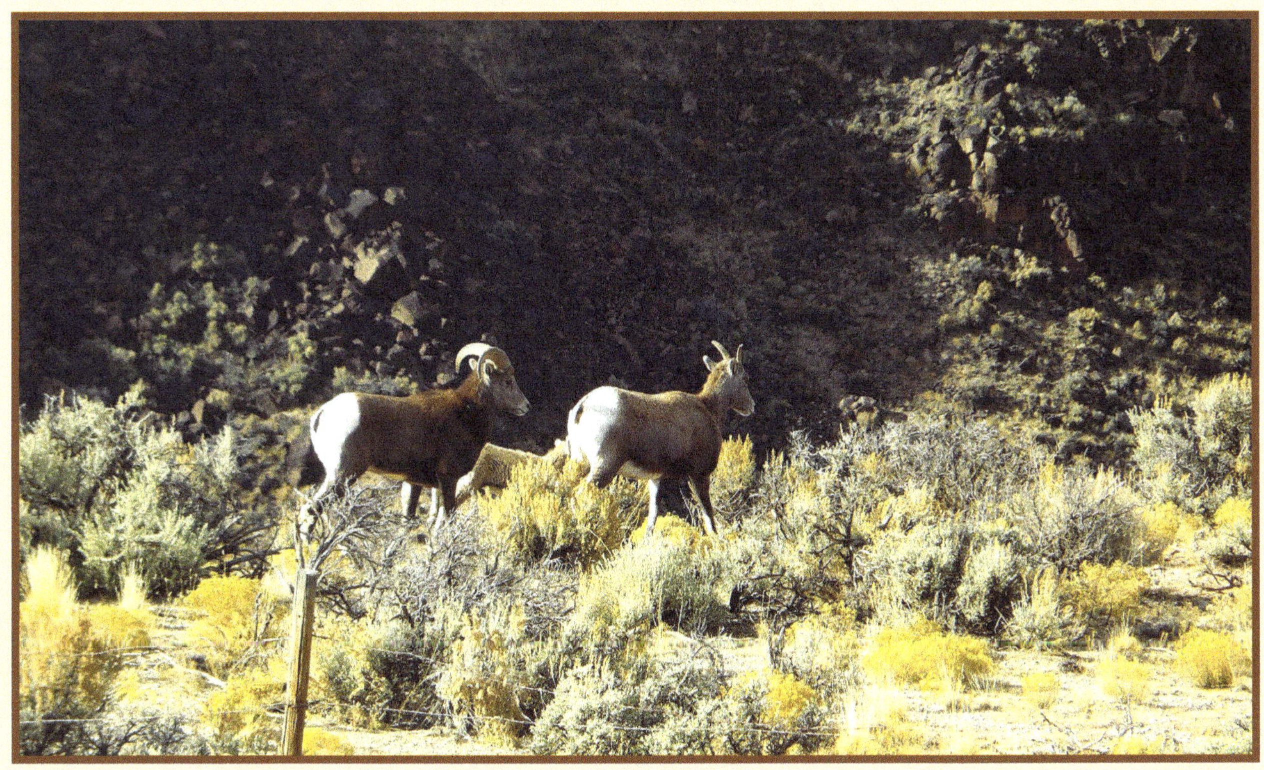

In the following photo series, a Rocky Mountain bighorn family ventures to the edge of the Rio Grande Gorge, where water lies below.

This species of bighorn sheep is the largest among the seven types of North American bighorns. Adults weigh over 200 pounds and have a shoulder height of 3 feet tall. The horns of a Rocky Mountain ram begin to curl at 10 years of age and weigh an average of 30 pounds.

The state allows hunting to manage populations. Rocky Mountain bighorns are in great demand as big game trophies. Hunting licenses are expensive due to limited numbers. For example, the N.M. Dept. of Game and Fish recently auctioned one Rocky Mountain bighorn sheep permit with bidding starting at $65,000. A winning hunting bid for a Rocky Mountain bighorn in New Mexico has reached a high of $157,000.

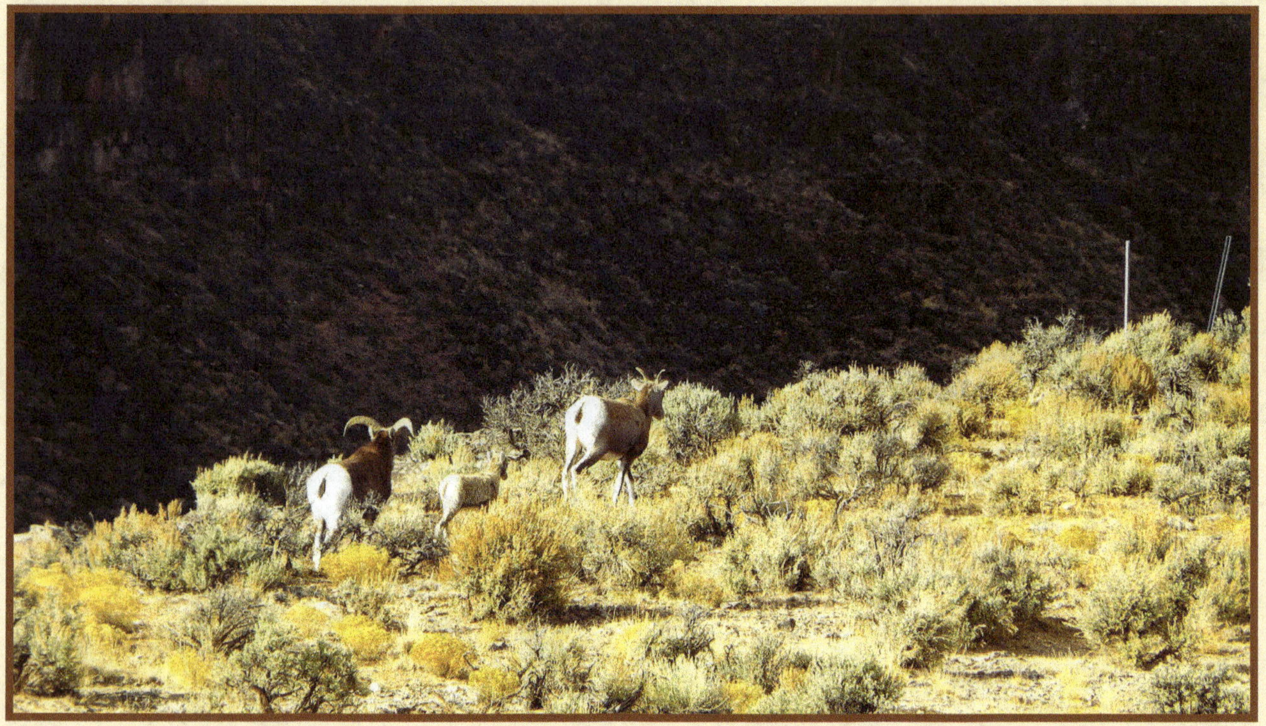

Although bighorns graze in open areas, they return to rocky terrain to digest their food.

An important part of their survival depends on mountainous terrain, which bighorns use to escape and hide from predators. Bighorns usually stay within 1,000 feet from cliffs, ledges, and rocky slopes that provide them with safe havens. Ewes and lambs, in particular, can be vulnerable prey for golden eagles in New Mexico. Other predators for the Rocky Mountain bighorns are bobcats, coyotes, and mountain lions. Born with keen eyesight, bighorns can easily spot predators in steep areas without trees, where they can better evade their natural enemies. Bighorns also have a strong sense of smell to detect the approach of danger. The canyons around the Rio Grande Gorge provide abundant escape terrain for herds compared to other areas where the bighorns live in the state. Today there are nearly 1,000 Rocky Mountain bighorns in New Mexico—compared to a population of less than 250 in 2003. The state has established 10 herds by capturing several dozen healthy bighorns from larger stable herds in alpine areas and transporting them for reintroduction into mountainous areas within the state.

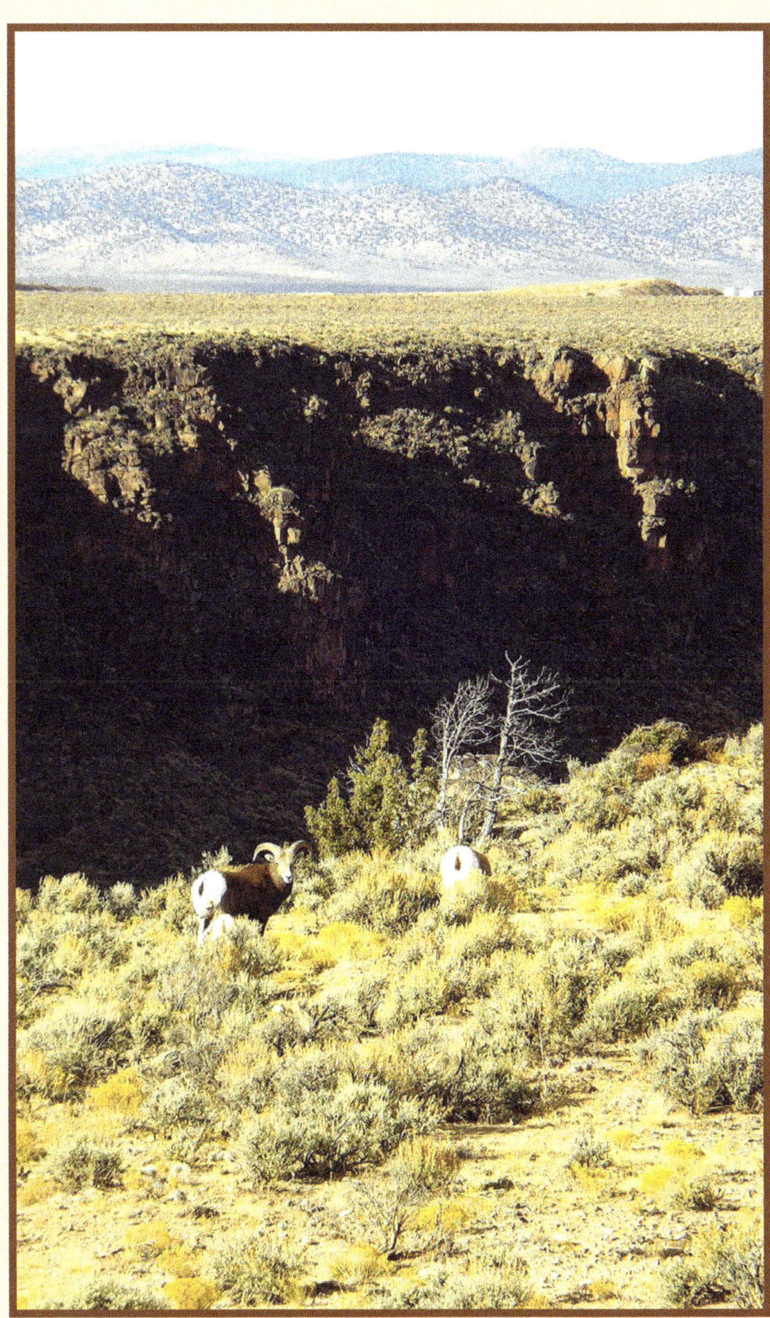

Although some Rocky Mountain bighorns fall to their death while climbing on steep rocky terrain, that is rare.

Bighorns have special hooves that are flexible and soft underneath, enhancing their ability to grip rocks and jump on rough, uneven surfaces. Bighorns are also excellent swimmers.

The ram, ewe, and lamb trot toward the rim of the Rio Grande Gorge.

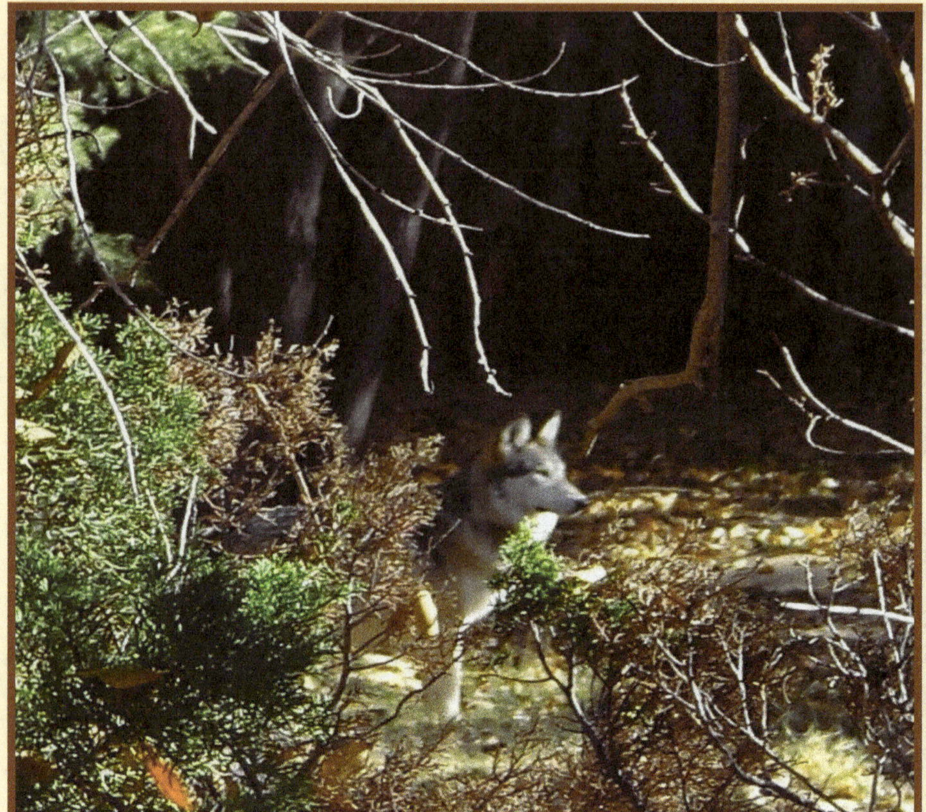

Mexican gray wolves, an endangered species, peer from foliage at the Rio Grande Zoo in Albuquerque in the following photo series.

Mexican gray wolves are part of a captive reproduction effort in a federal plan to reintroduce the wolves back into New Mexico and Arizona. These rare wolves are the most endangered mammals in North America. Until targeted for extermination by the U.S. government in the early 1900s, Mexican gray wolves roamed throughout most of New Mexico, including areas around the Rio Grande. They also inhabited Arizona and northern Mexico. An economic interest in protecting livestock from the wolves led to a federal program around 1905 to kill predatory animals in New Mexico and other Southwestern lands. U.S. reports indicate that in 1910 alone more wolves (71) were killed by forest rangers in the state of New Mexico alone than in the 11 Western states where the trappings and poisonings were encouraged. Government bounties were placed on hides (with higher amounts for wolves than coyotes) to encourage hunting. A U.S. Dept. of Agriculture report noted in 1918 that only 20 gray wolves remained in New Mexico compared to 300 in 1915.

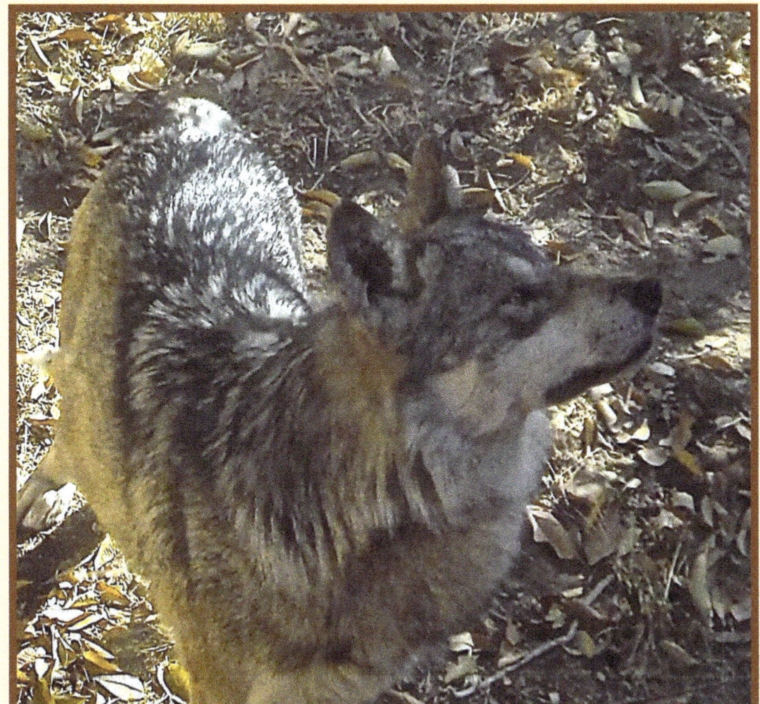

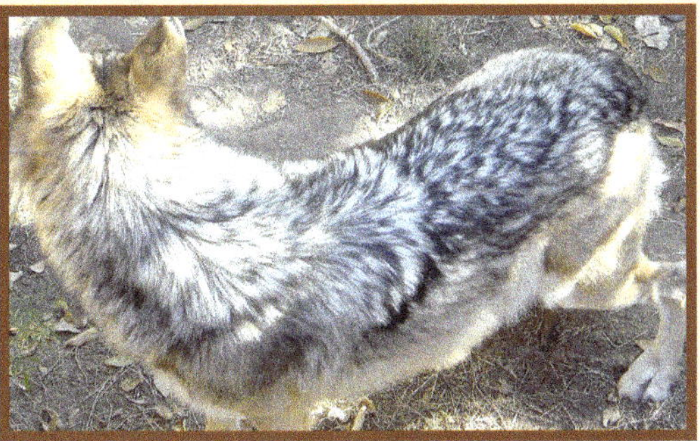

Mexican gray wolves in closeups.

Protected since 1976 under the Endangered Species Act, the Mexican gray wolf is the rarest subspecies of gray wolf in North America. Except for two reintroduction projects in the United States and Mexico, the Mexican wolf is extinct in the wild. The wolves were re-integrated into the wild for the first time in 1998 by the U.S. Fish and Wildlife Service. The Rio Grande Zoo was among the first facilities involved in the Mexico Wolf Species Survival Plan, in which some 284 captive wolves have been managed and bred through 50 zoos in the U.S. and Mexico. Two of the 3 facilities in the United States where the Mexican wolves are acclimated prior to release are in Caballo and Socorro, N.M. There the wolves have minimum exposure to people and develop healthy pack structure before they are freed in either a nearly 7,000-square-mile area in the Apache-Sitgreaves and Gila national forests, or in the Fort Apache Indian Reservation. Including 5 breeding pairs and 14 packs, only 83 Mexican wolves roam in eastern Arizona and western New Mexico. Some 100 reintegrated Mexican wolves died from 1998 to 2013. Of those, 55% were killed illegally (such as being shot with a gun or arrow) and 14% were hit by vehicles, noted a U.S. Fish and Wildlife Service report.

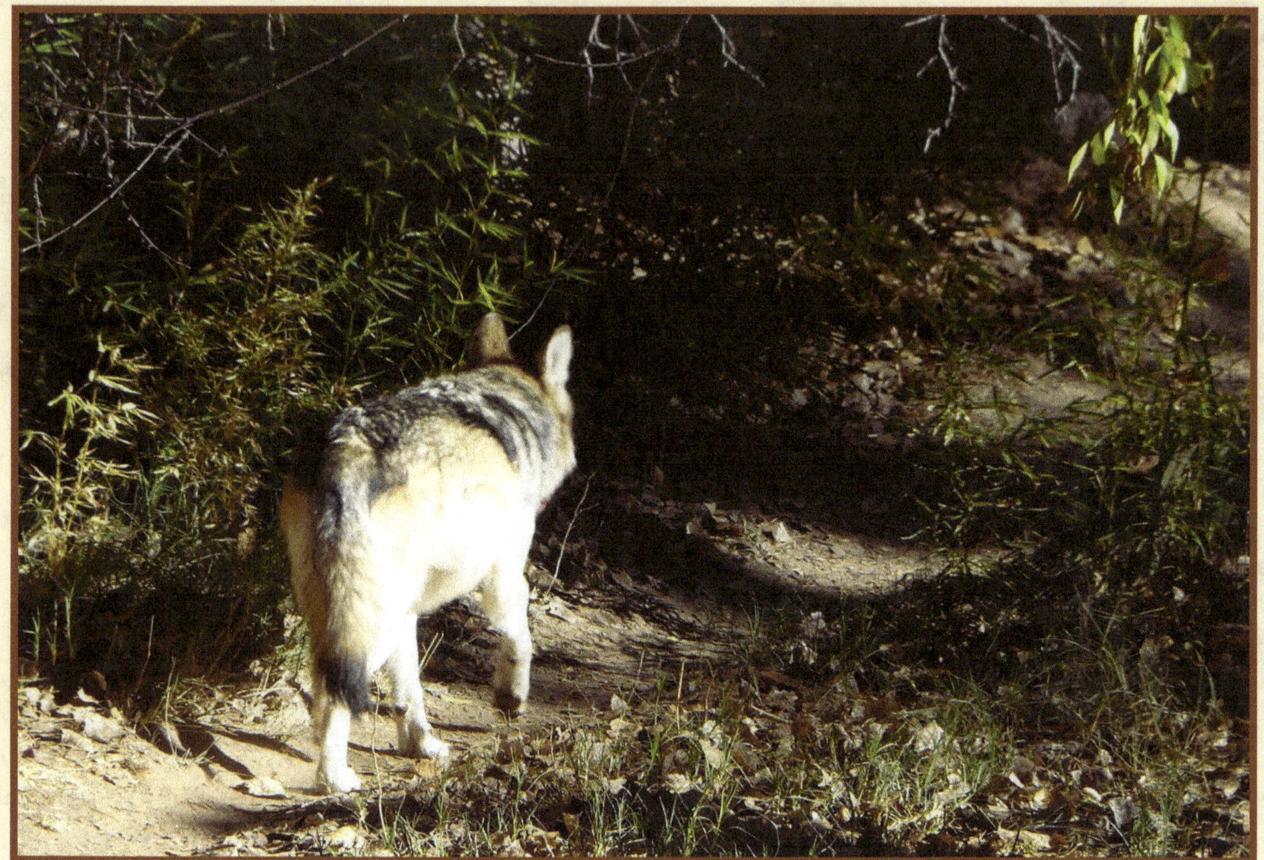

Known in Spanish as *el lobo*, the wolf is a much beloved mascot of the University of New Mexico.

The average male Mexican wolf weighs between 50 and 80 pounds, while females average 55 pounds. They live in packs of 4 to 8 wolves and hunt cooperatively within a territory that could span over several hundred square miles. They prey on elk, deer, javelina, and rabbits. Some livestock and dogs have been killed by released wolves. A trust fund has been established to pay for livestock killed by the Mexican wolves, with compensation ranging from $3,750 for a bull to $225 for a lamb. A new part of the wolf reintegration program is the compensation of livestock producers for possible negative financial effects of the Mexican wolves' presence in their vicinity (such as changes in herd behavior due to the presence of wolves and wolf territory overlapping on herd grazing areas).

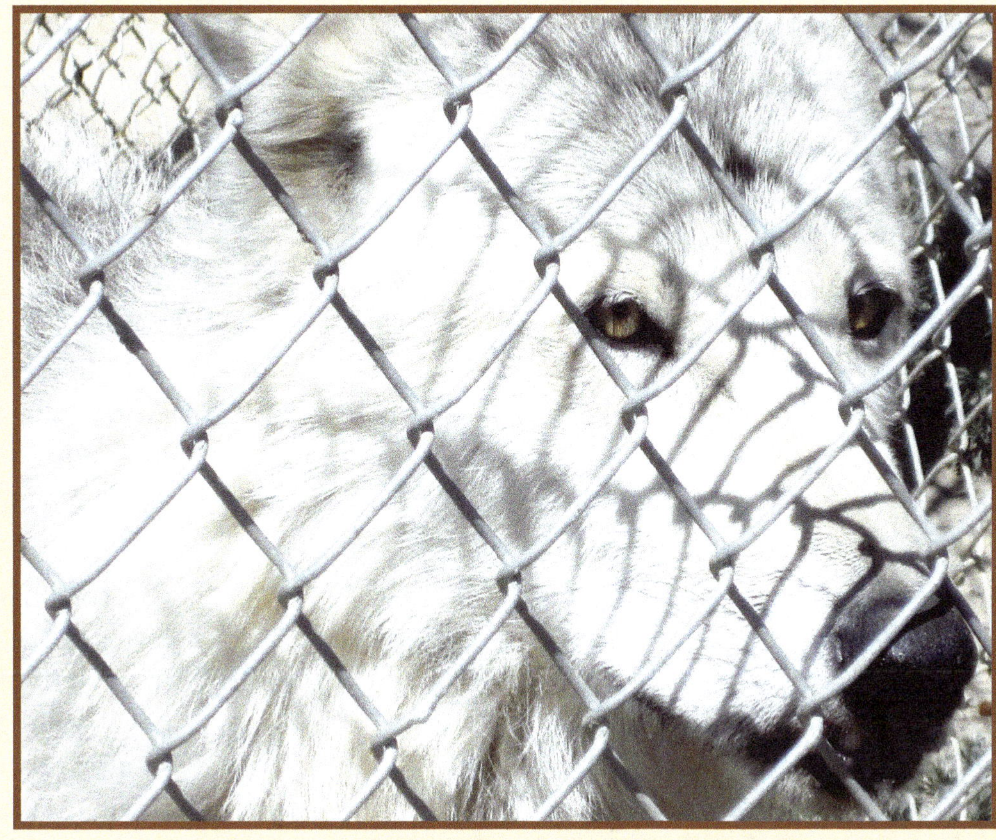

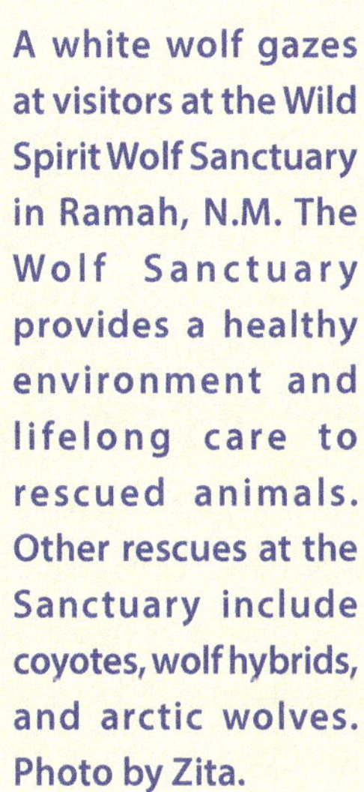

A white wolf gazes at visitors at the Wild Spirit Wolf Sanctuary in Ramah, N.M. The Wolf Sanctuary provides a healthy environment and lifelong care to rescued animals. Other rescues at the Sanctuary include coyotes, wolf hybrids, and arctic wolves. Photo by Zita.

Another major part of New Mexico's wildlife is the coyote. Coyotes are versatile hunters and scavengers that live in the high mesas, forests, and rural areas around the Rio Grande. It is easy to come across coyotes running near the Rio Grande in the early hours of the morning. Typically, coyotes are shy and will avoid people. However, they are notorious for killing house pets and will run off with any unattended dogs or cats they find outside in people's yards. Many people lose their pets to coyotes. Unlike wolves, coyotes are an unprotected species and are hunted for sport as well as for their pelts. Sometimes there are "coyote killing contests," which participants attempt to win by slaying the most coyotes. Protests have increased over coyote killing contests, and there are efforts underway by activists in the state to put an end to these contests.

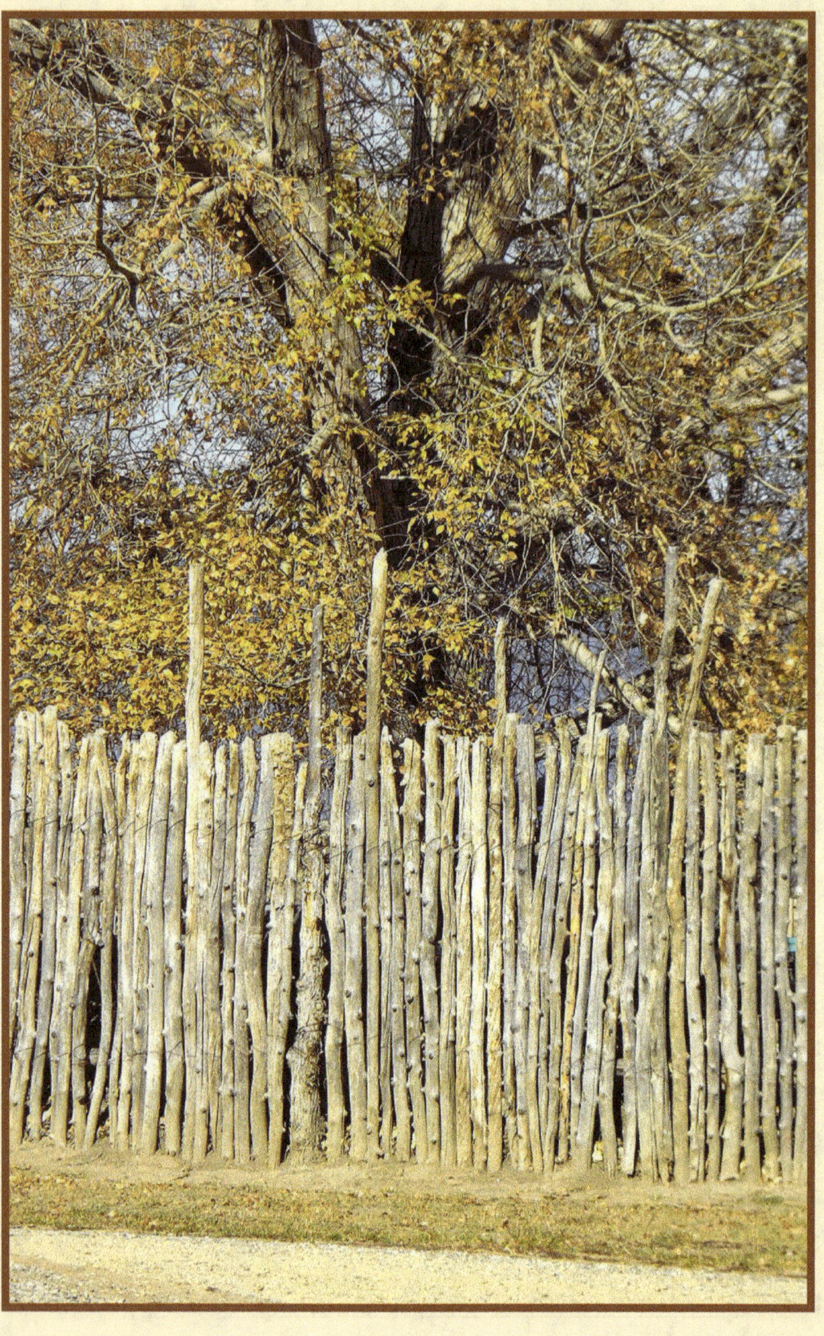

This coyote fence is typical of those constructed of wooden posts made of cedar, aspen, juniper, or fir. The narrow branches/posts are called *latillas.* They are bound together by hand with bailing wire. Some *latillas* are of a natural gray color; others are hand peeled and set deep into the ground.

These barriers are called coyote fences because they were invented to stop cunning coyotes from raiding people's farmyards. Coyotes are known to jump over small, ordinary fences or to dig tunnels underneath them.

My uncle, who takes morning strolls near the Rio Grande, has come upon coyote packs on the prowl near alfalfa fields and irrigation ditches. At night, high-pitched coyote howls can be heard along mesas and in neighborhoods near open spaces.

A coyote fence borders an *acequia.*

Chapter 7: Plant Life

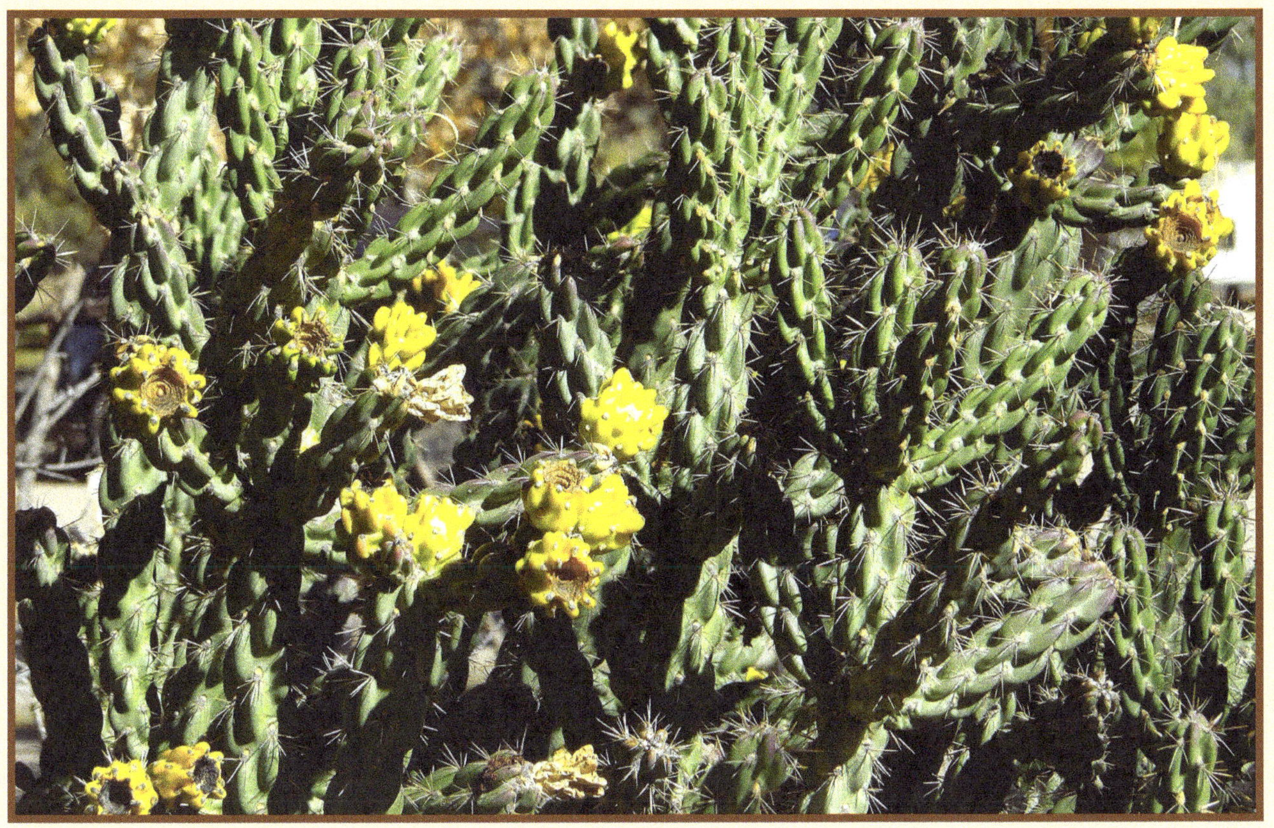

A close look at a cholla cactus, common along the Rio Grande and throughout the New Mexico.

Plant life around the Rio Grande is rich and diverse. Vegetation changes as the river descends from higher mountain elevations through forests and into lower elevation woods, grasslands, marshes, and desert areas.

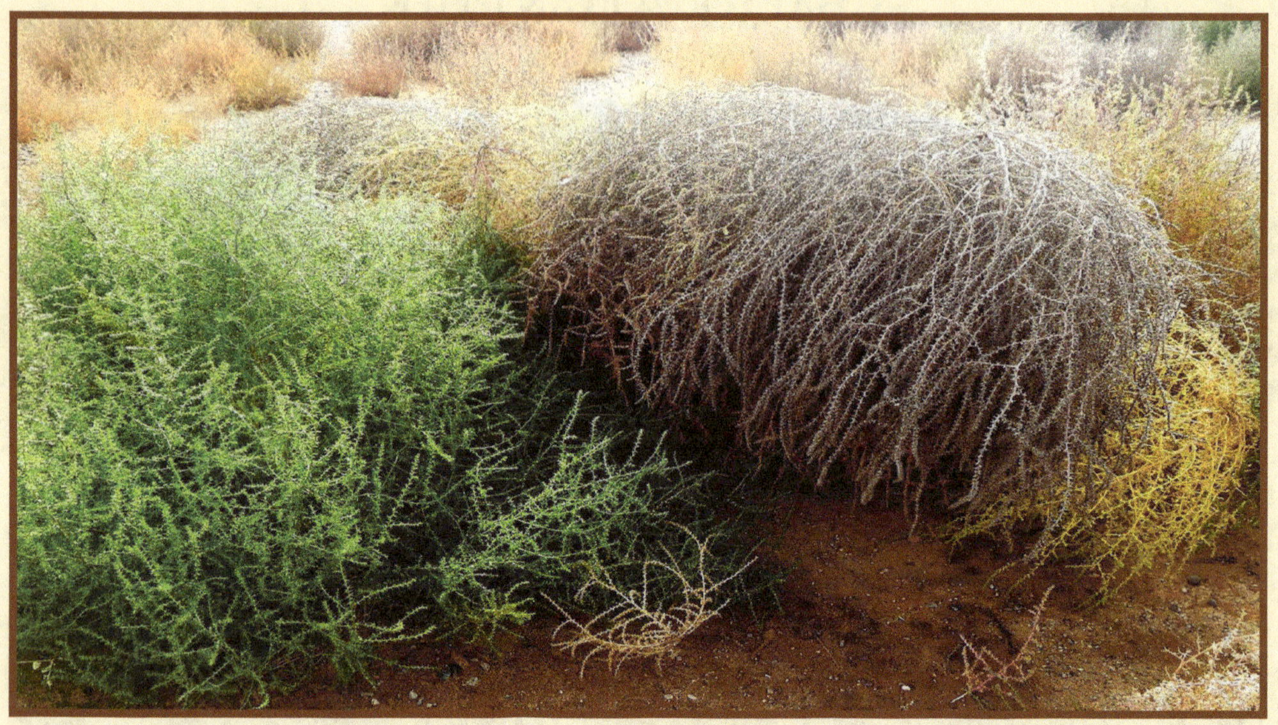

Colorful tumbleweeds adorn the ground on a mesa near the Rio Grande.

The green tumbleweed (left) is still growing, while the others are losing their colors as they dry. When they reach maturity, the plants break off at the root and roll away, dispersing as many as 250,000 seeds per plant.

Tumbleweeds were a cause for alarm in local newspapers and agricultural notices when the plants first appeared in the fall of 1894 in New Mexico. They were discovered growing in a wasteland near railroad tracks outside of Santa Fe, some 30 miles east of the Rio Grande. It had taken tumbleweeds 2 decades to appear in New Mexico. In 1874, Russian immigrants inadvertently brought tumbleweed seeds (Russian thistle) to South Dakota among imported flax seeds—marking the entrance into the United States of a desert weed that became a hallmark of the Wild West. Tumbleweeds spread southward drug by train wheels along the tracks of the Atchison, Topeka and Santa Fe Railroad through Albuquerque and into the remainder of New Mexico.

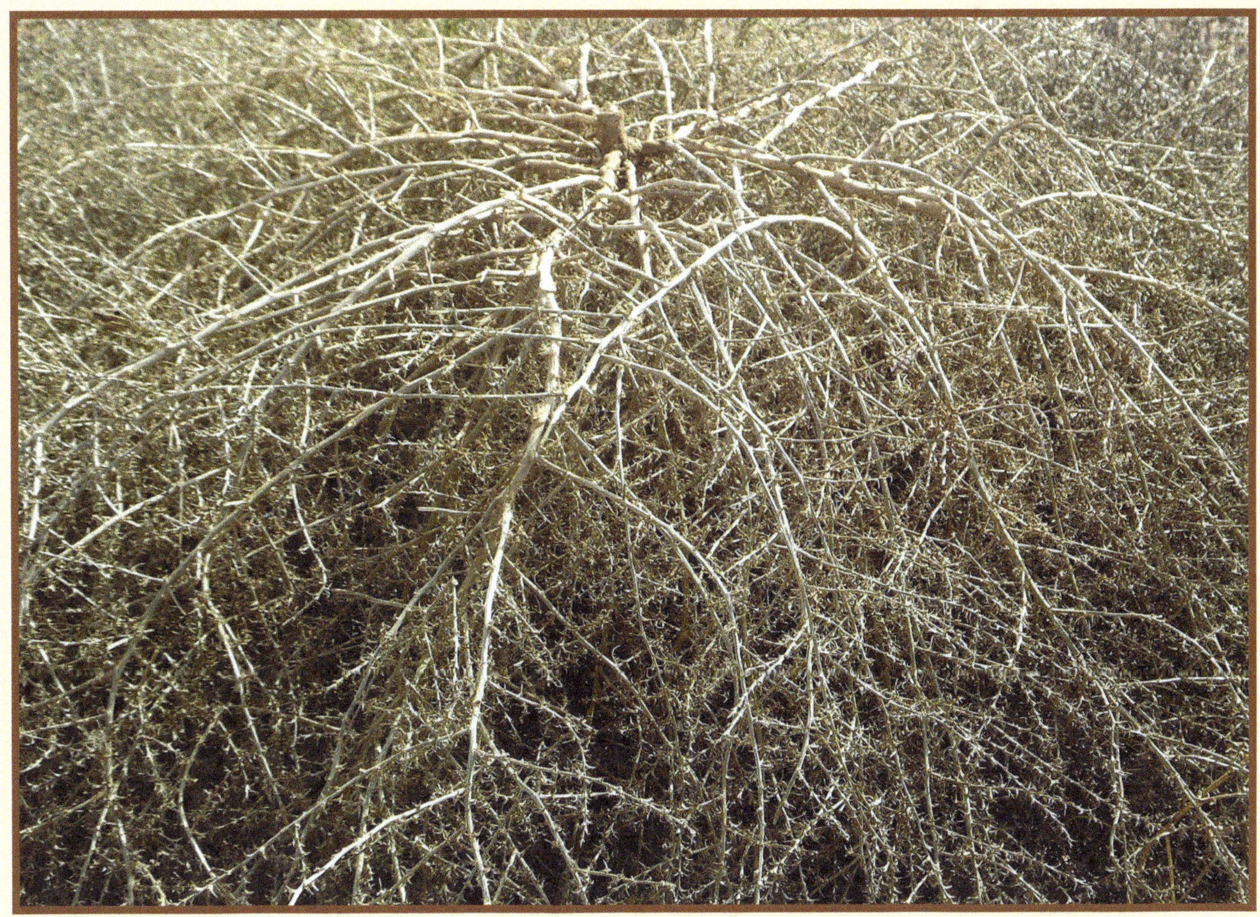

A large tumbleweed sits upside-down along the Rio Grande.

When they are still green and growing, tumbleweeds are favorite foods for prairie dogs. In addition, tumbleweeds are sometimes eaten by cattle, sheep, deer, elk, and quail. Tumbleweeds can grow as high as 2 feet tall and as round as 4 feet in diameter. The weeds pollinate in the fall and can cause seasonal allergies.

Tumbleweeds also can be hazardous, posing fire dangers, obstructing roads, blocking waterways, and hiding fences.

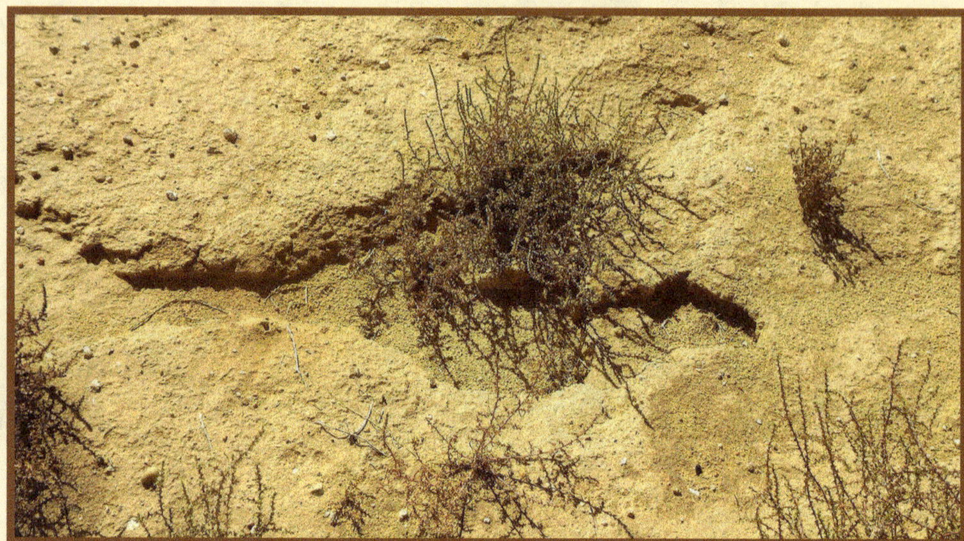

While New Mexico is home to various types of soil ranging from fine sand to red clay, the earth in the central Rio Grande Valley is composed of gravel, sediment, and sand.

Water erosion forms a footprint-like shape in the dirt near the Rio Grande.

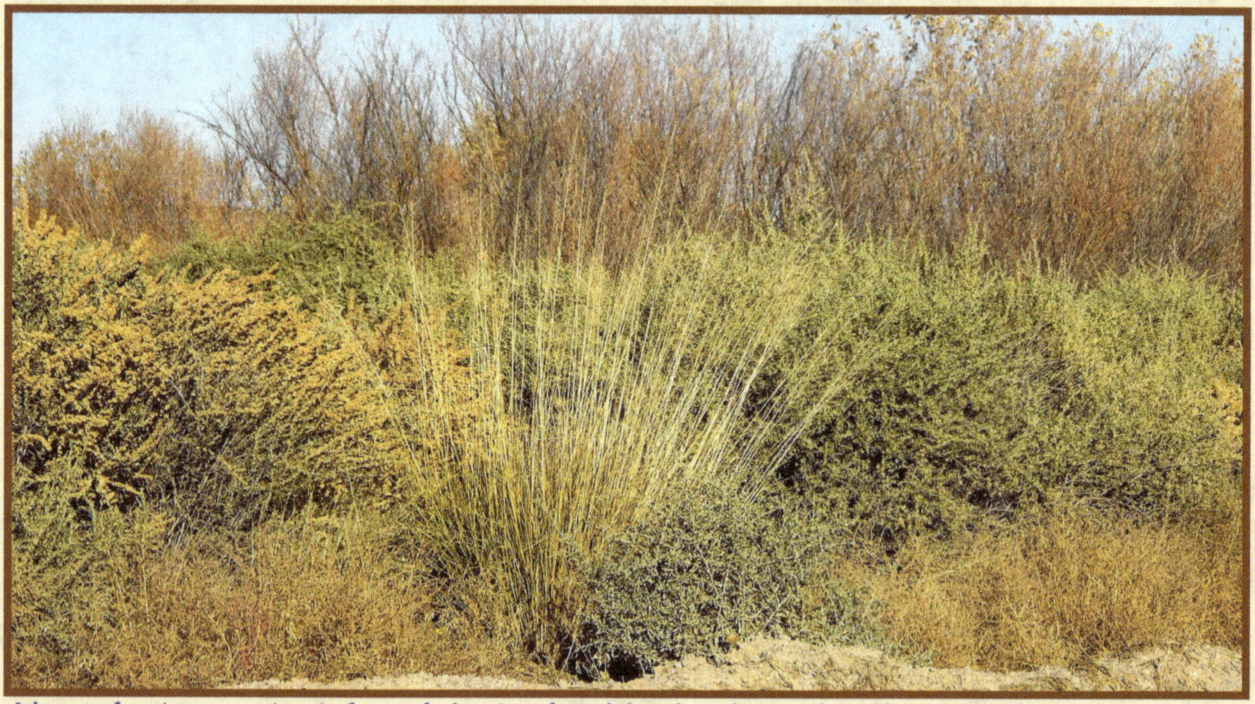

A burst of native grass rises in front of a barrier of scrub brush and trees along the river bank near Socorro.

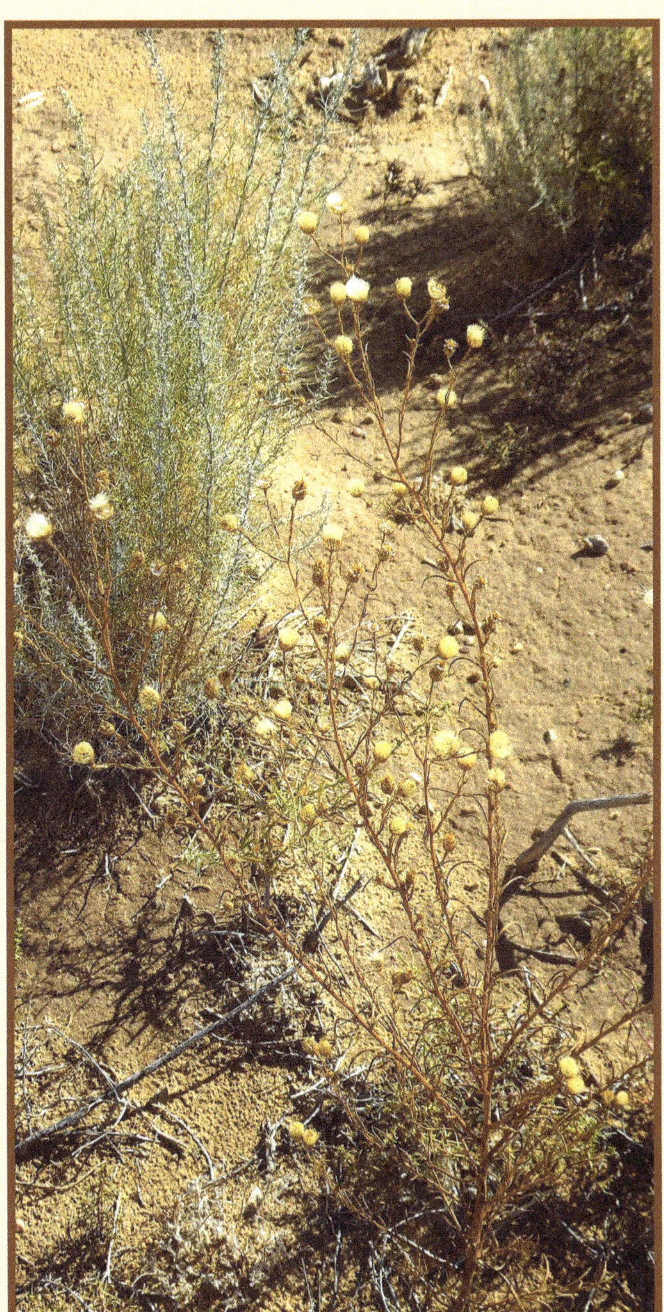

Most plants living on the 121,000 square miles that make up New Mexico—the 5th largest state in the United States after Montana, California, Texas and Alaska—are drought resistant. These include sagebrush, cacti, and many types of native grasses.

Dried yellow flowers top a bush that springs from soil near the river. Two blue sagebrush plants can be seen in the background.

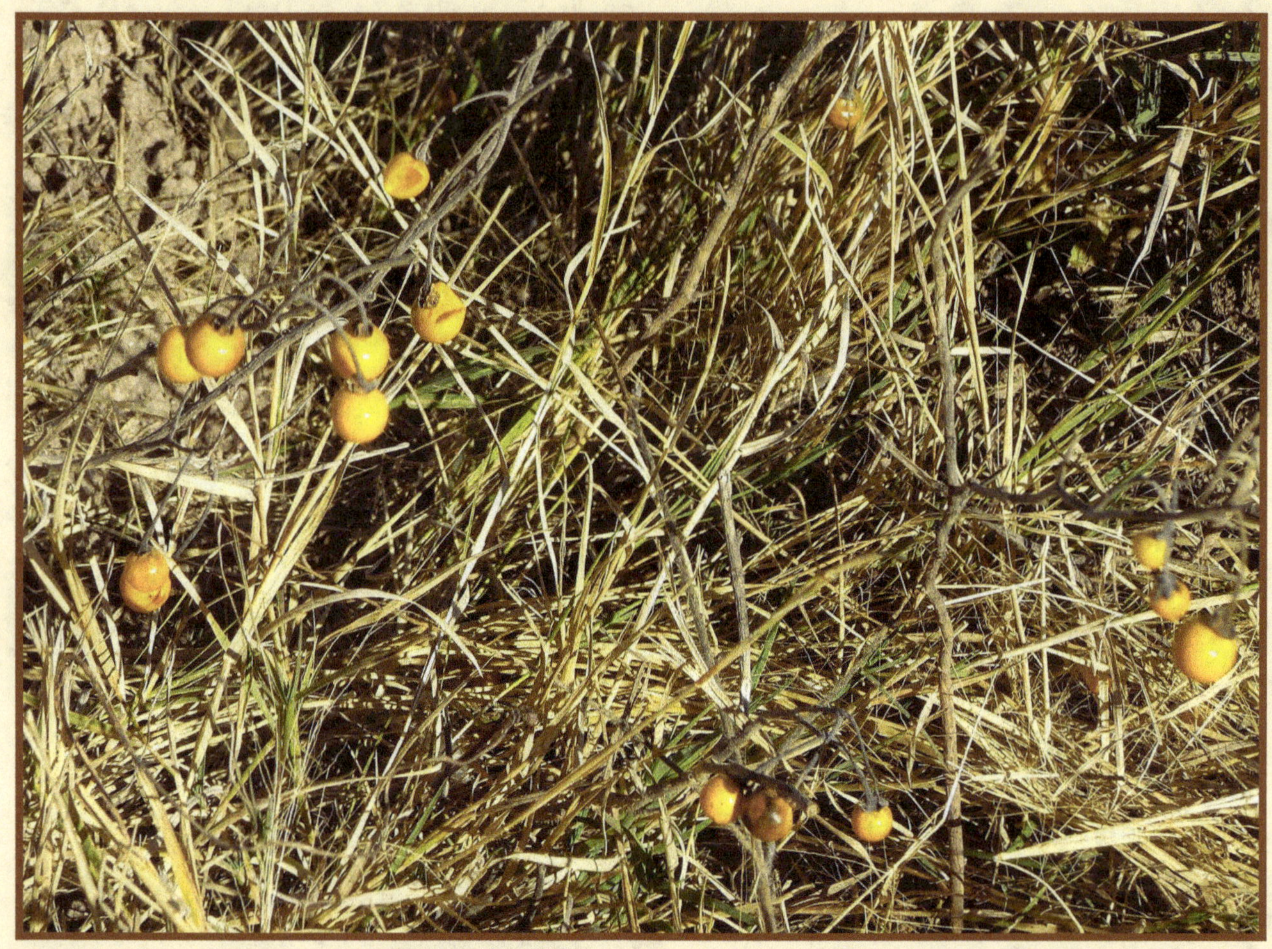

A dried horsenettle plant, with golden berries, withers among grass along the Rio Grande during an Indian summer.

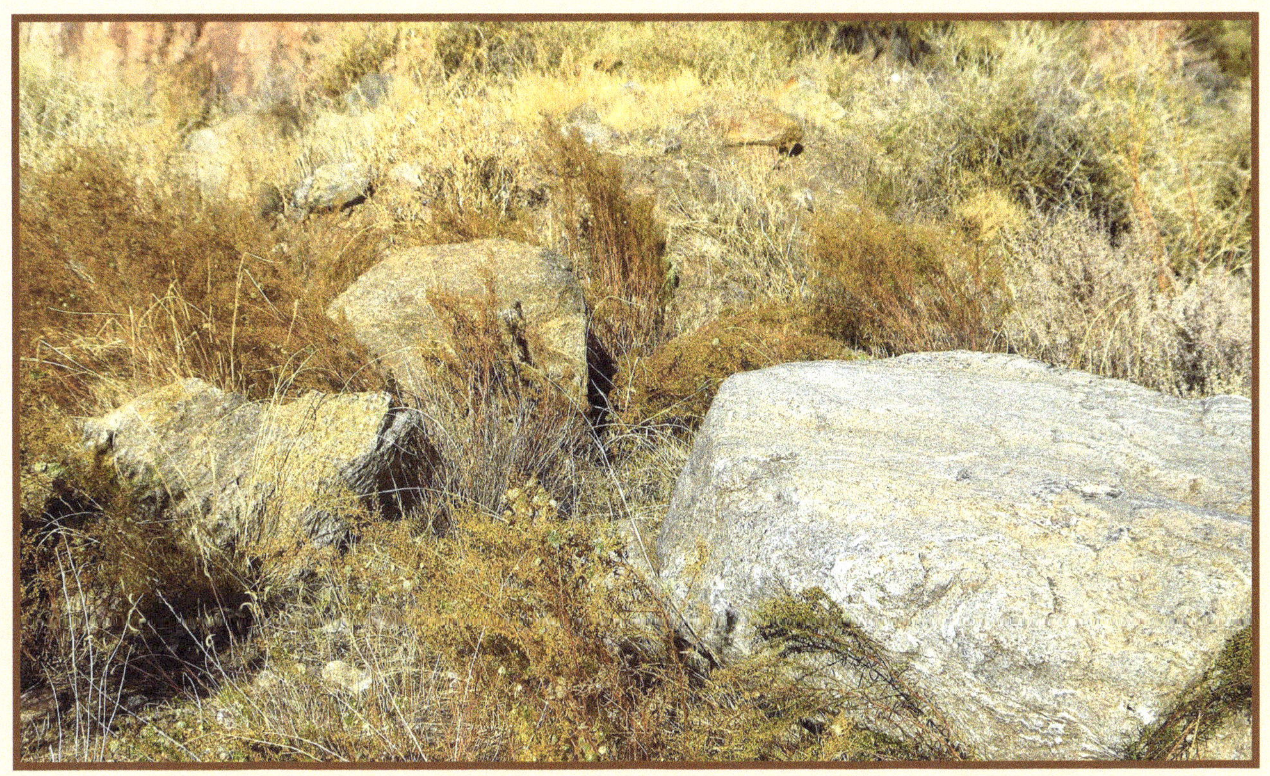

Dry desert grasses sprout around boulders near the bank of the Rio Grande.

Boulders are common in the waters of the Rio Grande and alongside its banks in northern New Mexico. The state is known for its many volcanoes and has a large diversity of volcanic rock types.

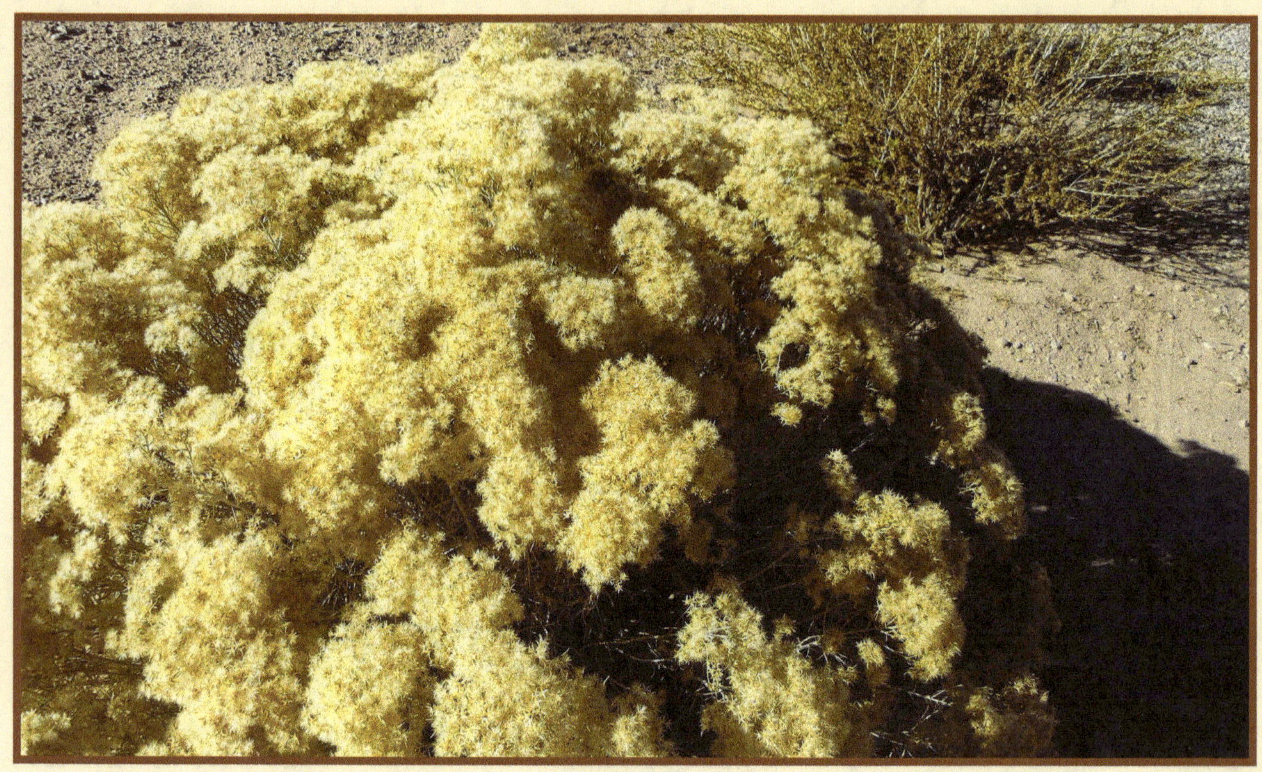

A native desert shrub blooms in autumn outside of Corrales near the Rio Grande.

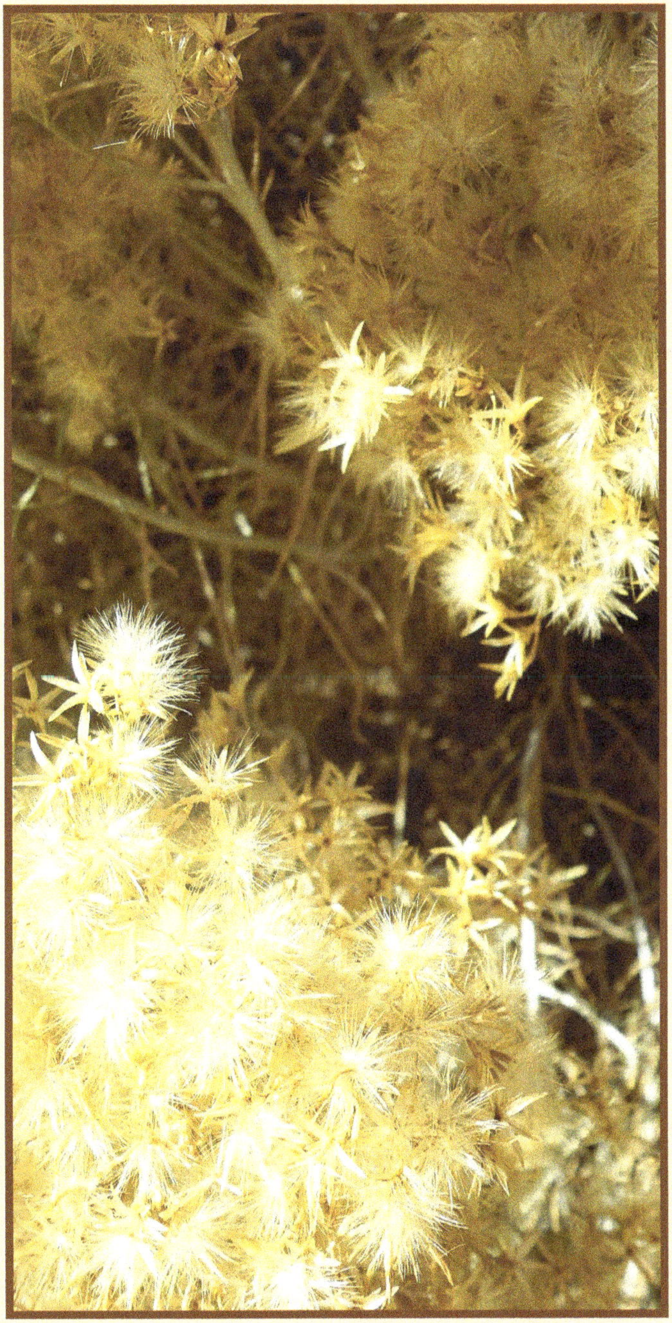

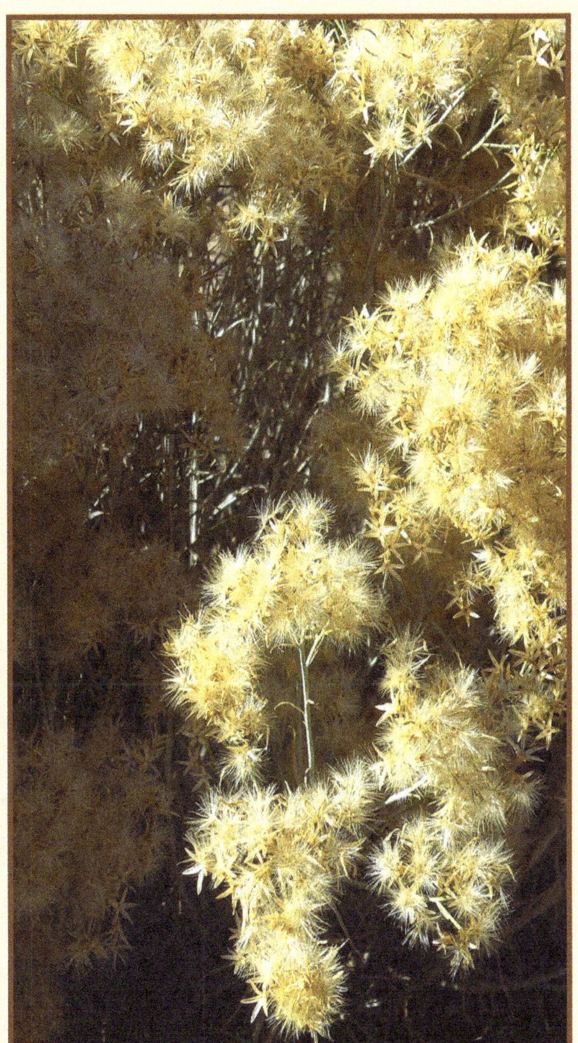

Delicate flowers can be seen in these closeup views of shrub blossoms.

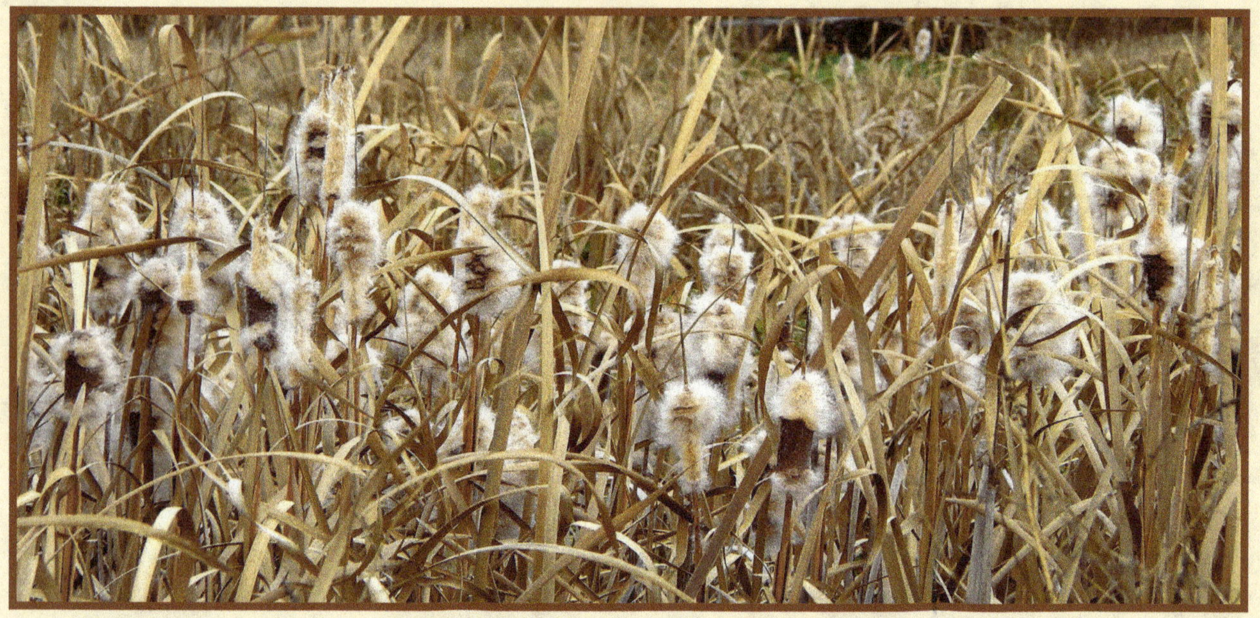

Cattail seeds disperse in fluffs next to a tributary of the Rio Grande in northern New Mexico.

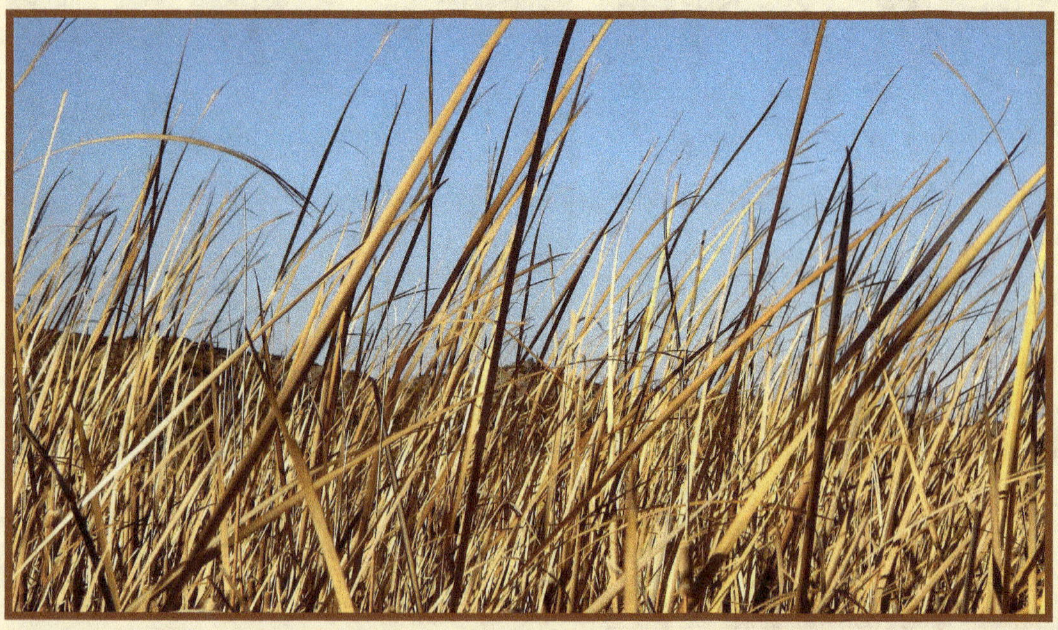

Dried reeds form a wall in a wetland region near the river in southern New Mexico.

Less than 1% of land in New Mexico is considered wetlands; this small area includes marshes around the Rio Grande.

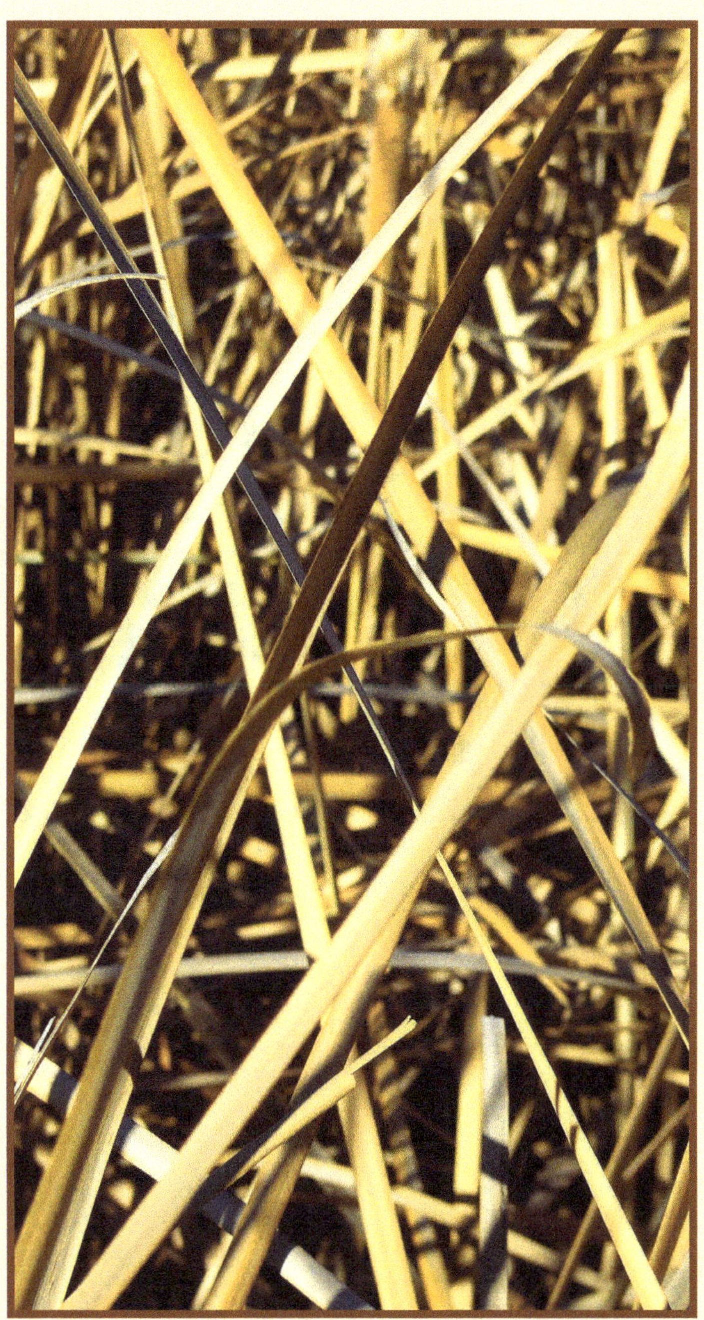

Reeds grow together densely. Thick vegetation in the wetlands provides a cover for migratory birds.

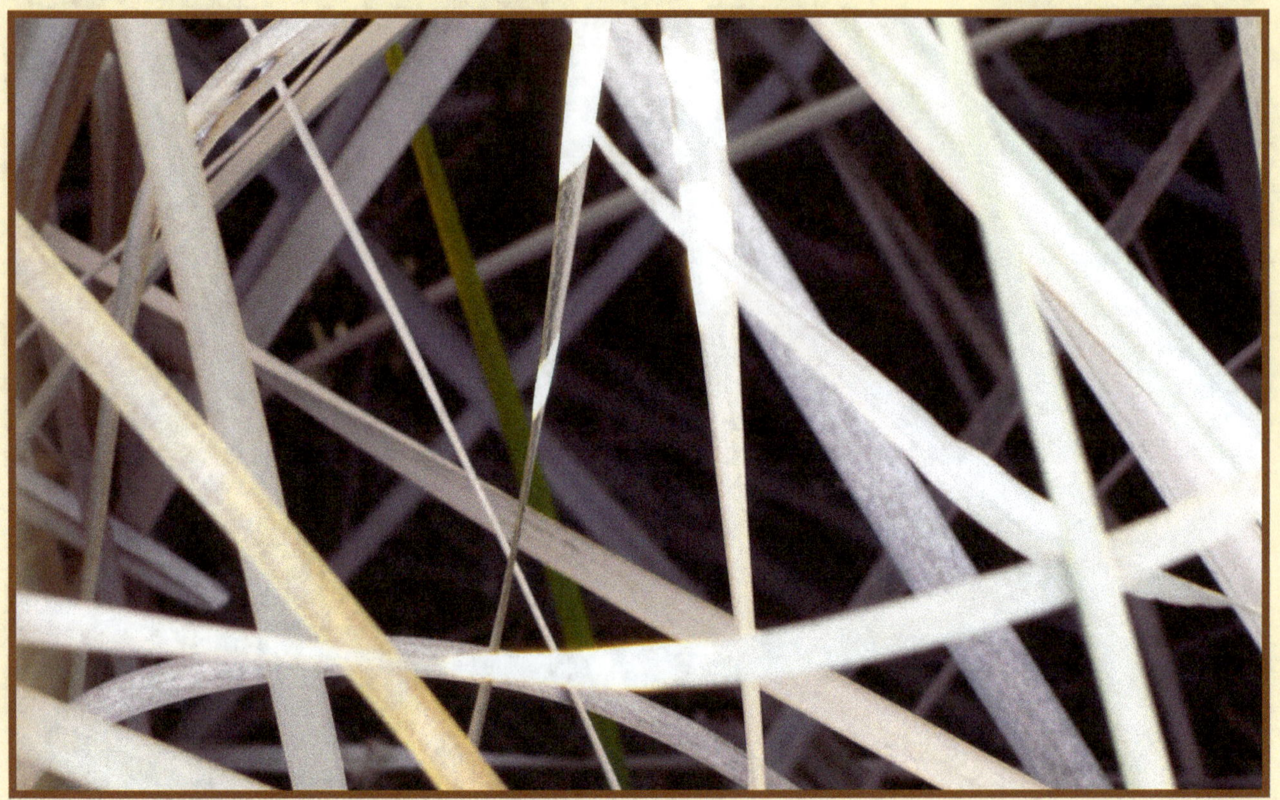

The leaves overlap in abstract patterns as they grow denser near the ground's surface.

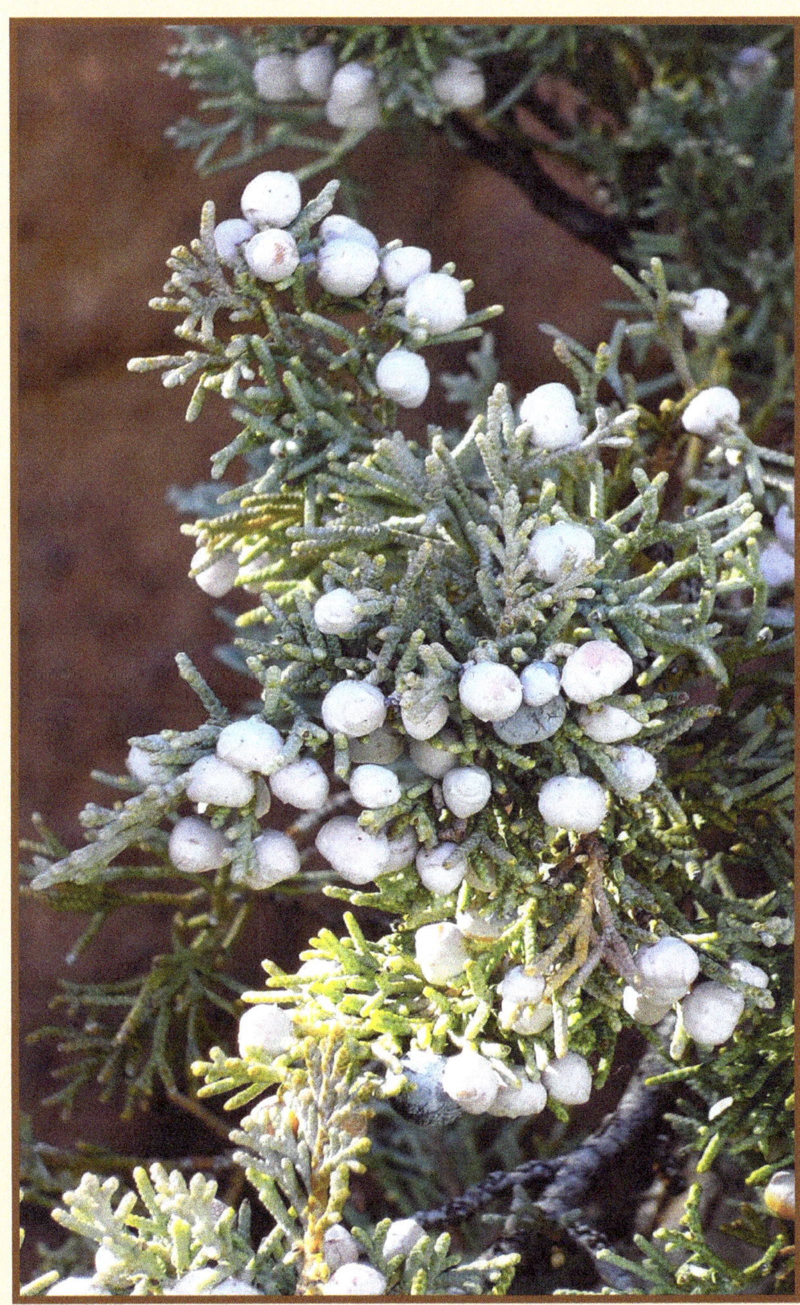

A branch from a juniper tree is weighed down with berries. Juniper trees are an important feature in the Rio Grande Gorge.

The Rio Grande flows through the base of volcanic canyons. The river is surrounded by ancient woodlands, which contain juniper and piñon trees that are over 500 years old.

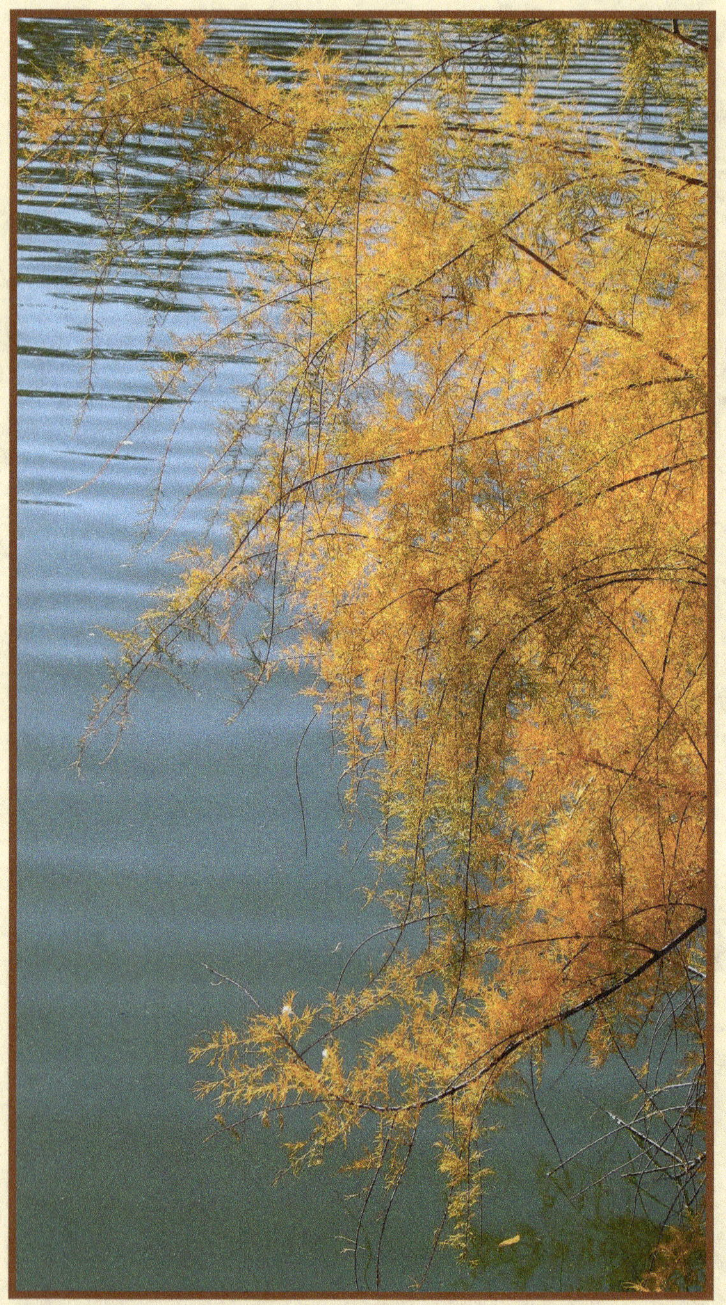

Salt cedars were imported into the United States in the 1820s from Eurasia as decorative plants. In the early 1900s, salt cedar shrubs were planted in Albuquerque and in some areas along the Rio Grande to control erosion.

A record flooding of the Rio Grande in the early 1940s transported salt cedar seeds to moist soil in new areas, which hastened the plant's expansion in the state.

Salt cedar is now the 3rd most common plant along streams in the Southwestern United States. It now dominates many plant communities along the Rio Grande, where millions of dollars have been spent to study salt cedar and eradicate it.

Delicate branches of a salt cedar (tamarisk) tree loom over the water near the Rio Grande. In the fall, the green leaves of the salt cedar transform into brilliant orange and red colors.

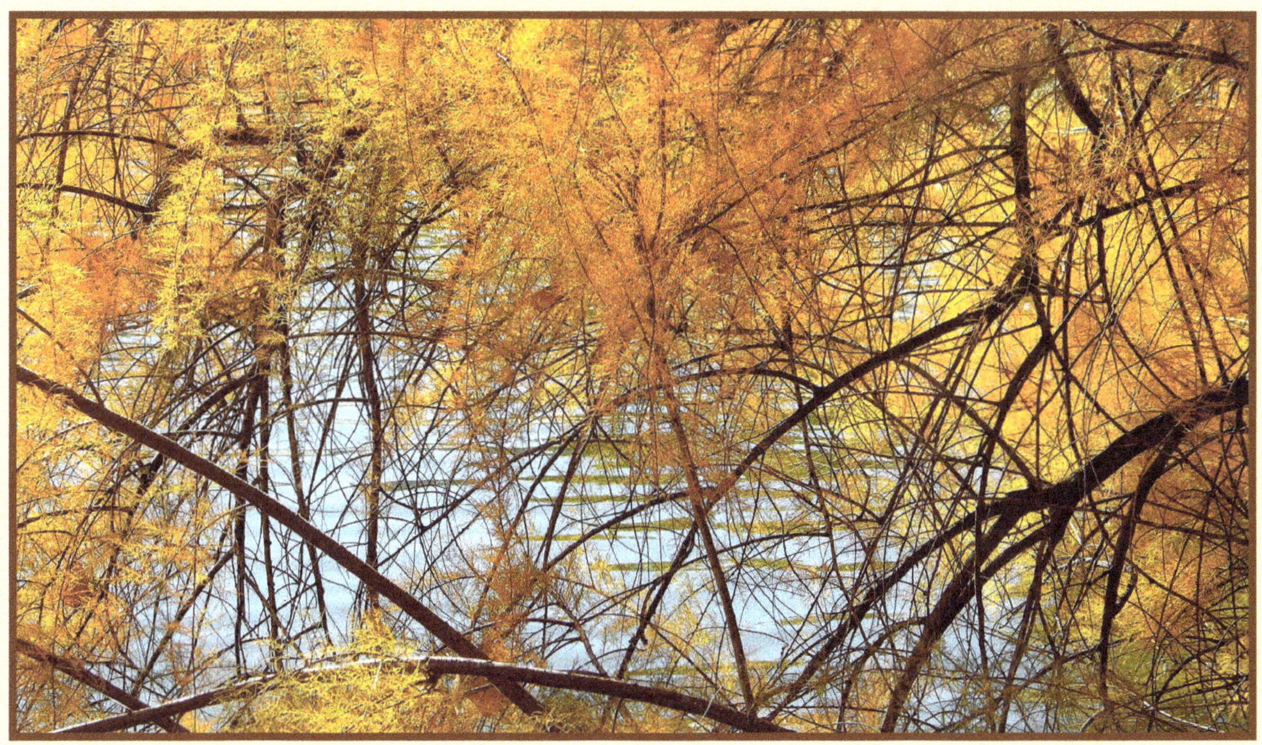

Salt cedar trees form a canopy over the water.

In New Mexico, salt cedar can thrive at elevations from 3,000 to 6,500 feet above sea level. Salt cedar is an invasive plant with deep root systems that reach into the water table and consume higher amounts of water than native plants. This is detrimental to traditional wildlife habitats.

Numerous federal, state, and local efforts are underway to eradicate salt cedar. It is estimated that a single tree can consume up to 200 gallons per day of water, a precious resource in New Mexico.

Removing salt cedar trees has been difficult and costly. Techniques in New Mexico have included spraying herbicides from helicopters, hiring crews to bulldoze the plants, and releasing leaf-eating salt cedar beetles as a biological control.

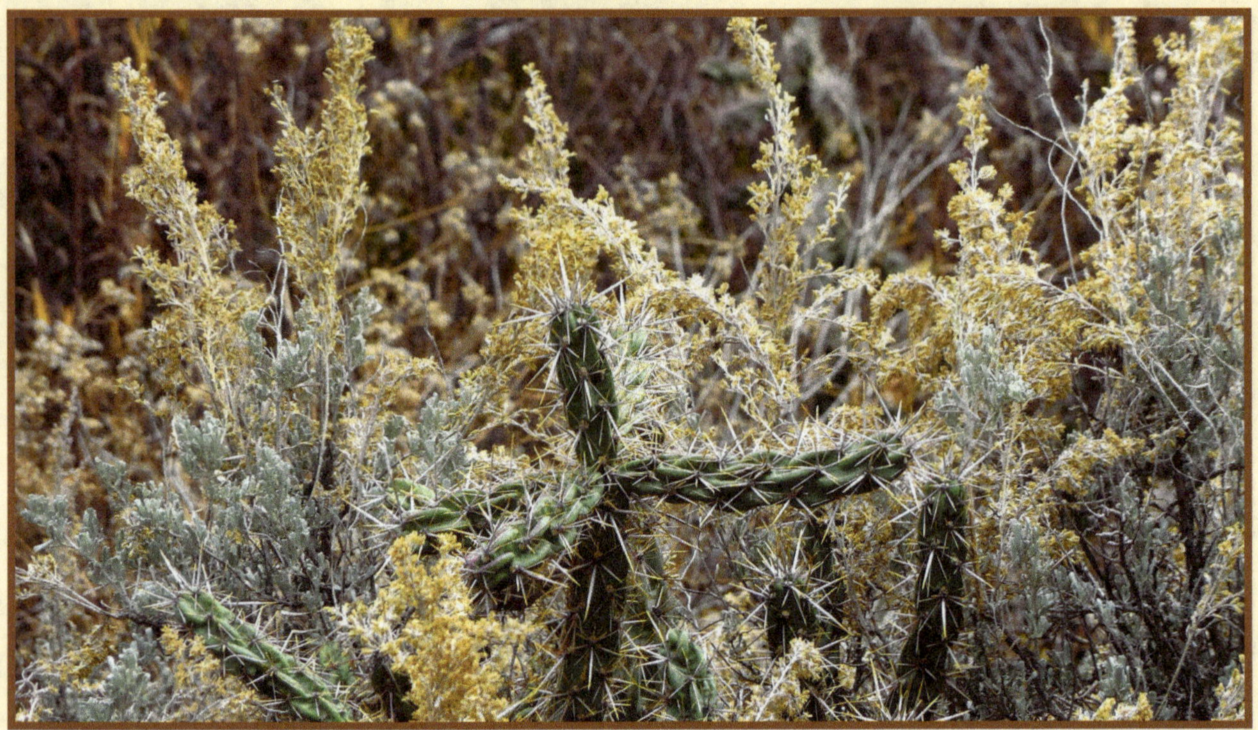

A green cholla cactus grows entangled among blue sagebrush and a chamisa (gray rabbitbrush) plant next to the Rio Grande.

New Mexico has the 3rd highest number of native cactus species (50) after Arizona (60), and Texas (100). Many varieties of cholla live in New Mexico and bloom in vibrant colors (such as magenta and yellow) in the spring and early summer.

Underneath the green fleshy tissue is a hollow woody cylinder stem with oval holes. Some dried wooden cholla stems are used by woodworkers to make canes, picture frames, and other objects.

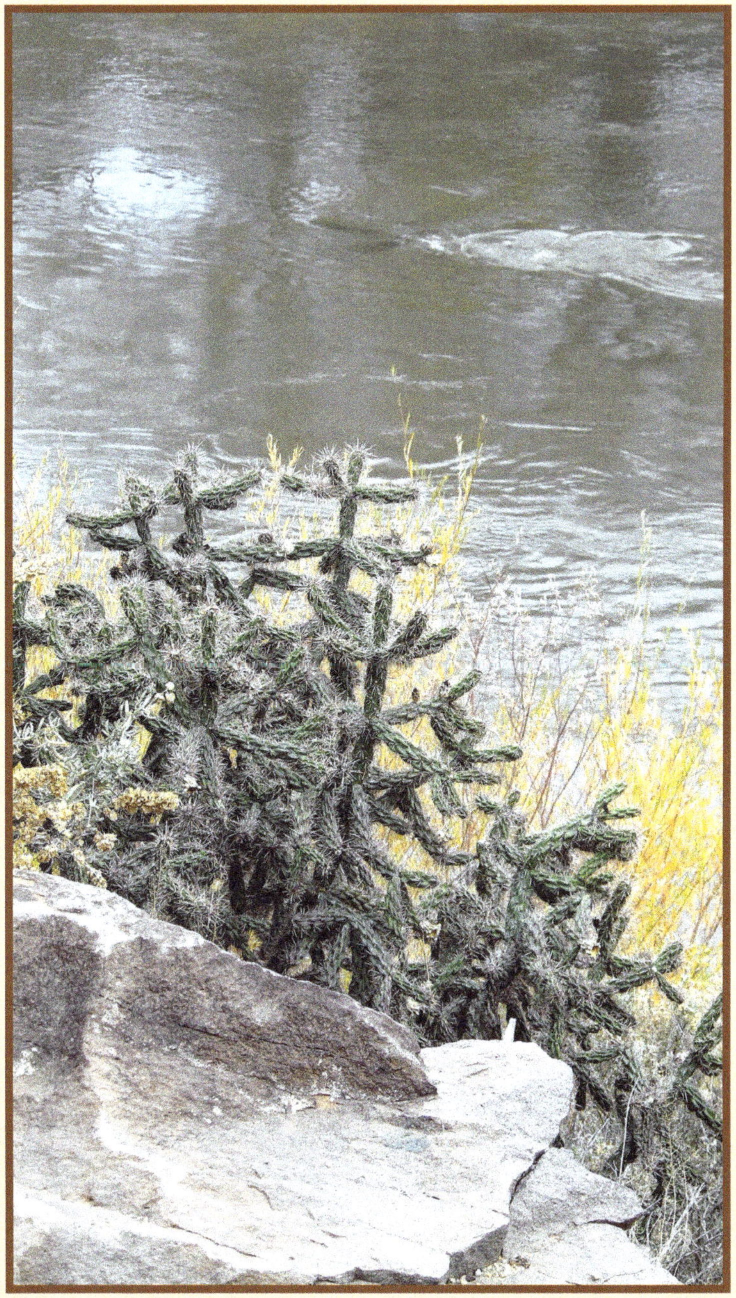

Cholla spines (needles) are legendary in New Mexico for being barbed and difficult to remove from skin and animal fur.

The spines average about 1 inch in length. Once the needles pierce the skin, the spines are likely to break off in your flesh when you try to extract them.

The spines can easily pierce through tennis shoes, jeans, and leather work gloves. Cholla spines also can become lodged in the heads of cattle and sheep.

A tall cluster of cholla grows between a boulder and willow on the bank of the Rio Grande.

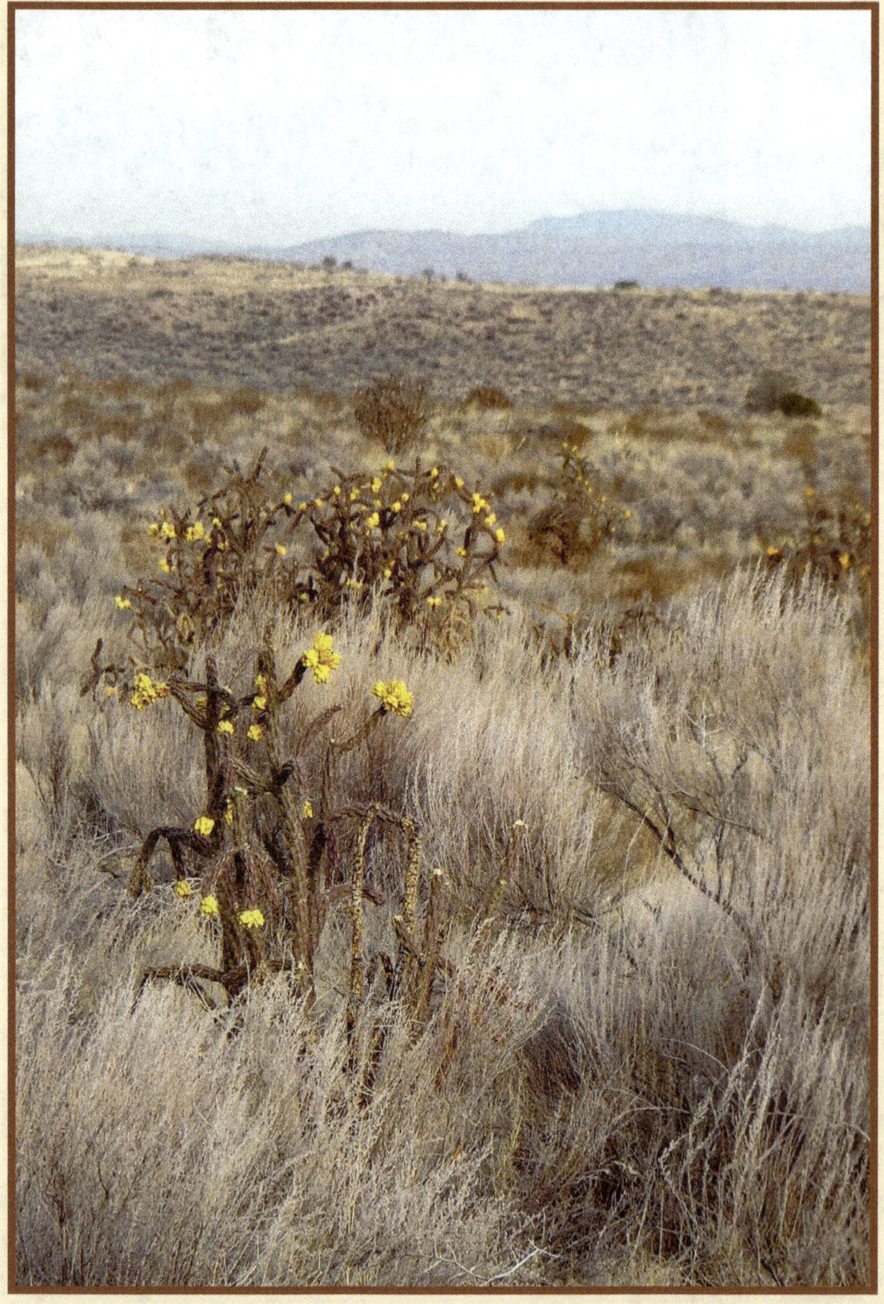

The spines have been described as being like fishhooks.

People familiar with the Southwest will avoid becoming entangled with cholla. Once the barbed spines break off inside skin, the needle fragments can fester and become infected.

A District Attorney in Albuquerque, who had many enemies, planted cholla cactus underneath all the windows of his home as a security system instead of installing a burglar alarm. I laughed when he told me about it, but he said he never had any problem with intruders.

Cholla plants rise above scrub brush on a mesa above the Rio Grande. Cholla can grow as high as a person's head— even over 8 feet tall.

Prickly pear cacti have edible green cactus pads and fruit. The fruit of the cactus can be used in jams. Coyotes are said to be especially fond of eating prickly pear fruit.

Prickly pear pads can be eaten raw, but are usually cleaned, freed from needles, and served cooked.

However, prickly pears, if handled incorrectly, can be very painful. As a child, one of my family members decided to eat a raw prickly pear while pretending to be a cowboy. He was inspired by a Western movie about cowboys who drank water from a barrel cactus. He dressed in his cowboy clothes, found a prickly pear in the backyard, cut off a piece, and tried to eat it without removing the needles. Later, a pediatrician had to remove needles from his inner lip and around his swollen mouth.

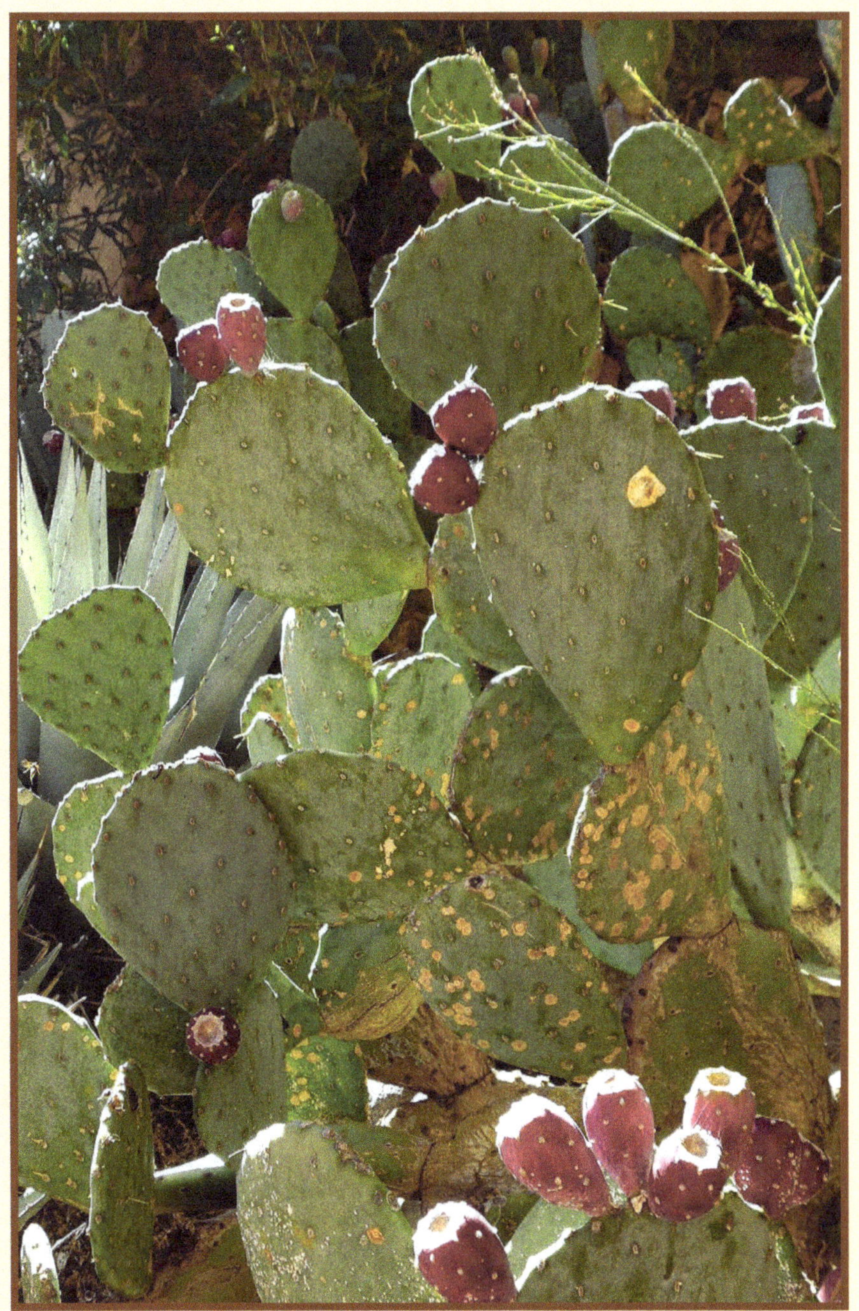

Prickly pear cactus grows in a cluster near the river in Albuquerque.

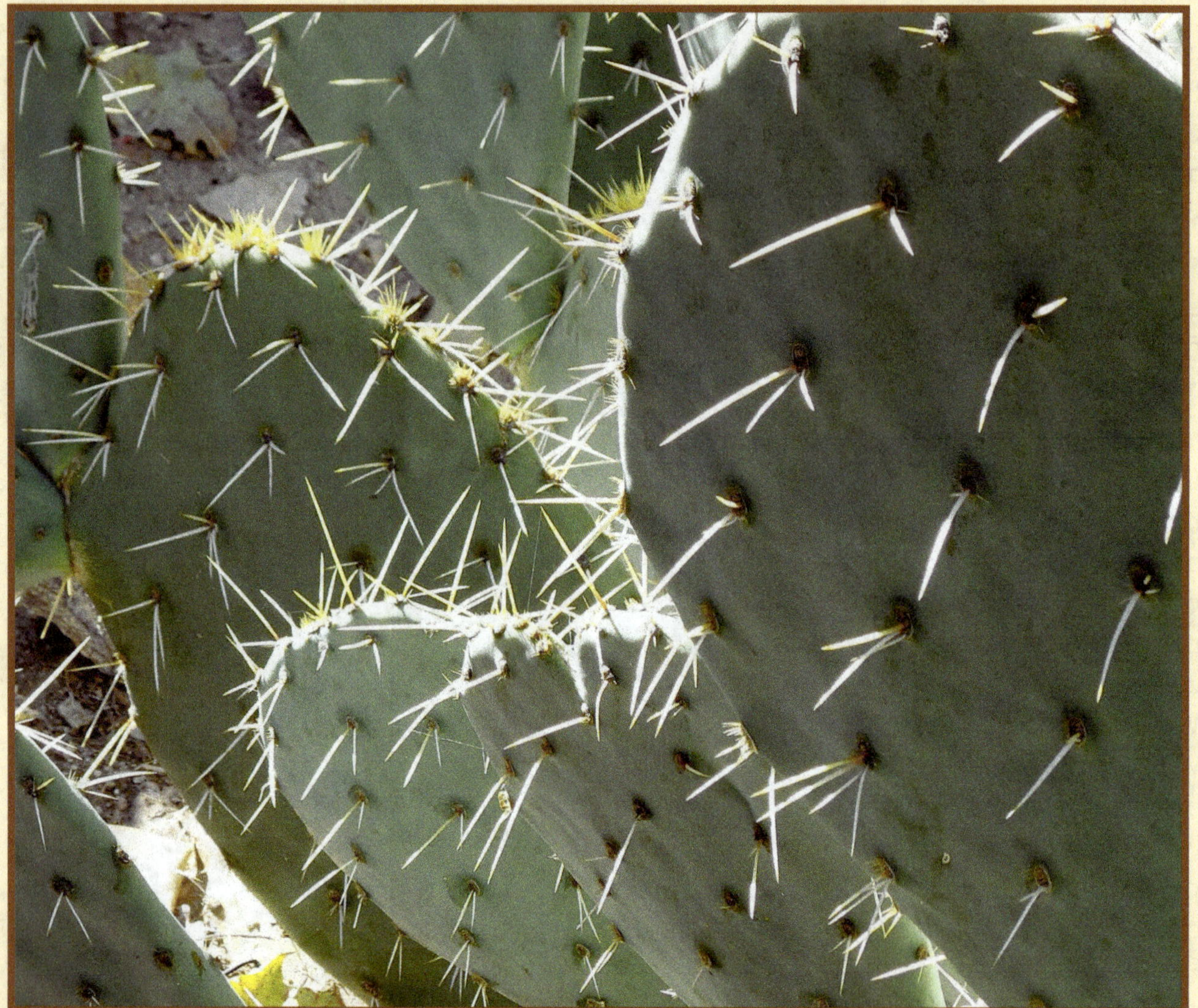

Bright sunlight glows on the needles of another type of prickly pear cactus found growing along a trail near the Rio Grande.

In New Mexico, many varieties of prickly pear can be found growing in dry sandy soil and gravel in elevations ranging from 3,500 feet to 7,500 feet above sea level.

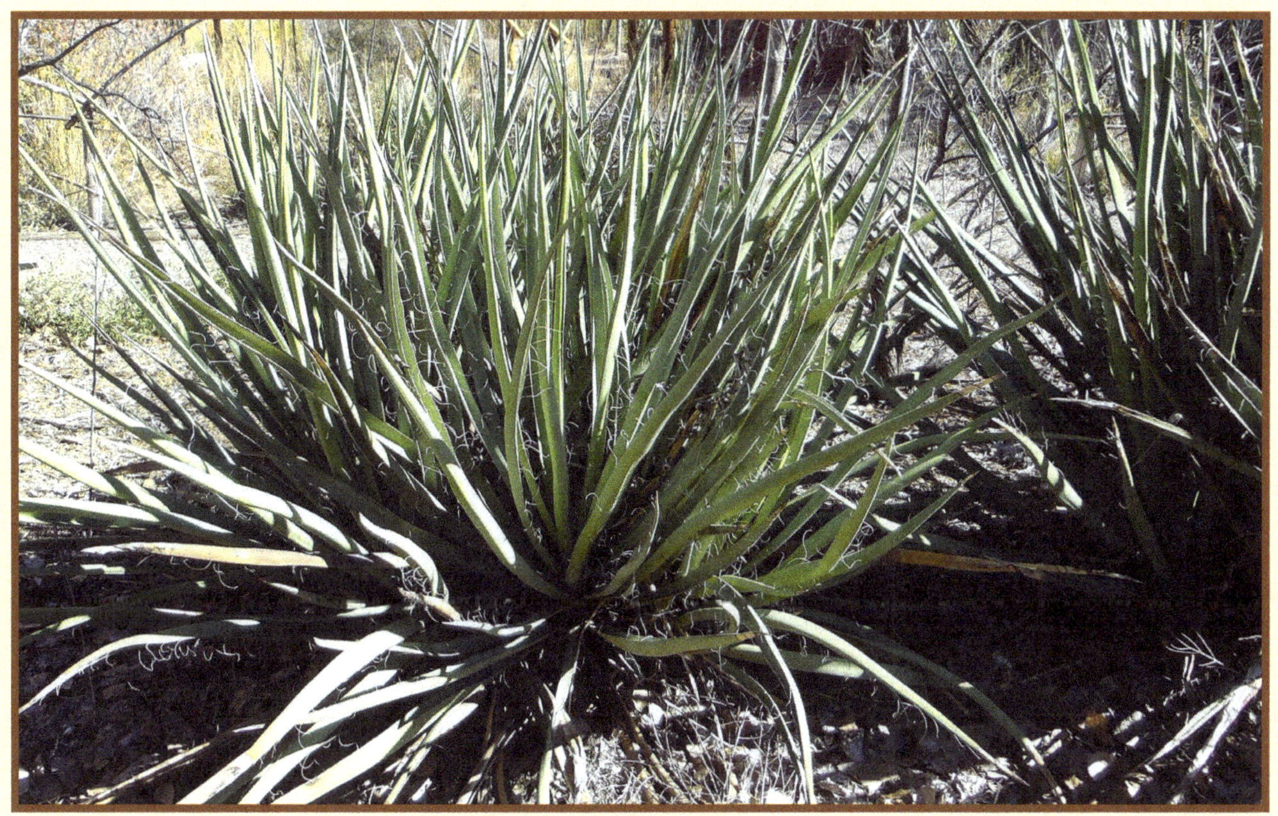

A group of yuccas line a trail in the Bosque along the Rio Grande.

There are many different types of yuccas in New Mexico. In fact, there are some 50 different species of yucca. So common are yuccas in New Mexico that they can be found growing in the higher elevation Sandia Mountains to lower-level grasslands.

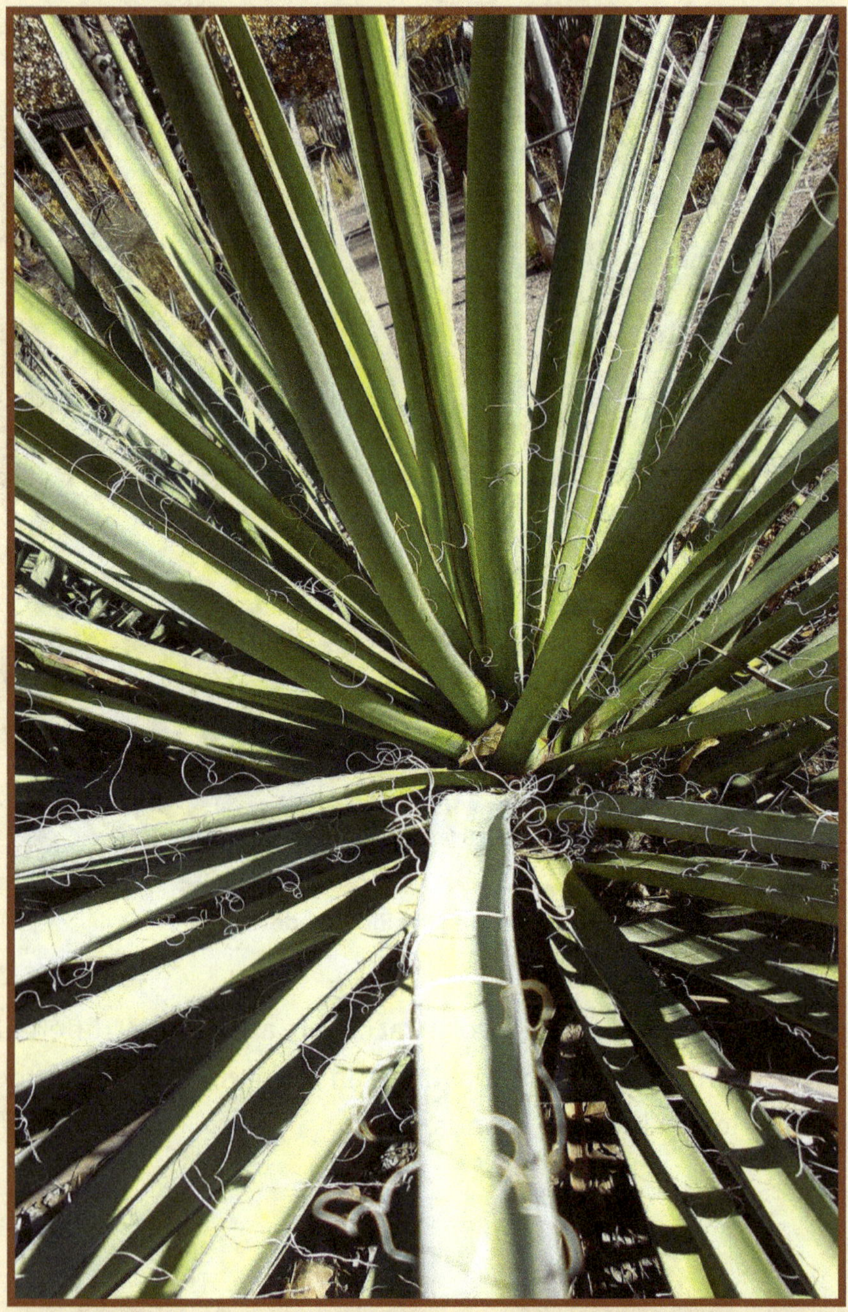

Yuccas have stiff leaves of varying widths. If you accidentally walk into the sharp tip of a yucca, it can easily pierce your clothing and stab into your skin.

The leaves are so sturdy and straight—and don't bend easily—that you can be stabbed by them inadvertently if you're not careful when passing by them.

It's no wonder that some types of yucca have been given names like Spanish bayonet, Spanish dagger, and sword-leaf yucca.

Sharp tips and curling rims of another species of yucca grow next to the Rio Grande.

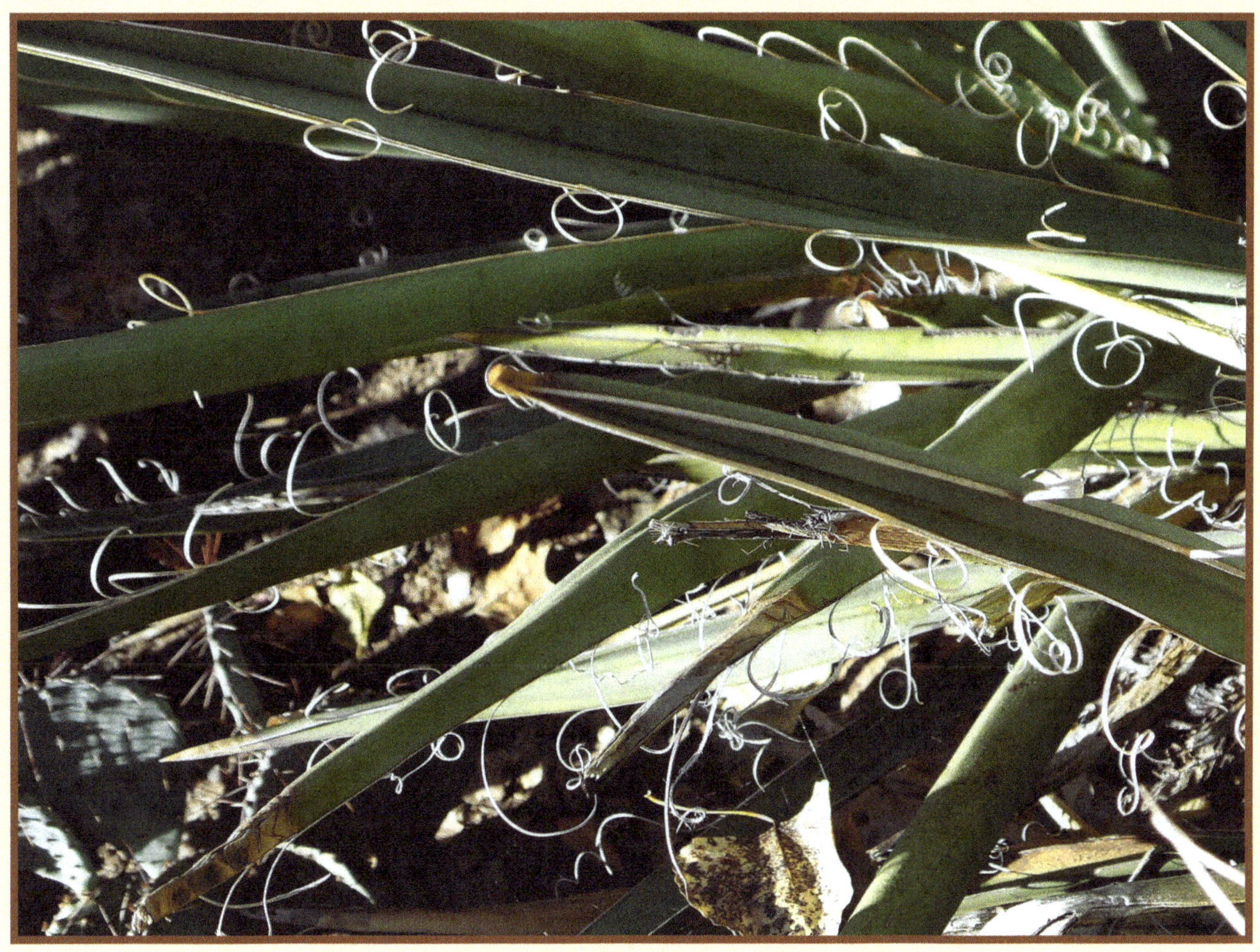

Chapter 8: Rio Grande Gorge

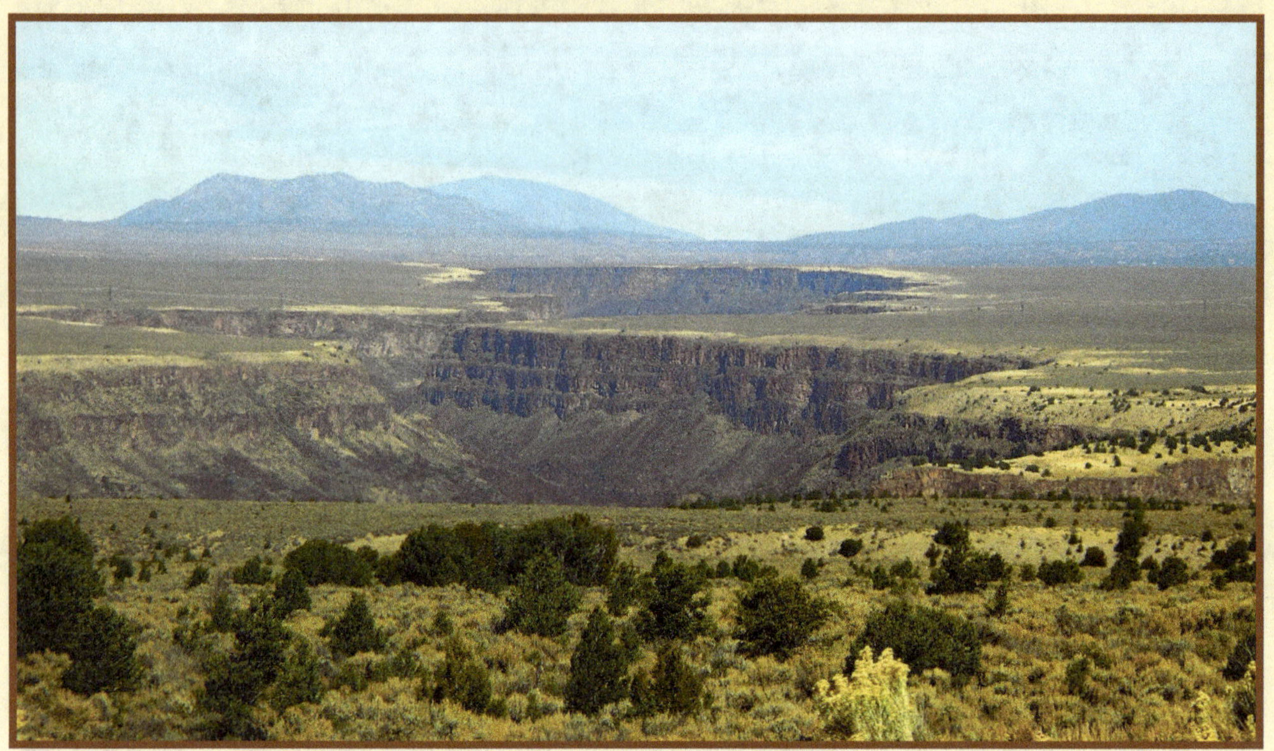

The Rio Grande Rift cuts a path through volcanic canyons, which interrupt the flat plains south of the Rio Grande Gorge outside Taos, N.M.

New Mexico is home to unique geologic features, including volcanic landforms and a rare continental rift formed 30 million years ago in the Earth's surface. The 800-mile-long Rio Grande Rift, which continues to widen by 2 millimeters annually, attracts scientists worldwide because it is among the few rifts that are still active. Most rifts are found in the middle of the ocean. This rift resulted in the Rio Grande Gorge, located at the base of a volcanic valley. Natural waters flowing down from mountainous areas created the Rio Grande, which follows along the rift's north-south course.

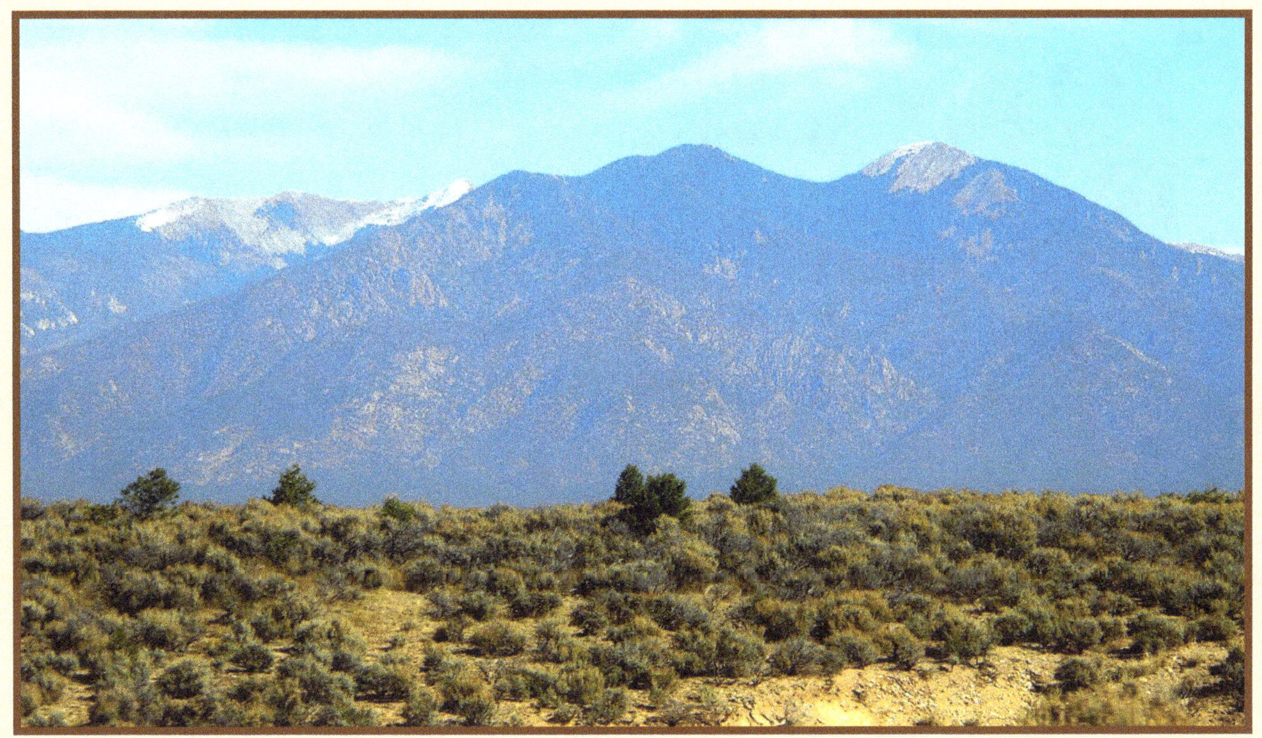

Opposite the Rio Grande Gorge rises Wheeler Peak.

At an elevation over 13,000 feet, Wheeler Peak is the highest summit in New Mexico. It was named after famed Southwest surveyor and cartographer George Montague Wheeler, a U.S. Army officer who supervised a federal government survey of the Southwest in the mid-1800's.

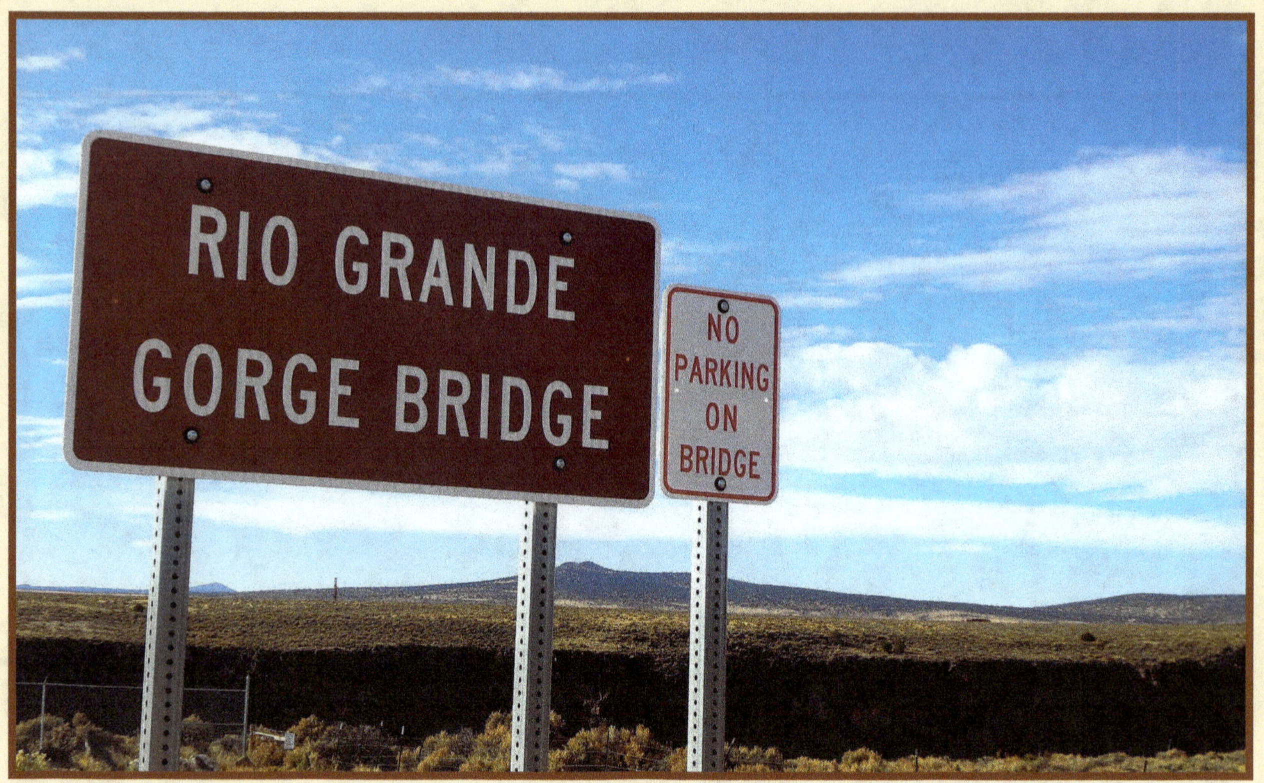

Signs mark the entrance to the 10-mile-long suspension bridge spanning over the Rio Grande Gorge.

The dark canyon rim, seen along the base of the photo, is a huge crack in the ground formed by the gorge in otherwise flat plains on either side of it.

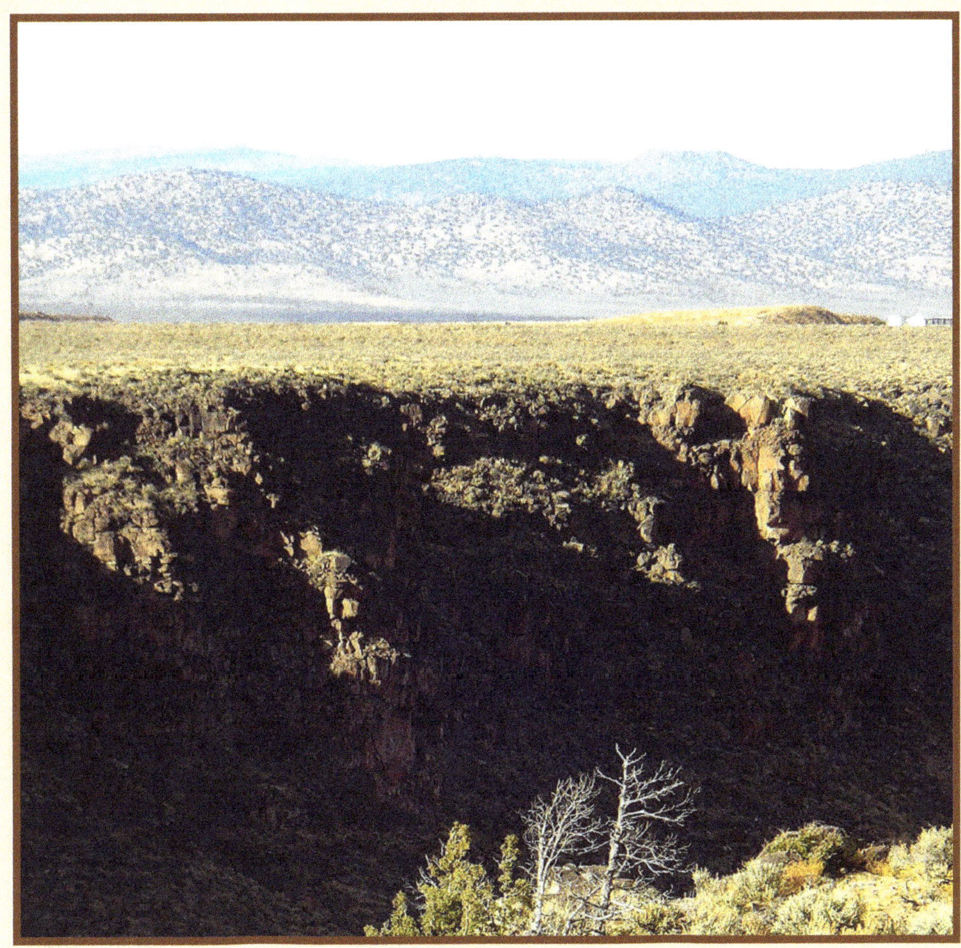

Basalt cliffs face the eastern rim of the Rio Grande Gorge, which descends 800 feet to the river below.

The gorge is located 6 miles from Taos Pueblo, whose inhabitants are one of 22 Native American tribes who have lived in New Mexico for centuries. The state has 19 Indian pueblos (settlements) along the Rio Grande and 3 reservations (2 Apache and 1 Navajo). Native Americans account for nearly 10% of the population in New Mexico, according to the U.S. Census. The state has the 2nd highest population composition of Native Americans after Alaska. Ancient Indian petroglyphs have been carved into boulders in the gorge and are visible from hiking trails. One example is the Big Arsenic Trail, a steep 1-mile-long trail that drops 680 feet in elevation to cold water springs and offers views of ancient Indian petroglyphs.

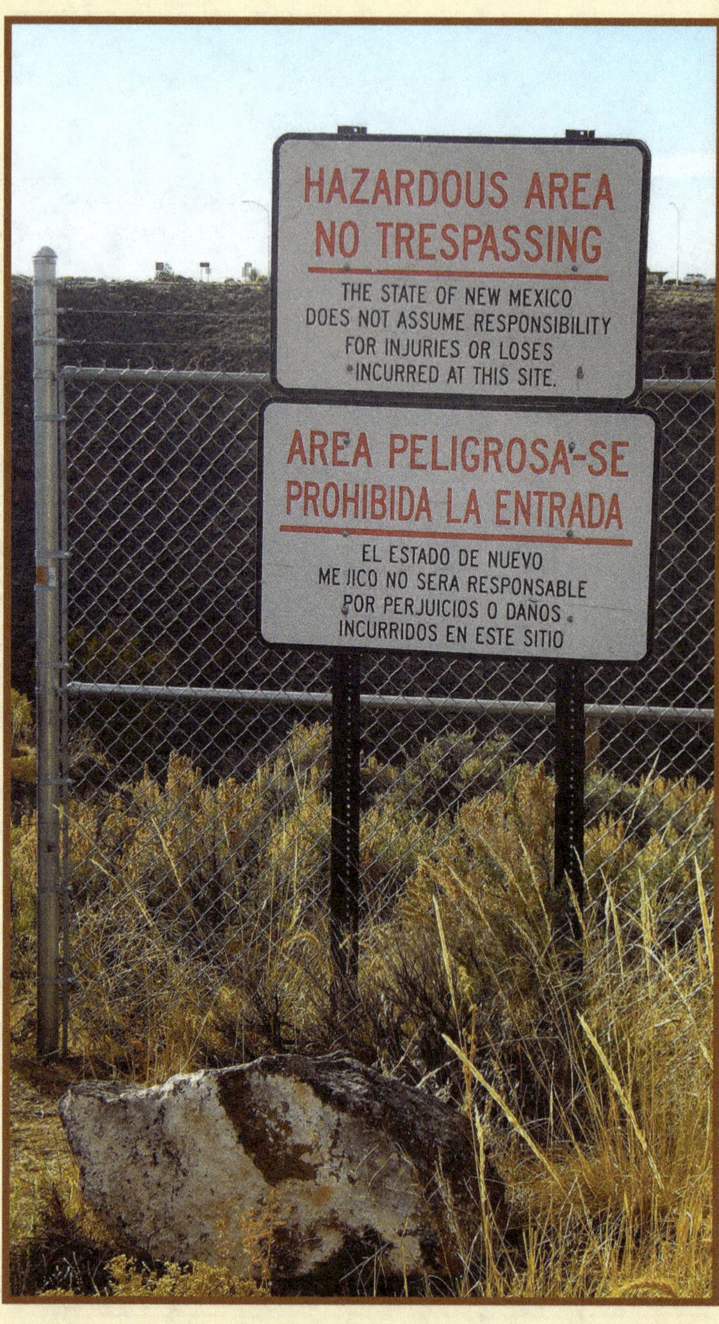

Many people have lost their lives in and around the Rio Grande Gorge. Areas around the gorge's cantilever bridge are heavily fenced.

Signs provide warnings to visitors of the Rio Grande Gorge.

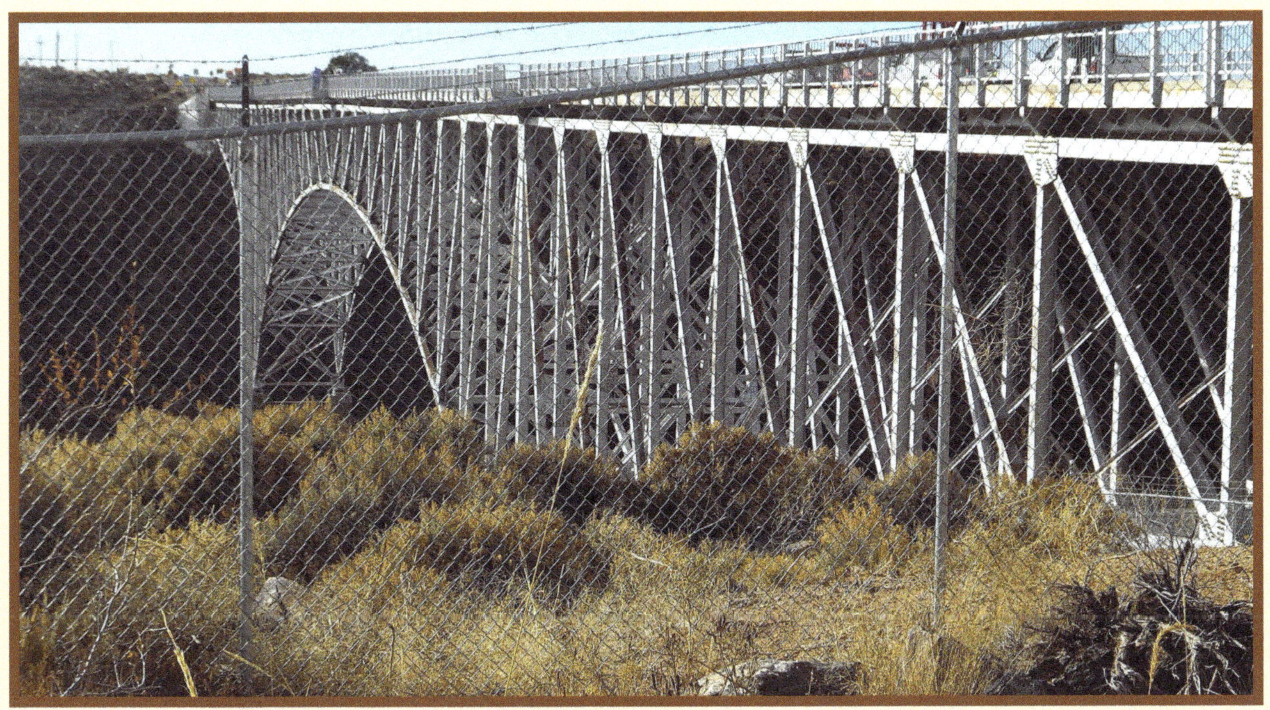

A side view of the Rio Grande Gorge suspension bridge masks the immense drop at the top of the canyon to the river below.

The Rio Grande Gorge Bridge spans 1,280 feet in length. It is the 7th highest bridge in the United States and 82nd highest in the world. It was completed in 1965 after two years of construction. It earned the "Most Beautiful Steel Bridge" award by the American Institute of Steel Construction in 1966 in the "long span" category. The bridge has been featured in 7 major Hollywood movies.

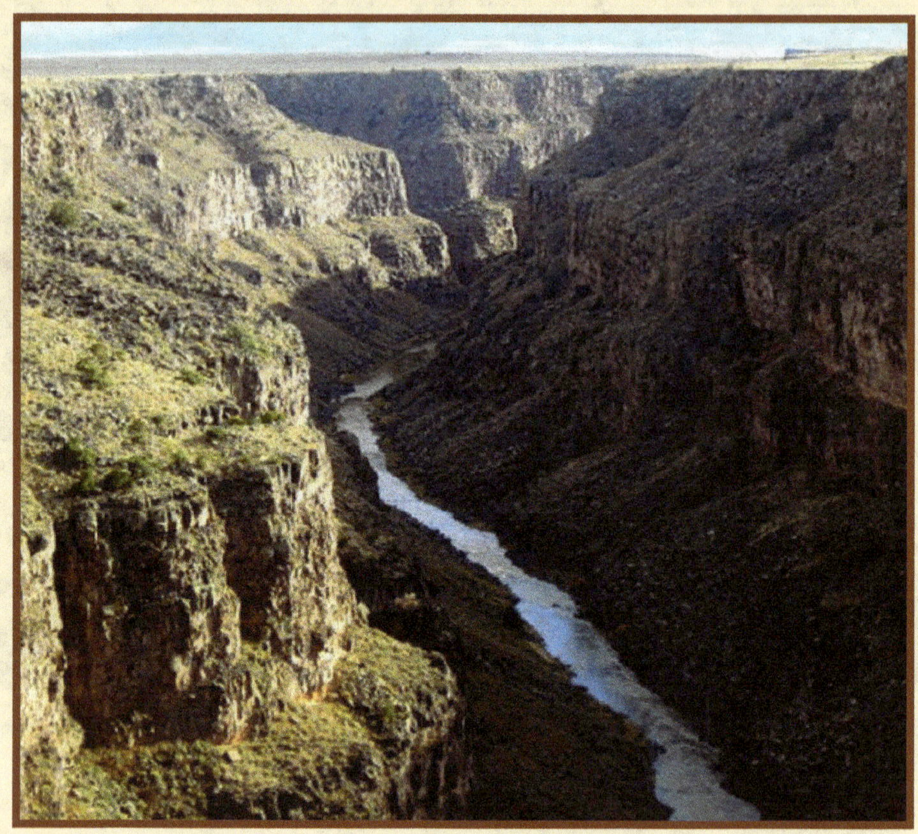

The Rio Grande curves through the base of the gorge.

This photo and the following four were taken while walking over the shaky Rio Grande Gorge Bridge and standing in its center to capture the images.

The waters of the Rio Grande are unpredictable, with dangerous rapids that flow through rugged terrain. Depending on the time of year, the water temperature may be cold enough to cause hypothermia.

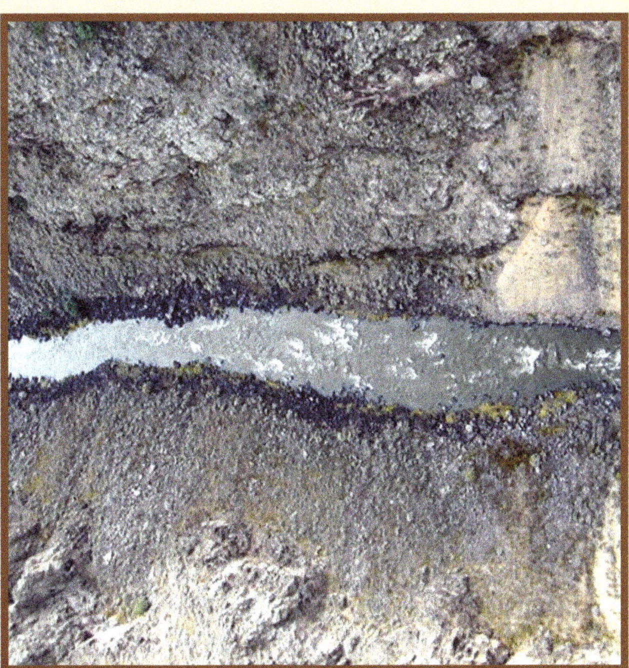

Whitewater rapids form in an isolated box canyon in the gorge called the Taos Box, a 17-mile area that attracts adventurous rafters. Experienced rafters have given the boulders in the river names such as Fishhook Rock, Sharkfin Rock, and Camel Rock. The rapids there are listed as Class 4+ due to dangerous hazards and a potentially high risk of injury for swimmers. Several people have died in boating accidents around the Taos Box.

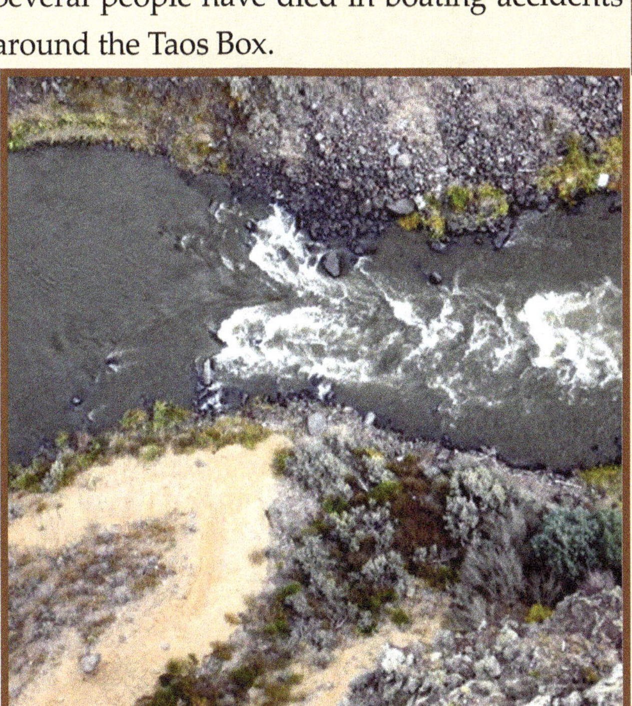

These two views of the river were taken looking straight down from the gorge bridge at the water 650 feet below.

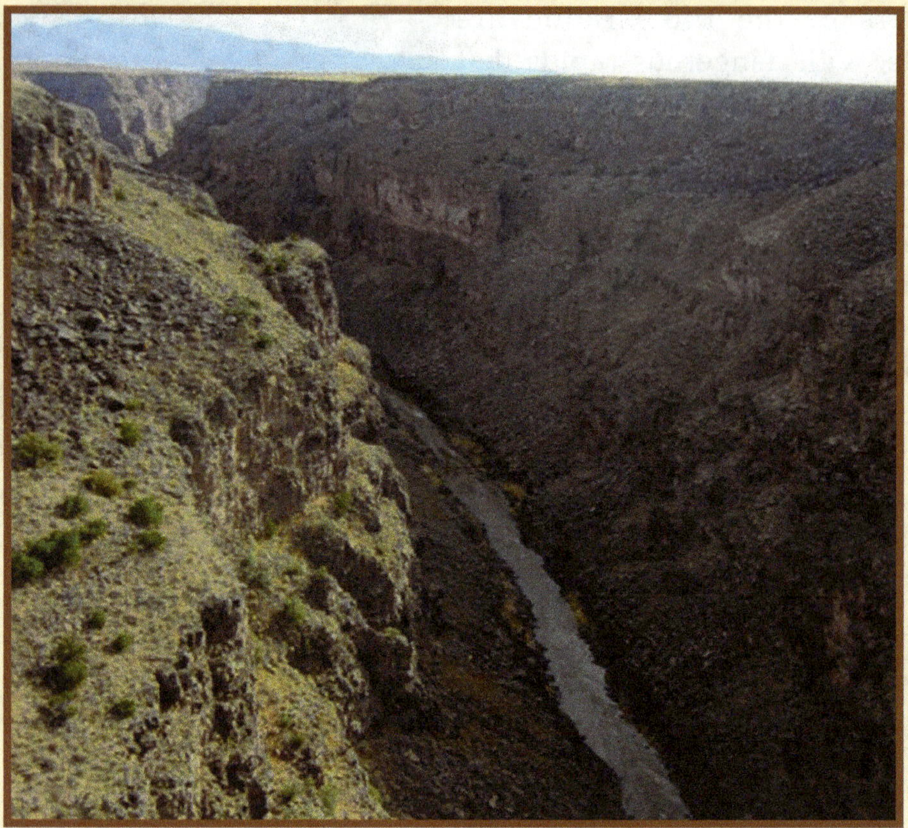

The Rio Grande Gorge cuts through massive thick sheets of lava and basalt in the Taos Plateau volcanic field.

The elevation of the Rio Grande inside the gorge is about 6,000 feet. The Bureau of Land Management has two recreational areas—the Wild Rivers and Orilla Verde—within the gorge that include places for camping and picnicking as well as hiking trails. Ancient magma eruptions formed several types of volcanic rock such as andesite, basalt, dacite, and rhyolite. The geology within the canyons of the gorge showcase dissected lava flows. Volcanic boulders lay scattered in and around the Rio Grande as it passes through the natural drainage basin formed at the base of the rift valley.

New Mexico is famous for numerous extinct volcanoes that are remarkably preserved. The volcanoes are accessible. The state has every main kind of volcanic landform, including:

- 16 volcanic fields (clusters of small volcanoes);
- many major volcanoes, such as the Jornada del Muerto, the Sierra Blanca, the Sierra Grande, the Tome, Black Butte, and Los Pinos volcanoes;
- the Capulin Peak lava dome (about 4,500 years old);
- cinder cones;
- fissure eruptions;
- exposed interior necks of young volcanoes that look like dark peaks; and
- craters (such as the 12-mile-in-diameter Valles Caldera).

Located in the upper Rio Grande Gorge area is Ute Mountain, the cone of an extinct volcano that borders the river.

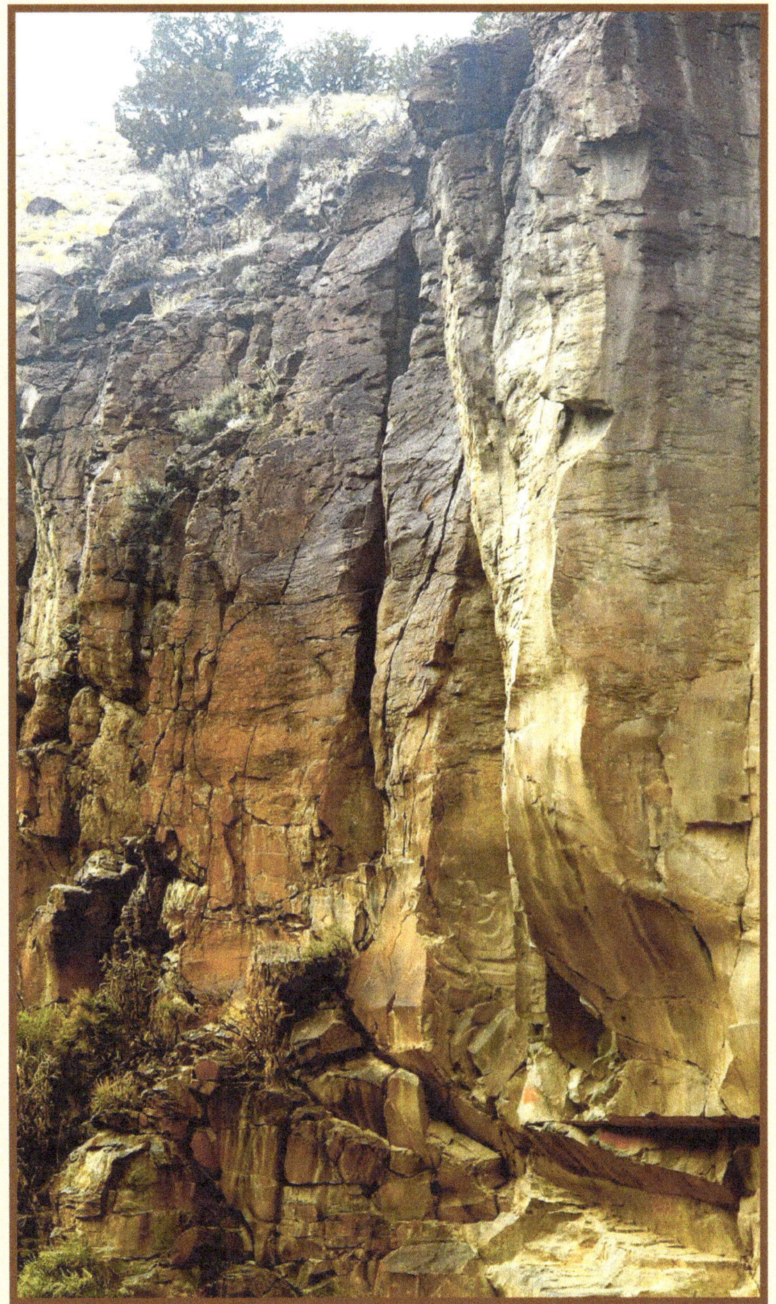

A majestic rock canyon next to the gorge provides a stunning view of the interior geologic structure that lies below grassy plains visible at the top of the photo.

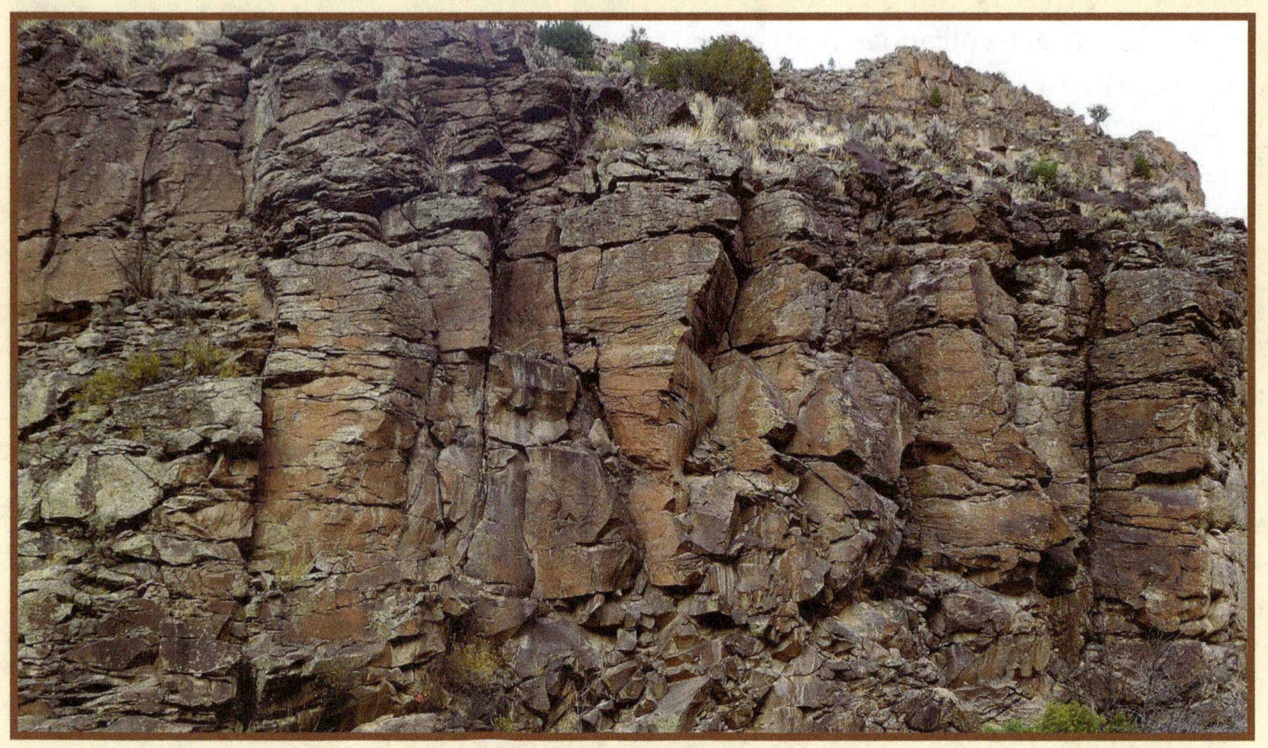

Basalt cliffs such as these, which line the Rio Grande Gorge, are popular for rock climbing.

Two designated rock-climbing locations around the gorge are Dead Cholla (near the West Rim Trail) and John's Wall (close to the John Dunn Bridge). Visitors to the gorge also can take advantage of two natural hot springs.

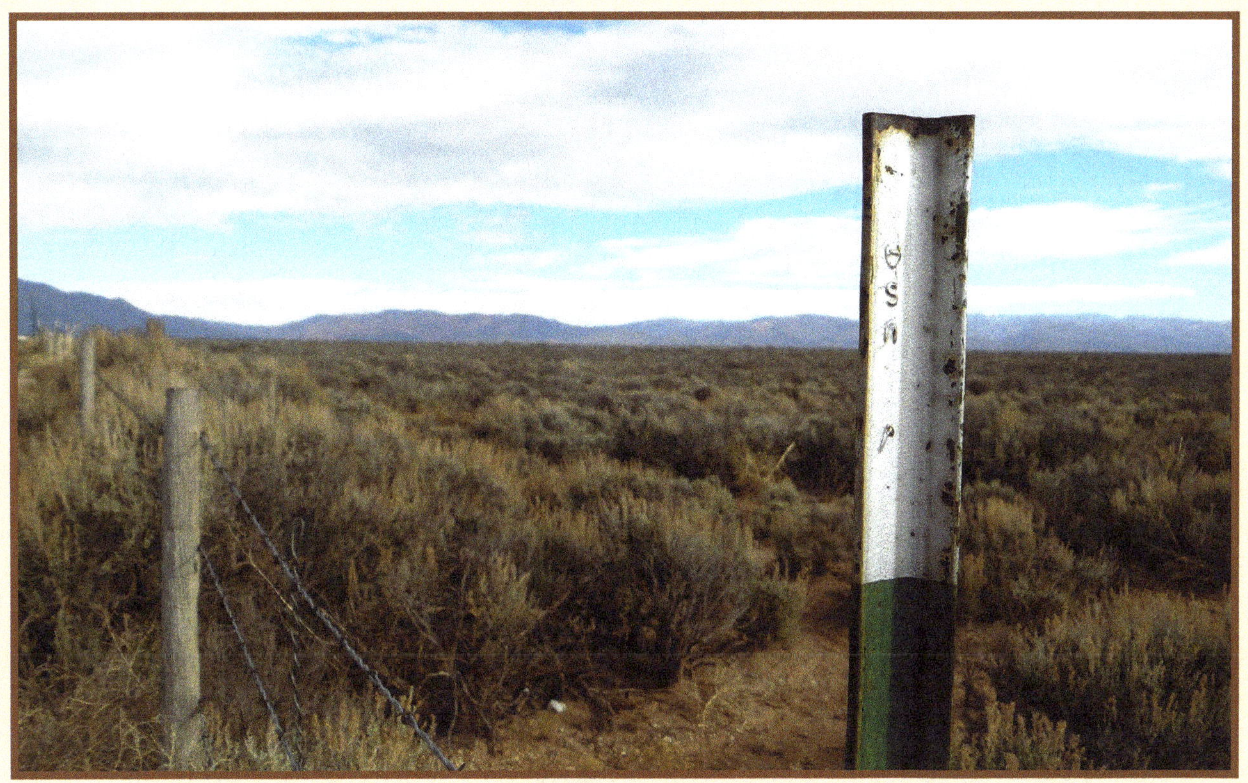

A barbed wire fence blocks public access to land around the Rio Grande Gorge.

Beyond the Rio Grande Gorge are open spaces dotted with sagebrush that have remained unchanged for centuries. It is unclear when barbed wire fences first came to New Mexico after the first U.S. barbed wire patent was granted in 1867.

Evidence of early interest in the use of barbed wire in New Mexico can be seen in newspaper ads from as early as 1879. The advertisements promote the benefits of the strength and durability of barbed wire fencing to farmers and ranchers in the eastern part of the state.

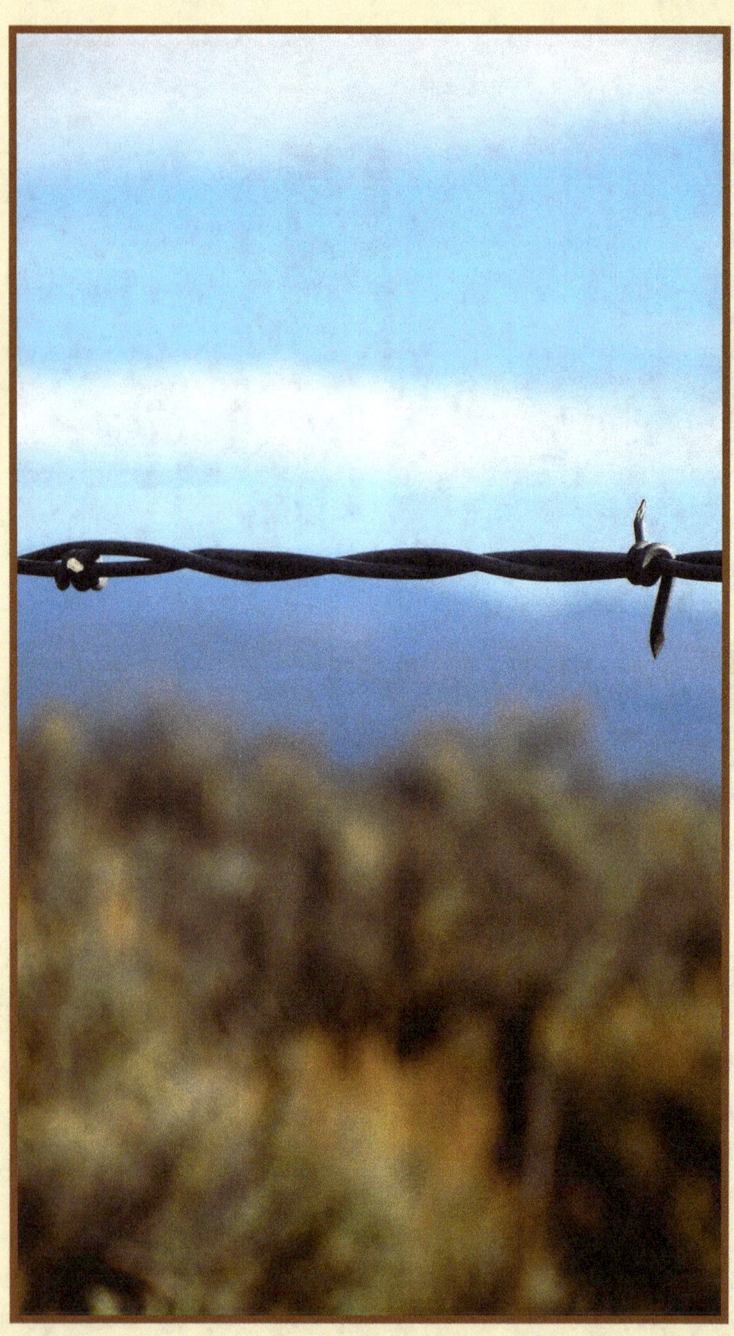

The introduction of barbed wire fencing was controversial in New Mexico as in other Western states. Barbed wire fences ended open-range cattle ranching and started violent range wars.

Fence cutters in New Mexico were imprisoned and sometimes shot to death in gun battles for cutting fences erected by the government.

One of New Mexico's most famous range wars occurred in 1878 in the Lincoln County War that involved legendary outlaw Billy the Kid, who was later killed and buried in Fort Sumner, N.M.

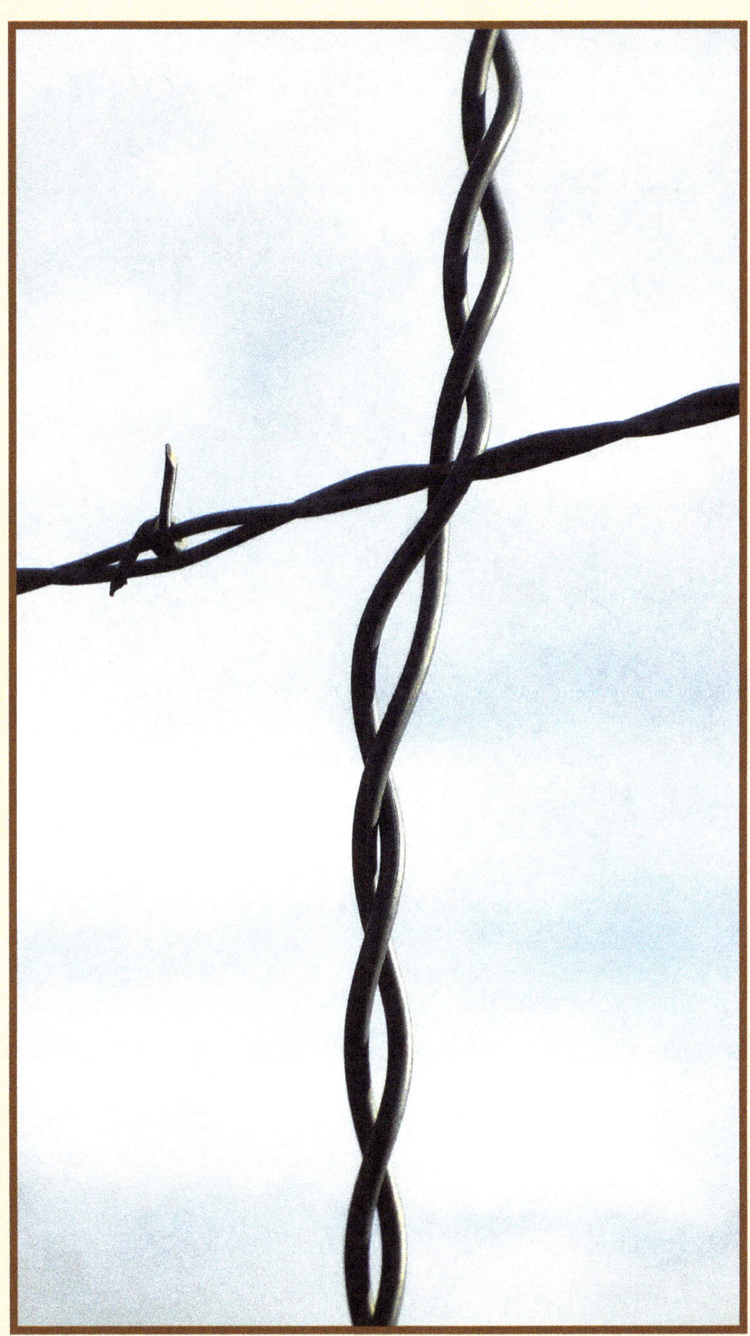

Closeup views show twisted cable and 2-point barbs in barbed wire fencing along the Rio Grande Gorge.

CHAPTER 9: BOSQUE DEL APACHE

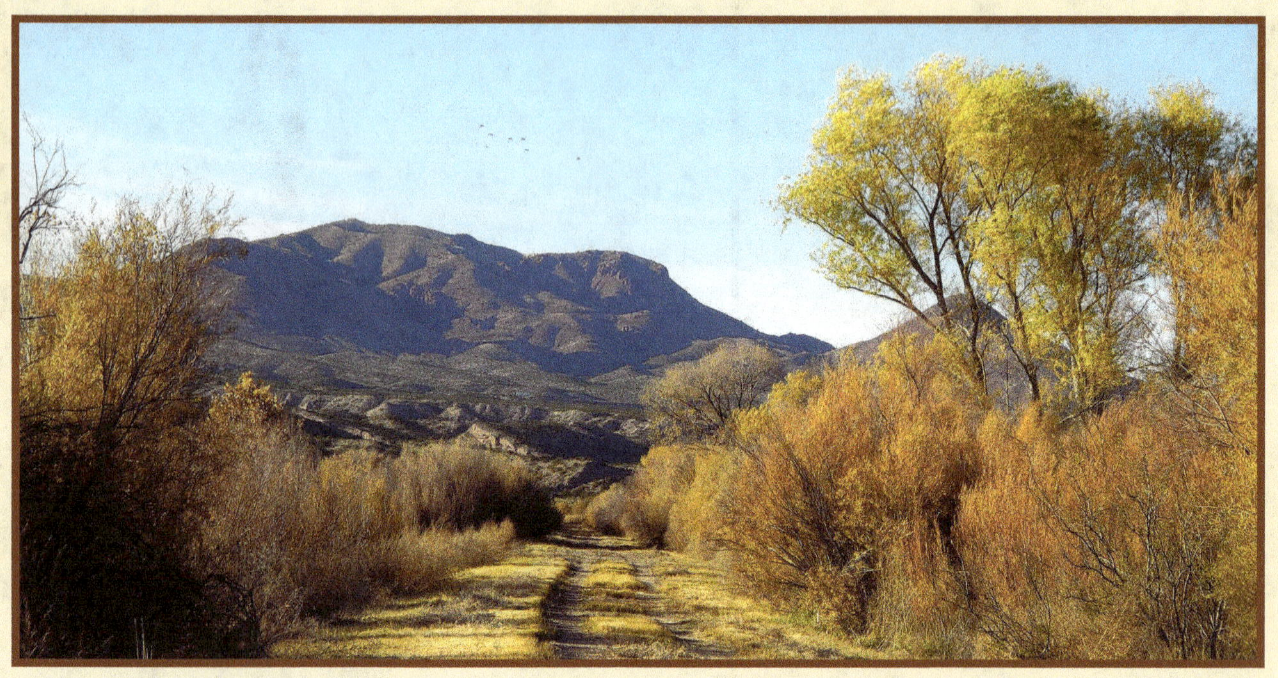

Birds fly overhead in the distance at Bosque del Apache National Wildlife Refuge. Photo by Zita.

The waters of the Rio Grande enable wetlands to flourish in a 57,300-acre sanctuary for migratory waterfowl in the Bosque del Apache National Wildlife Refuge outside Socorro, N.M.

More than 377 bird species have been observed there since 1940. Over 100,000 birds can roost in the refuge in a single week during the winter.

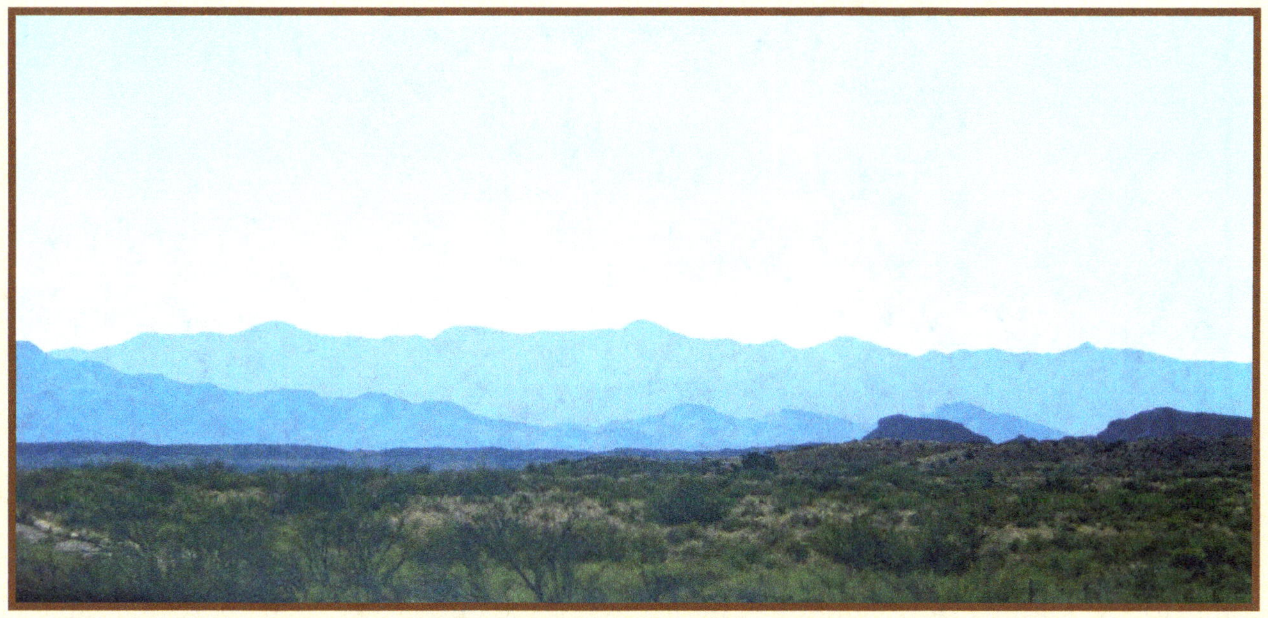

The ridge of the Sierra de las Ladrones (Mountain of Thieves) rise from the high desert plains outside Socorro near the Bosque del Apache National Wildlife Refuge. Photo by Zita.

My great-grandfather Abenicio Perea and his family members tracked cattle rustlers and horse thieves to the Ladron mountains, located 10 miles east of the Rio Grande. Criminals and outlaws often fled to its caves and canyons to conceal themselves with stolen goods and livestock. Apaches and Navajos used the Ladron mountains as hideouts after attacks on travelers on the Camino Real and raids on settlements along the Rio Grande.

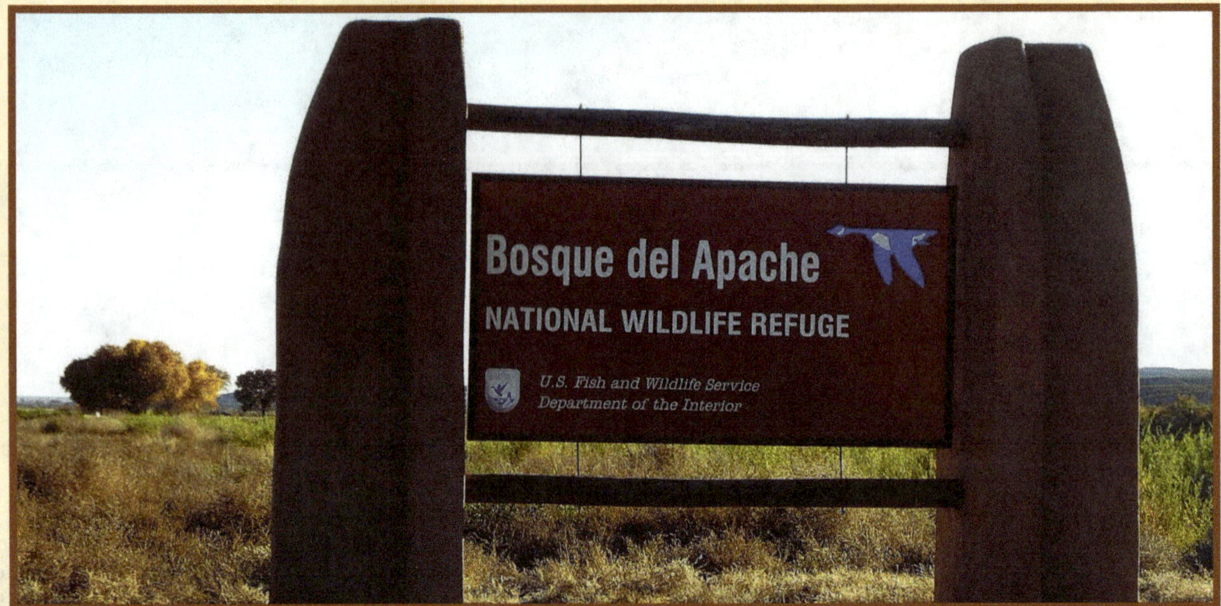

Managed by the U.S. Fish and Wildlife Service, the Bosque del Apache refuge was established in 1939 around the site of an 1845 land grant bearing the same name.

The refuge features viewing platforms and touring areas that provide numerous vantage points to see wildlife. Dawn and dusk fly-ins, when the birds leave their roosts in search of food and return for the evening, are popular for spectators. The best months to view migratory birds are from November to February, when the greatest numbers of birds are living there. Biologists at the refuge regularly conduct scientific surveys to estimate how many birds are there as part of managing the habitat. Although the numbers fluctuate, a weekly bird count in December estimated there were:

- 61,300+ snow and Ross geese;
- 27,200+ ducks;
- 12,400+ sandhill cranes;
- 470 water and shorebirds;
- 360 Canada geese, and
- 50 raptors.

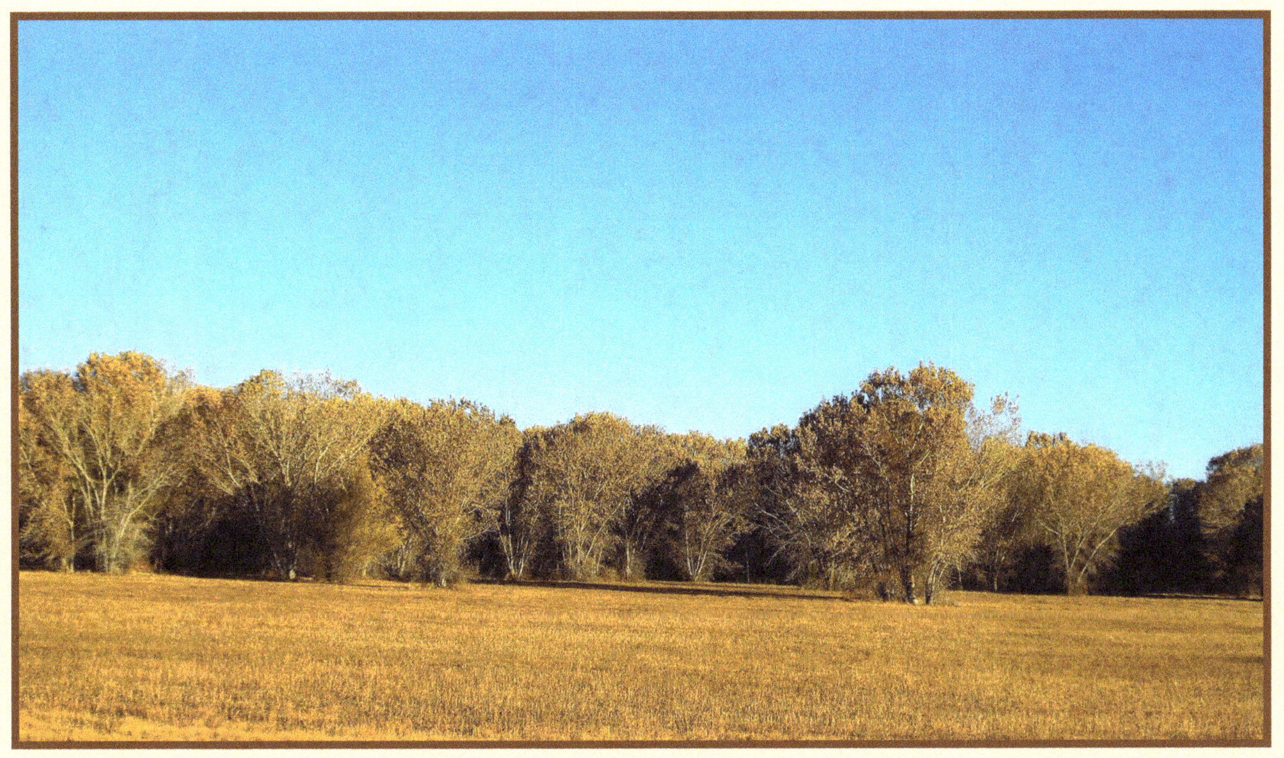

Cottonwood trees line the riverbanks at Bosque del Apache (Apache Woods), which takes its name from the Native Americans who established camps there along the riverbanks.

Spanish conquistadors recorded that the Piro Indians were living in a pueblo community near the present-day wildlife refuge along the Rio Grande in the 1500s. But the Indians abandoned the village in the late 1600s. Later the Apaches moved into the area. The Rio Grande in that area was divided among three Apache territories: the Chiricahua, west of the river extending into Arizona, and the Mescaleros on the east. To the south of the river lived the Mimbreño Apaches (people of the willows). The U.S. Army fought the Apache Wars in the mid-1800s in parts of New Mexico, Arizona, and Texas with various tribes, whose famous leaders included Mangas Coloradas (Red Sleeves), Cochise, Victorio, and Geronimo.

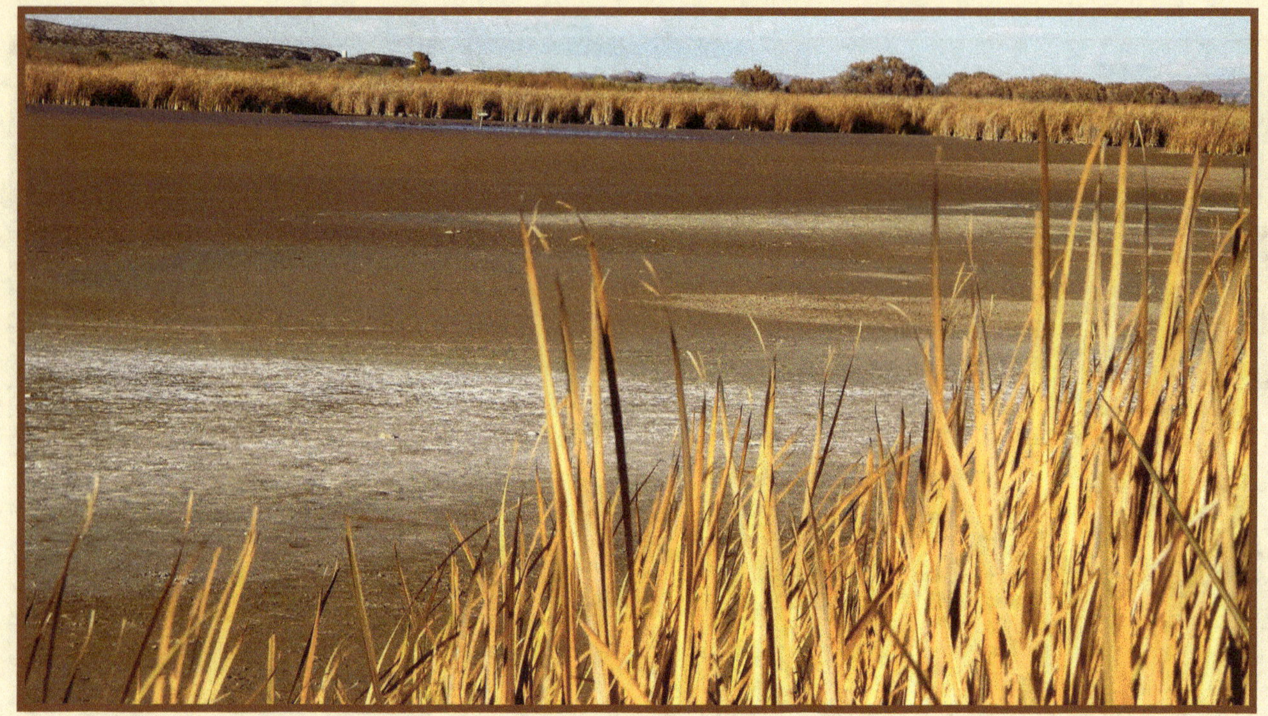

A mud flat shows the rugged isolation of the Bosque del Apache area.

Located down the road some 20 miles away on the west bank of the Rio Grande is Fort Craig. The fort was built in 1854. It was among 8 forts along the Rio Grande valley established to protect travelers and settlers from Apache, Navajo, and Comanche raids. In the decade that followed, Fort Craig became the largest U.S. fort in the Southwest. From 2,000 to 4,000 infantry and cavalry soldiers, including African-American Buffalo Soldiers, were garrisoned there at different times.

Fort Craig played important roles in the Civil War and the Indian Wars. Military campaigns from Fort Craig were conducted against Apache leaders Nana, Geronimo, and Victorio.

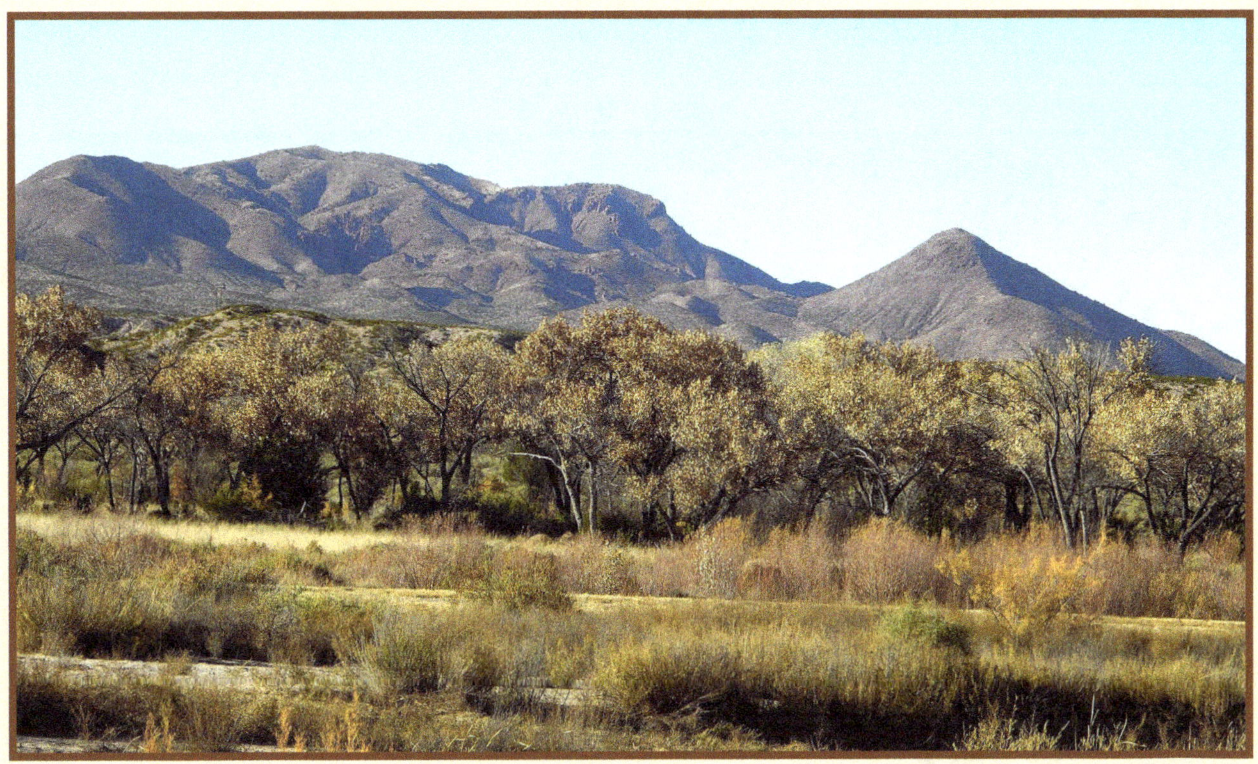

The Chupadera Mountains stand behind cottonwood trees on the west side of the Bosque del Apache Wildlife Refuge.

The mountain ranges around the refuge were important to the U.S. government when New Mexico was still a Territory and U.S. geologists and businessmen were evaluating natural resources to exploit. Mining in the area has a long history. Spanish conquistadors mined the area from the late 1500s to mid-1600s. Mining resumed there in the late 1880s for gold, silver, lead, and copper ore. In the late 1800s, old Spanish mineshafts could still be found in the Ladron mountains.

In 1893, the New Mexico School of Mines opened in Socorro to provide expertise to capitalize on the silver and lead ores mined in the nearby Magdalena mountains. The school, known today as the New Mexico Institute of Mining and Technology, continues to be an important center for mining in the state and has two geophysics research centers.

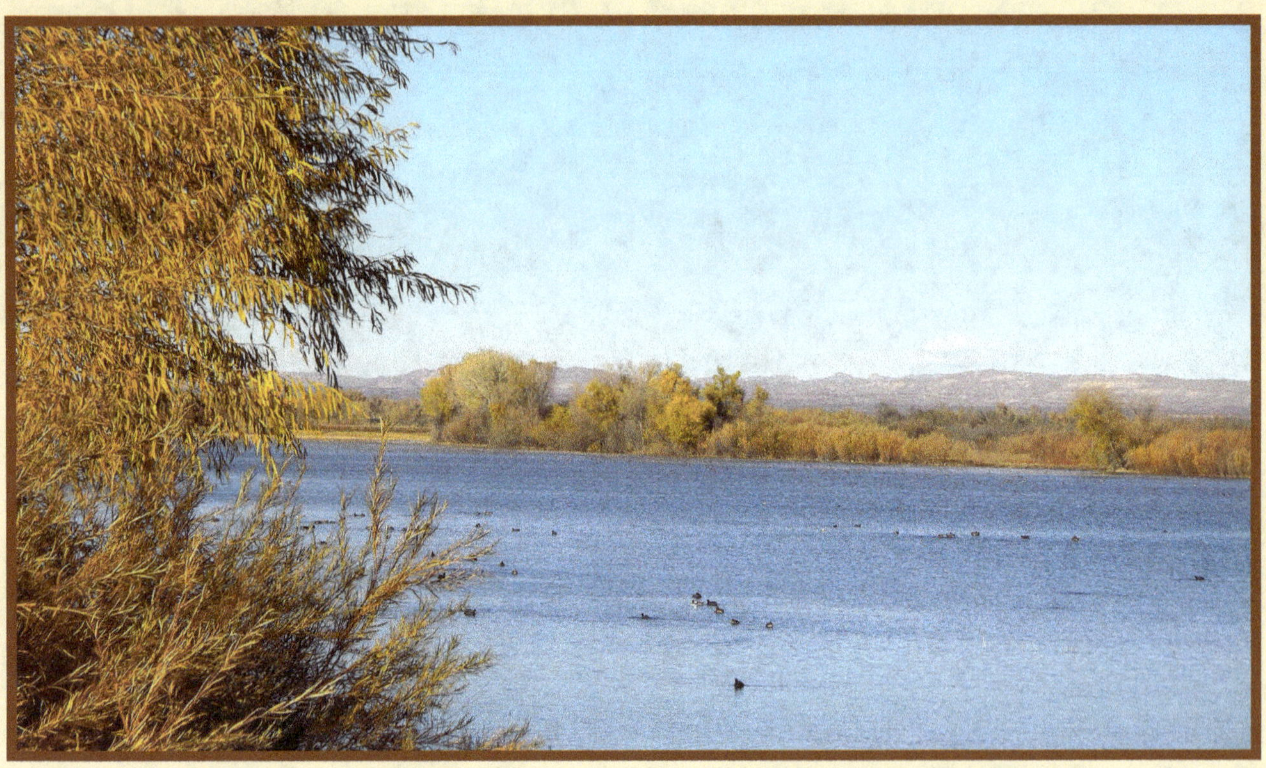

Ducks and geese swim through the cool waters of the refuge facing the San Pascual Mountains on the east.

Each November, the refuge hosts the Festival of the Cranes to celebrate the winter migration of the sandhill and whooping cranes. Birdwatchers from all around the United States and from overseas journey to the Bosque del Apache for the popular event.

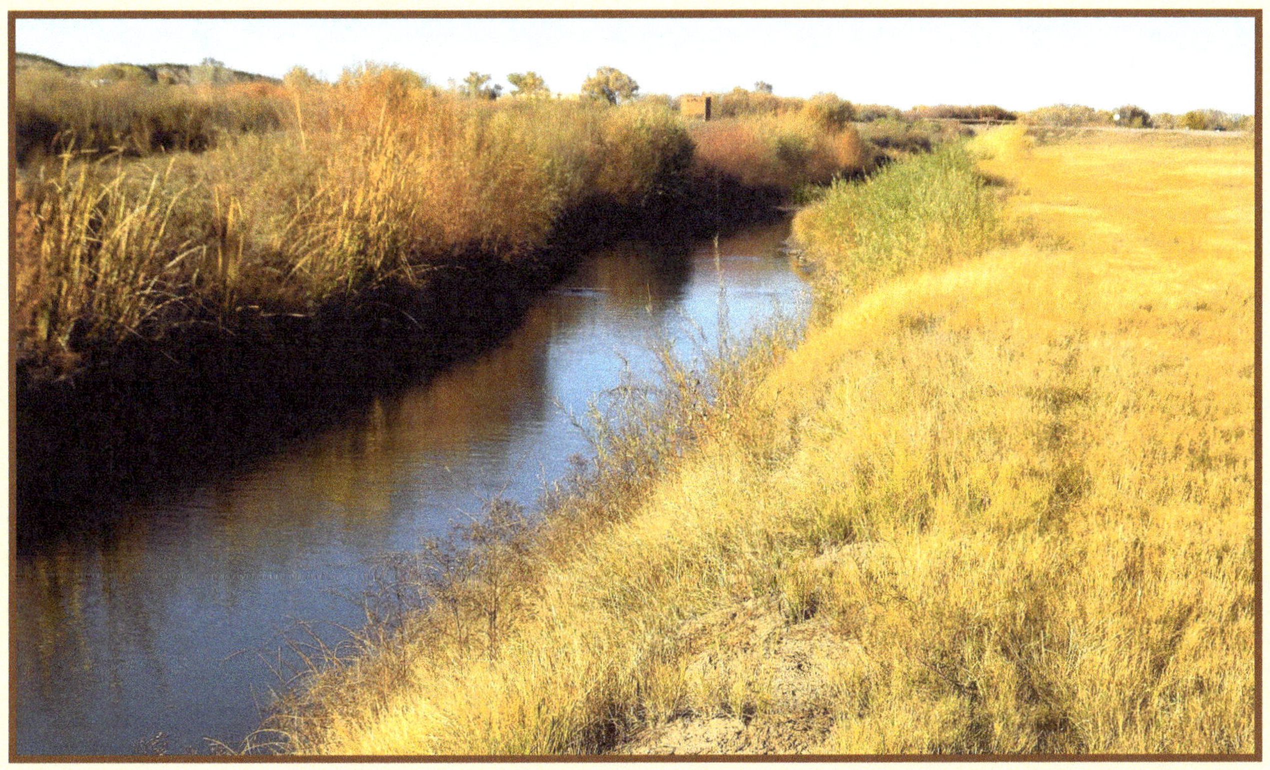

Water from the Rio Grande is diverted into a ditch on the Bosque del Apache Wildlife Refuge.

This river water will flow into wetlands, marshes, and ponds to create important habitats for migratory and year-round wildlife.

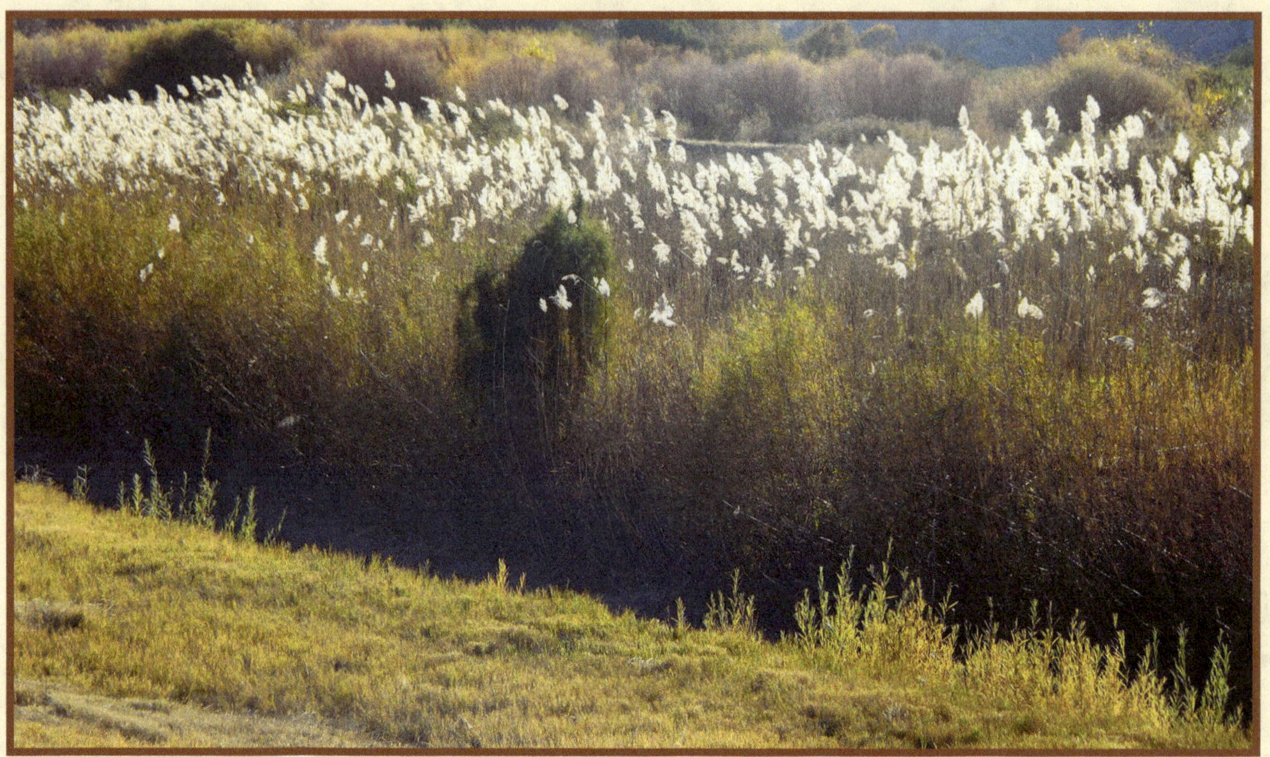

Native grass flutters along a ditch bank in the Bosque del Apache.

Horses, cattle, and sheep feed on 15 types of indigenous grasses that cover New Mexico's mesas, valleys, and mountain plains. Blue Grama grass, an important food source for foraging cattle, has been designated as the state's official grass since it is found in all 33 counties that make up New Mexico. It is a thin-bladed grass that grows in bunches from 6 inches to over a foot tall. When the fuzzy seeds mature at the tips of the stalks, they resemble curved eyebrows.

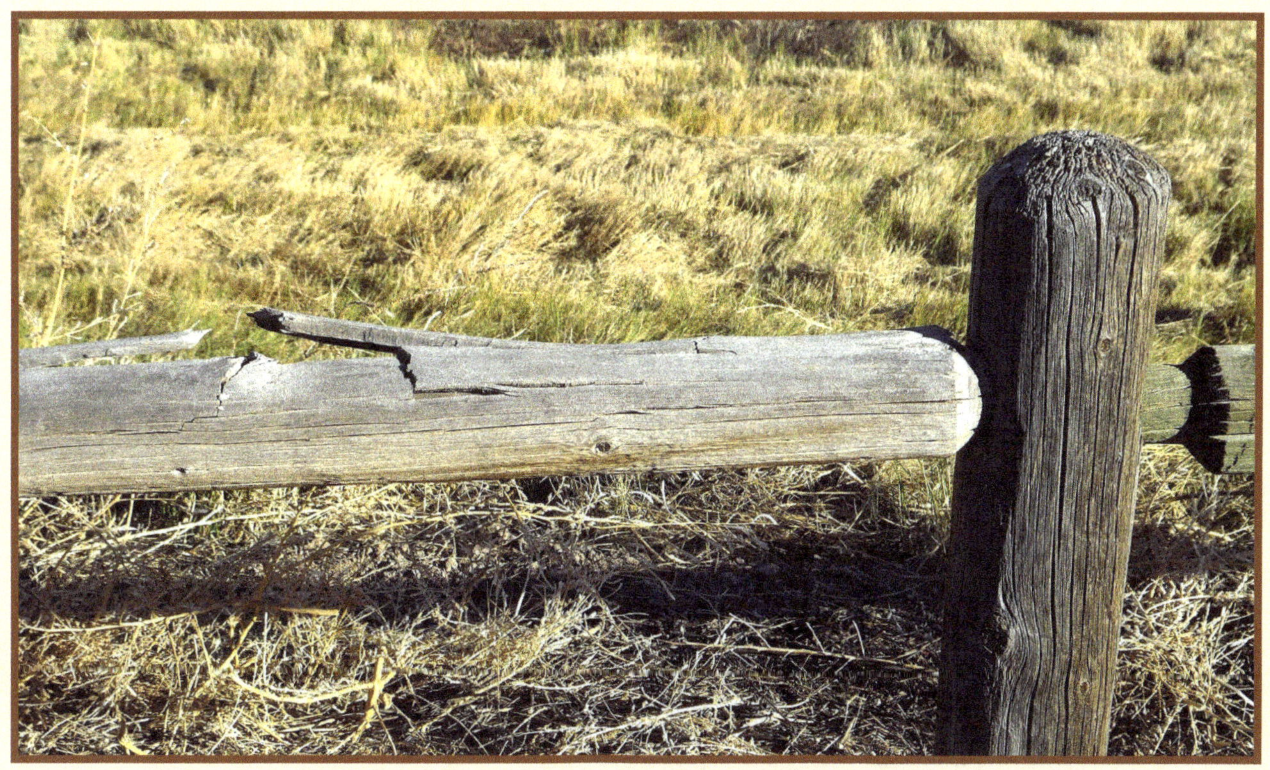

A weathered fence forms a corral enclosure to keep visitors out of some wildlife areas in the refuge.

Another mission of the national refuge is to provide members of the public with educational experiences about the wildlife there. Visitors have several choices about viewing the birds and animals. There are hiking trails and several tour loops of varying lengths for travels by car. The refuge also has three wilderness areas:

- Chupadera Peak Wilderness Area—spanning 5,440 acres in a rugged area, with a hiking trail nearly 5 miles long.
- Indian Wells Wilderness Area—covering 5,100 acres of foothills covered with wild grasses, cacti, and juniper trees. There are places to hike and watch wildlife.
- Little San Pascual Mountain—nearly 20,000 acres of rolling land in a desert habitat with limited hiking.

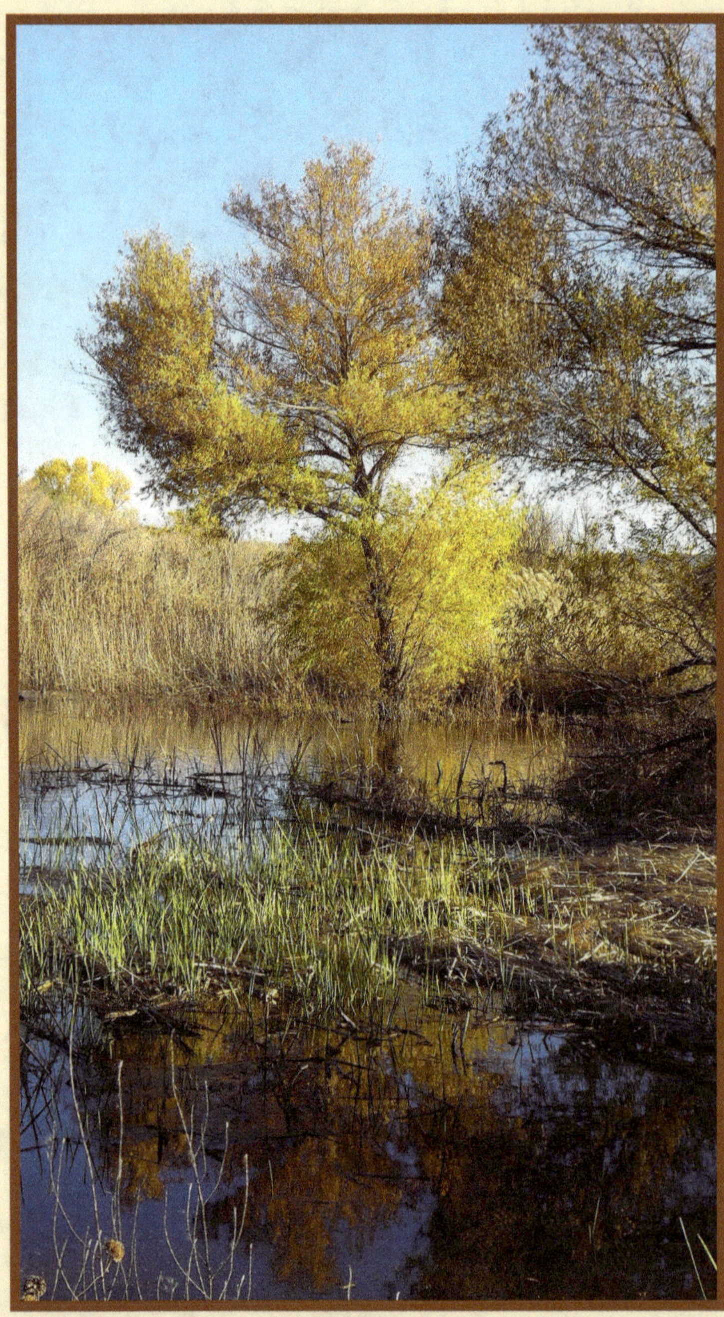

Autumn trees are reflected in the waters of a pond.

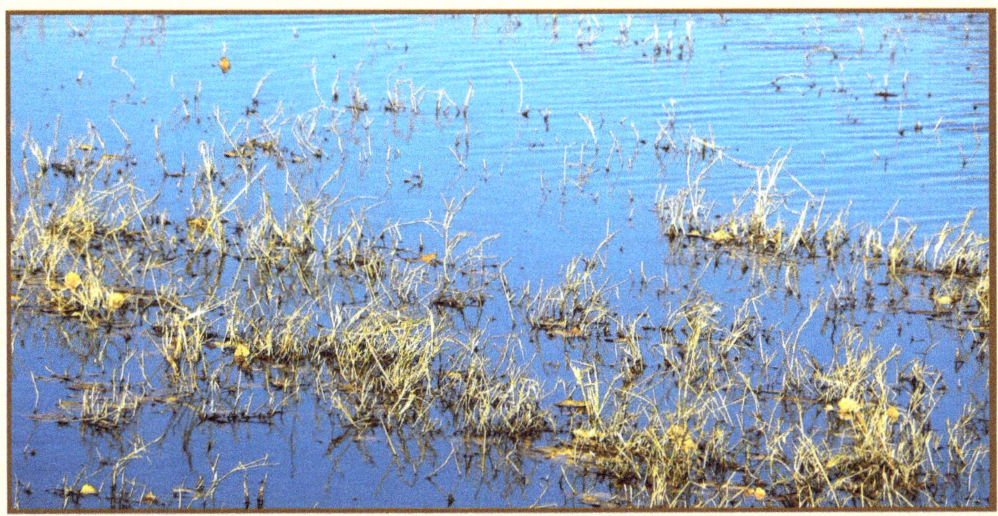

Wild grass grows in brilliant blue waters in a lake inside the refuge. This grass is an important part of the wetland environment for migratory birds.

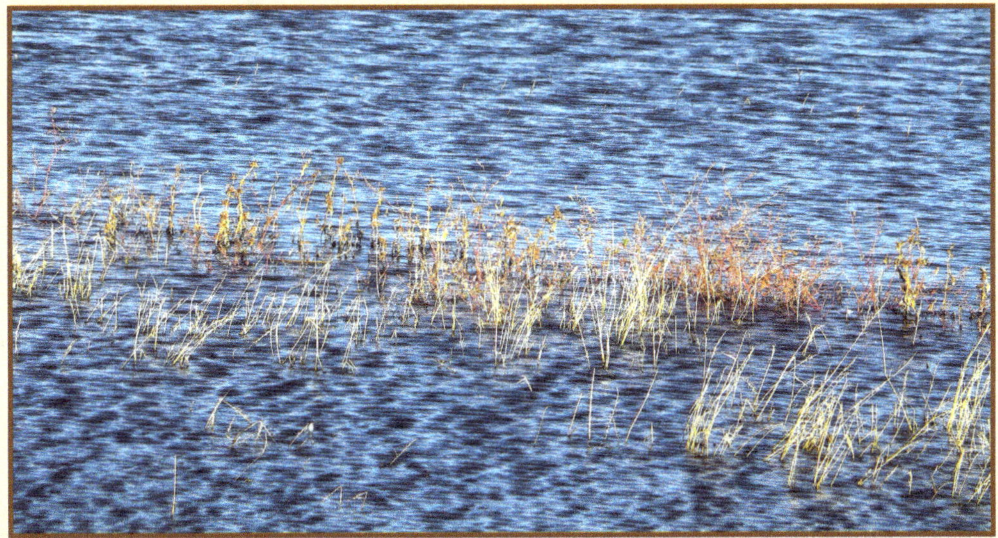

Native grasses of many varieties can be found in the wetlands of the refuge.

Some waterways within the refuge can be used for recreation. Fishing for carp, catfish, largemouth bass, and sunfish is approved in certain places from April to September 30, until a few minutes after sunset. Frog hunting is permitted for bullfrogs from June through September.

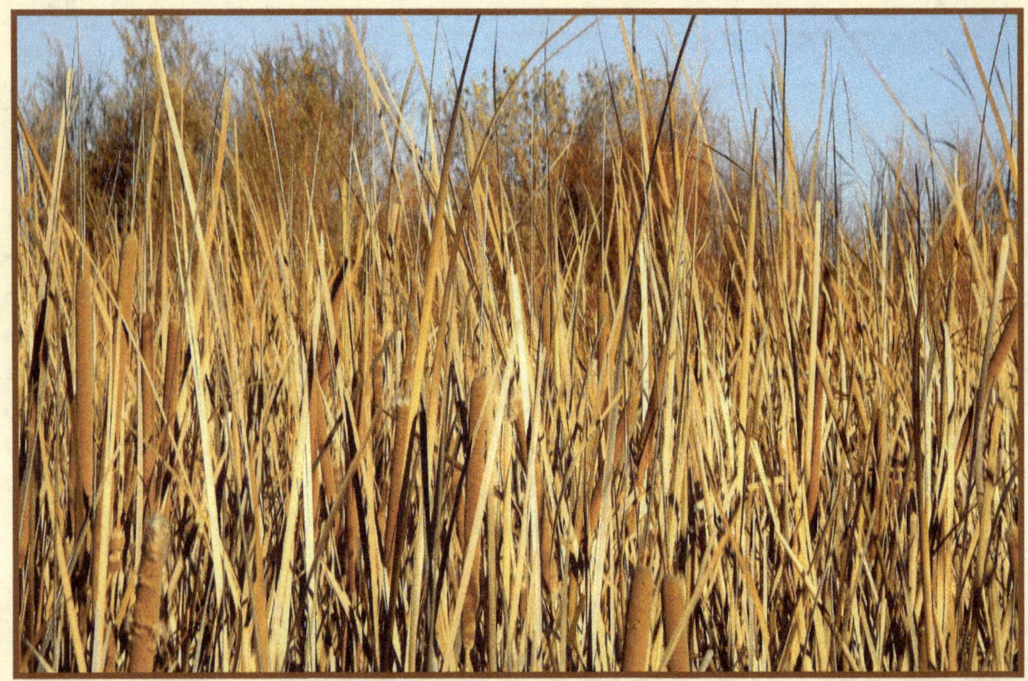

A thicket of cattails creates a golden wall of vegetation in a quiet marsh.

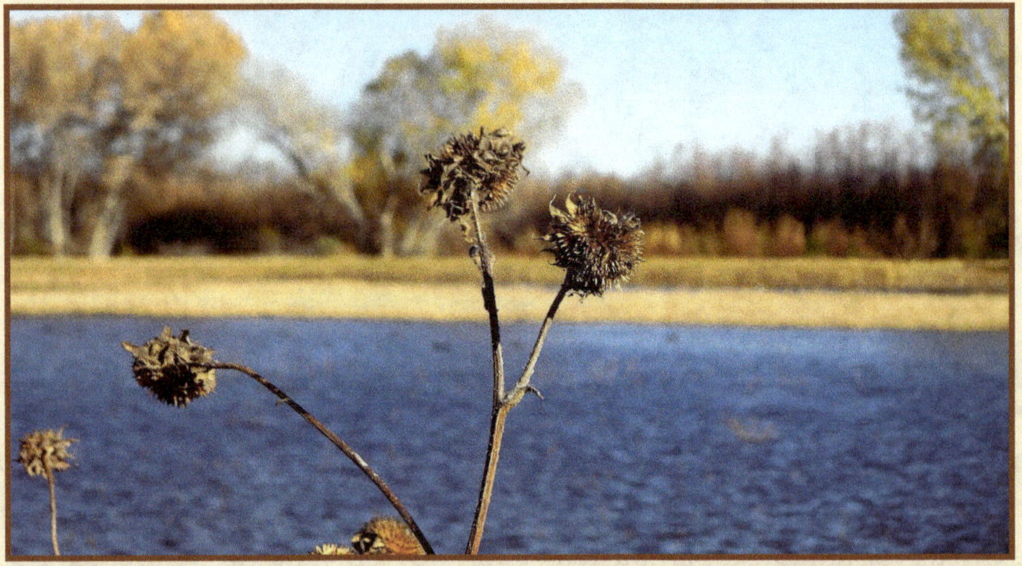

A dried sunflower bush overlooks the banks of a waterway at the refuge. The refuge also provides shelter to other creatures besides birds, including elk, mule deer, and coyotes.

The Bosque del Apache refuge is located within the northern edge of the Chihuahuan Desert, which covers territories in Arizona, Texas and northern Mexico.

The Chihuahuan Desert is considered a rain shadow desert, with mountain ranges and higher precipitation than other deserts. The Rio Grande runs through its center.

The desert extends over 175,000 square miles, making it the largest of 4 deserts in North America. With over 1,500 species of plants within its U.S. portion, the Chihuahuan Desert has a greater diversity of plant life than other deserts.

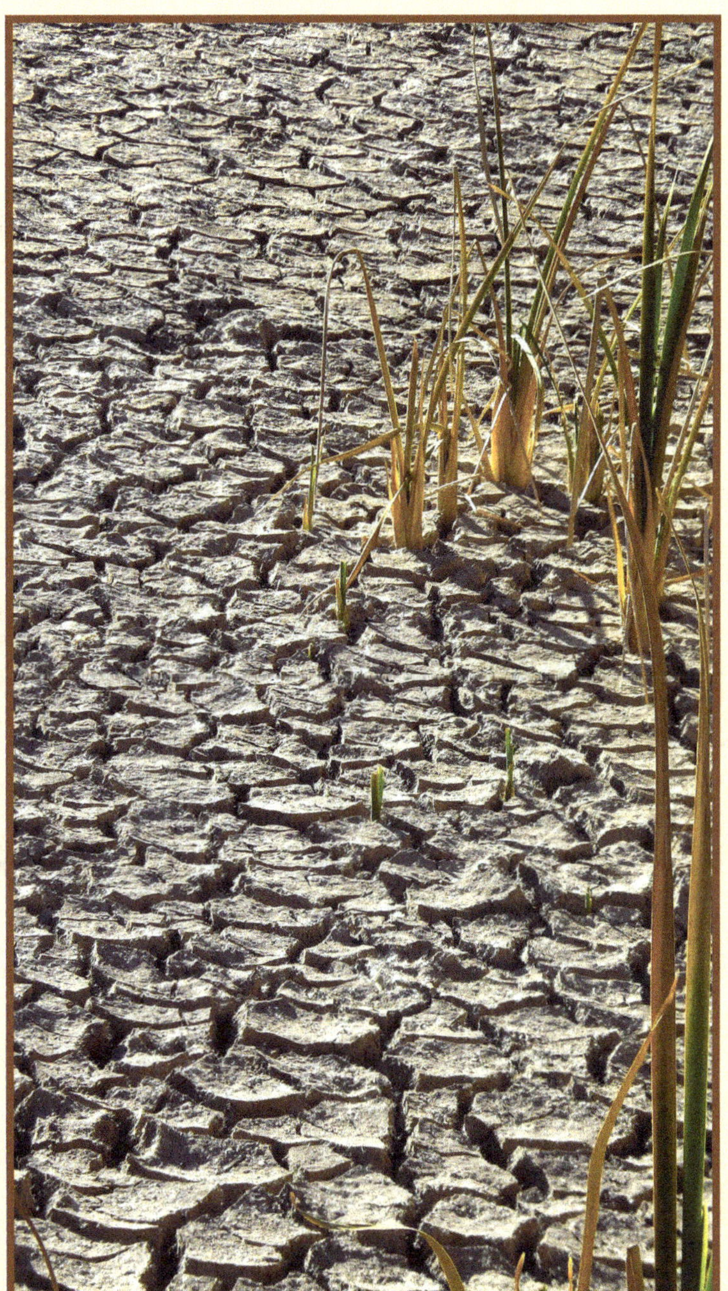

Vegetation is sparse in a dried pond.

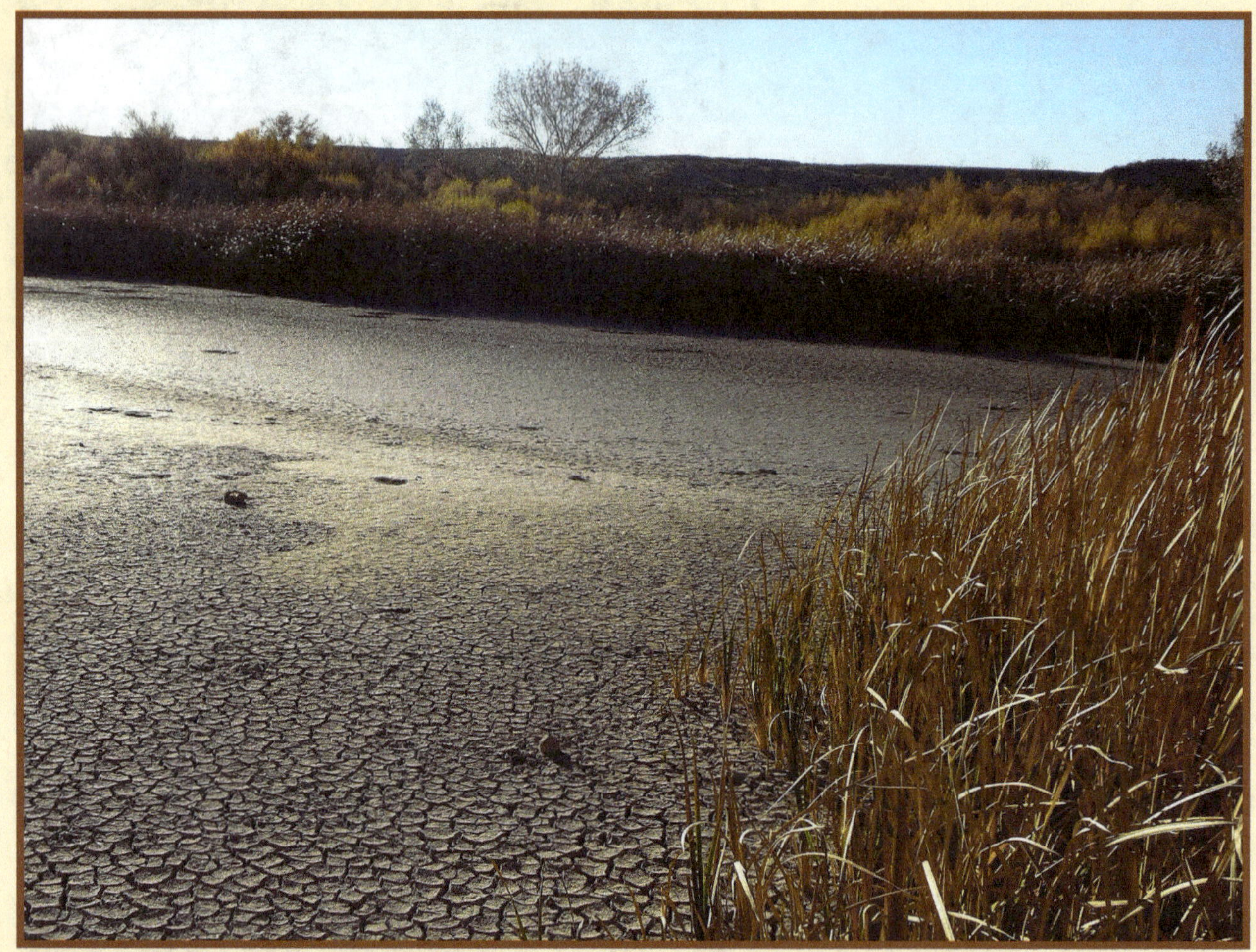

Dried mud forms a pattern at the bottom of an empty pond.

The desolate landscape surrounding the refuge has changed little since June 1598, when Juan de Oñate and the first colonists from Spain marched through the area. Upon reaching an Indian settlement adjacent to the Rio Grande (some 6 miles north of the refuge), the Spaniards named the town Socorro (meaning, "succor," or help in hardships) in recognition of the Indians' gifts of corn, water, and generous hospitality. This encounter with the Indians, who were unafraid of the strangers, was recorded in Oñate's official expedition records.

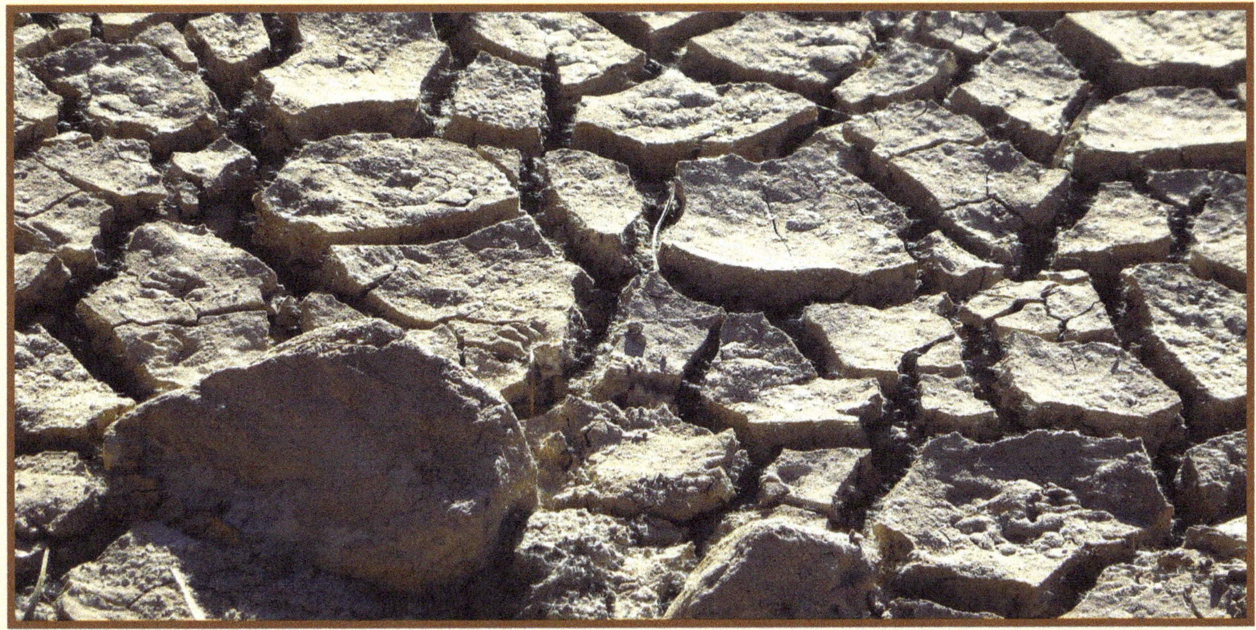

Sun bakes the earth in an arid section of the refuge.

A deadly part of the Camino Real is south of the refuge near Fort Craig called Jornada del Muerto (Dead Man's Journey)—a 90-mile-long strip of desert east of the Rio Grande where people died of thirst. Travelers along the Camino Real avoided suffering under the harsh sunlight by crossing the desert at night in 3 marches. Santa Fe trader Josiah Gregg wrote this about the Jornada del Muerto in 1844: "We generally find a great advantage in traveling through these arid tracts of land in the freshness of the evening, as the mules suffer less from thirst, and move on in better spirits—particularly in the season of warm weather." He continued: "Early the next morning we found ourselves at the Laguna del Muerto (Dead Man's Lake) where there was not even a vestige of water. This lake is but a sink in the plain of a few rods in diameter, and only filled with water during the rainy season...nothing but the firmest and driest tableland is to be seen in every direction. To procure water for our thirsty animals, it is often necessary to make a halt here, and drive them to the Ojo del Muerto (Dead Man's Spring) ...in the very heart of the mountain ridge that lay between us and the river. This region is one of the favorite resorts of the Apaches, where many a poor *arriero* [muleteer] has met with an untimely end."

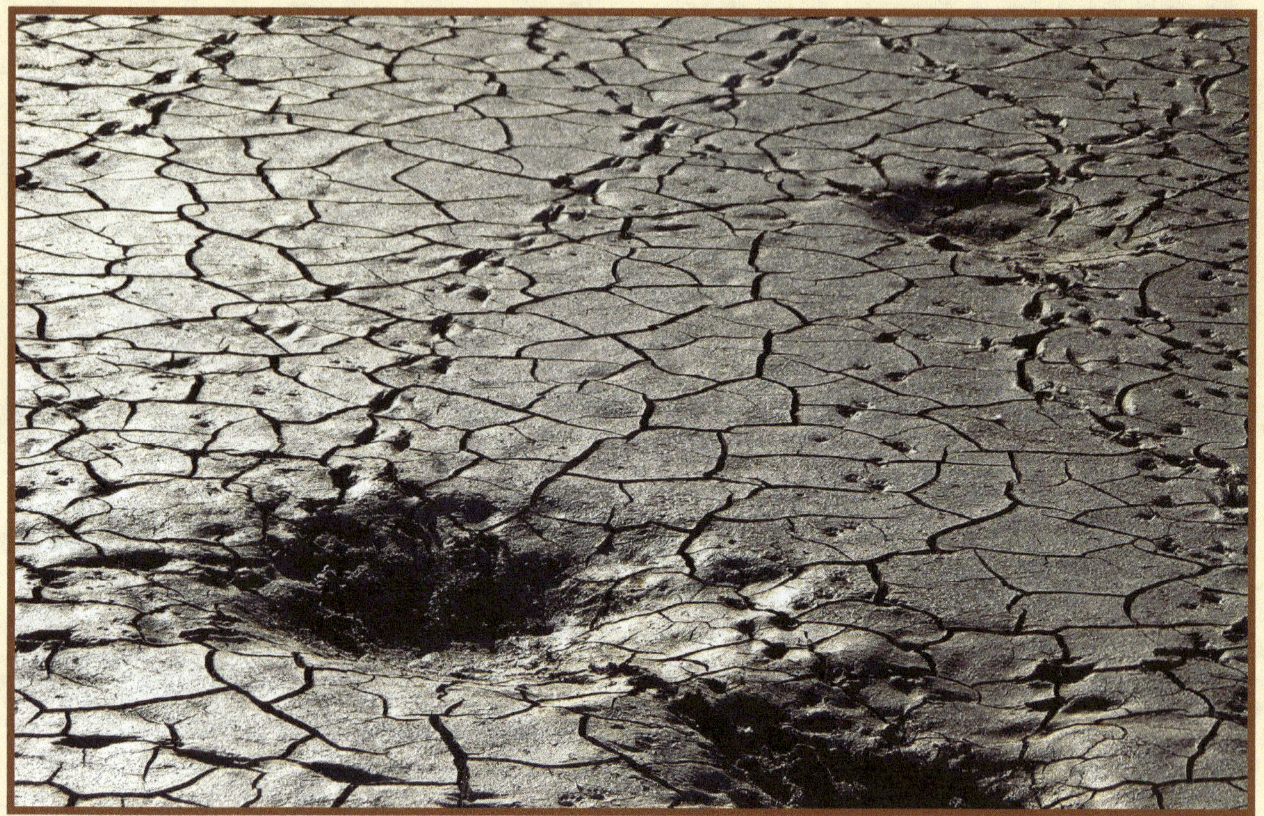

Animal tracks glint in the sunlight in mud at the wildlife refuge.

A first-hand account of traveling across the dreaded Jornada del Muerto, located not far from the refuge, was penned in 1847 by Frank S. Edwards, of the 1st Regiment of Missouri Mounted Volunteers. "Near to the middle of it is a large hollow in the ground, which, if rain has fallen lately, usually contains water. A Spaniard who had just come through informed us that this was dry," recalled Edwards. "Some of our men, thinking to avoid the usual suffering for water on this trip, got rather tipsy just before entering the Jornada, calculating that, with a canteen full of whisky, they could keep in that state all the way across. Some did so, but others having used their canteens too freely, exhausted their stock the first night and suffered terribly from thirst."

Fortunately, the waters of the Rio Grande in the nearby Bosque del Apache provided relief and much-needed water for the travelers and their animals.

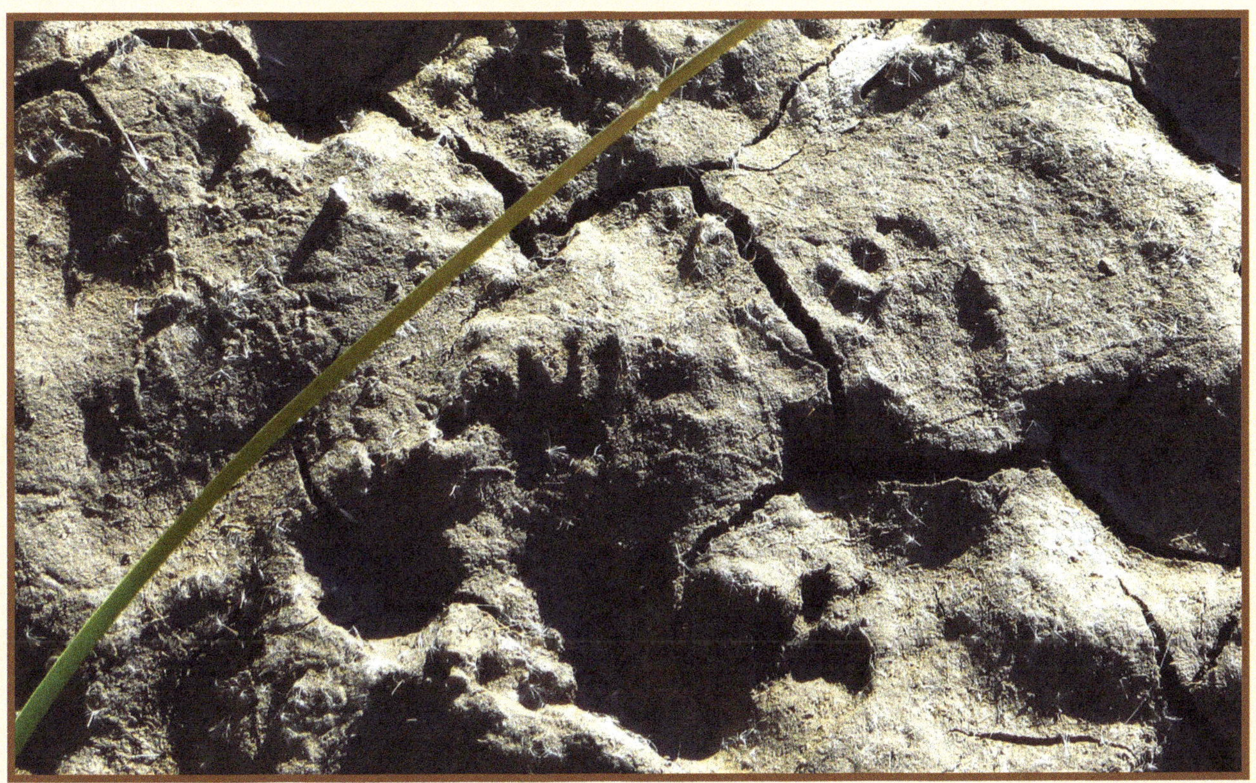

Animal footprints leave imprints in the mud in a dried marsh at the Bosque del Apache National Wildlife Refuge.

Many small mammals make their homes in the refuge and depend on the waters of the Rio Grande for survival.

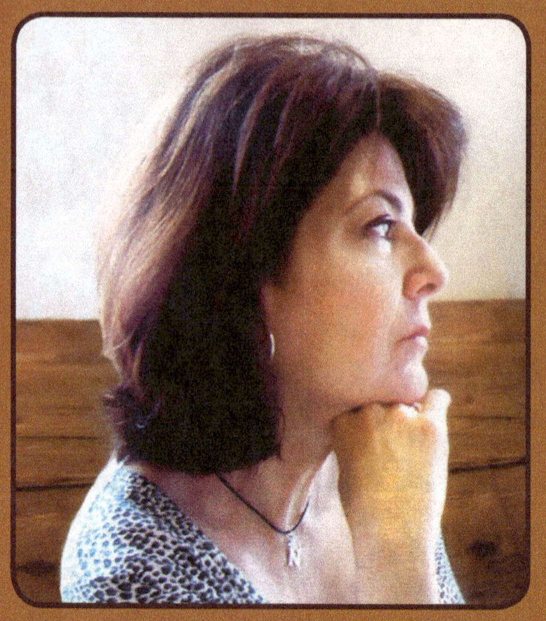

Chapter 10:

About Noël Fletcher

Noël Fletcher is an innovative writer, graphic artist, and photographer. She inherits a zest for life and a strong will from her Spanish conquistador ancestors, who braved travel on ocean vessels and rode on horseback across unexplored frontiers to build their futures despite the unknown.

She is proud of her diverse heritage. She is from New Mexico, a land rich in rugged beauty and the Southwestern cultural blend of Native Americans, Hispanics, and Anglos.

Her Hispanic ancestors came as Conquistadors to the Rio Grande valley and settled there. Among them were the Perea family of Spanish-Arab origin, who helped found the famed Santa Fe Trail and served in government roles under the Spanish crown, the Mexican era, and the American acquisition.

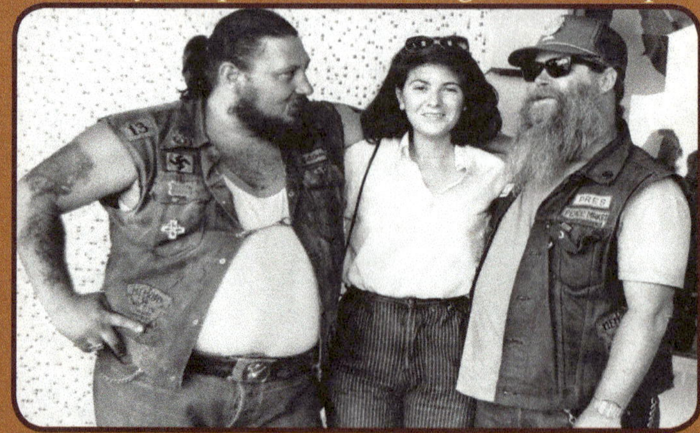

Two members of the Vagos Motorcycle Club pose with Noël after she conducted a newspaper interview with them at a Palm Springs restaurant.

On her father's side, her Fletcher and Ballinger relatives were early East Coast settlers from England; some from Virginia served in a volunteer militia under the Continental Army during the Revolutionary War.

Setting her sights on a career in journalism, Noël put herself through college at San Francisco State University and launched her news career in California, where she wrote TV news and worked on newspapers.

Noël worked through the trenches of daily news coverage at the *Desert Sun* newspaper in Palm Springs, an interesting locale of intrigue and affluence.

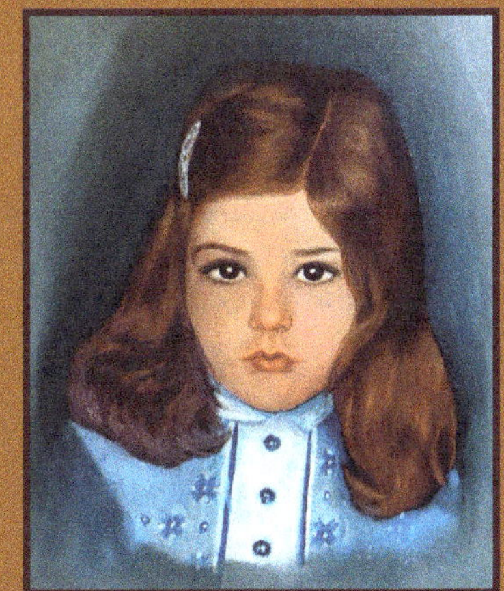

Art has been part of her family for generations. One of her aunts painted this portrait of Noël at age 5.

A few years later, she left on a whim to Hong Kong—with one suitcase in hand, $200, and the names of four people she'd never met—to become a foreign correspondent in Asia. Within two weeks, she landed a job at the *HongKong Standard* newspaper covering the Supreme Court, a.k.a. the "High Court." She learned the ropes of the British legal system by reporting on a world populated by red-coated High Court justices, wigged barristers, black-frocked solicitors, and prisoners in the dock. She covered white-collar crime and sensational murder trials as well as the Court of Appeals.

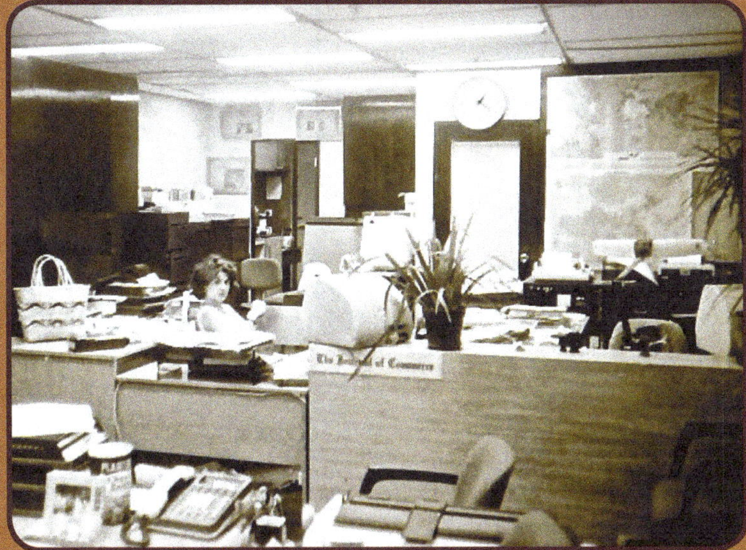

Noël sits at her desk in the newsroom in Hong Kong.

Moving up the ranks as a foreign correspondent, Noël focused on business and financial news, thereby becoming part of an elite American press corps. Her beat was Asia.

She lived and worked in China,

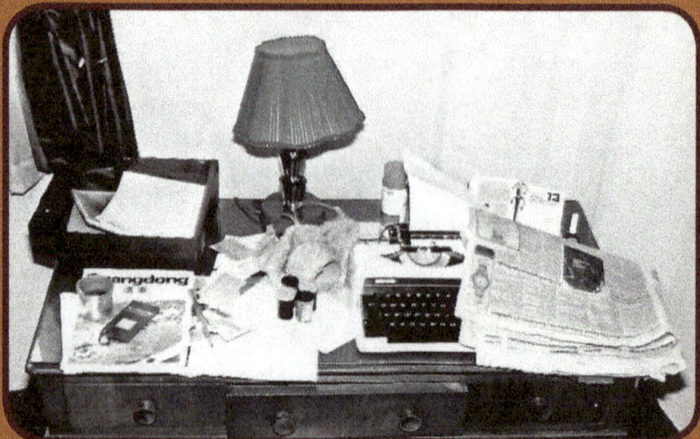

Press credentials, a portable typewriter, a magazine on Guangdong, China; a newspaper; rolls of 35 mm film; a knitting project and papers cover Noël's hotel desk in Guangzhou (Canton) while she was on assignment interviewing and creating news reports.

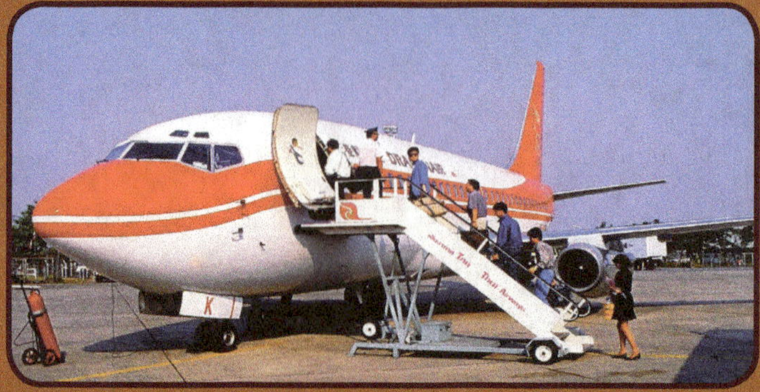

Noël' boards a Draigonair flight in Thailand.

Hong Kong, and traveled through many other Asian countries including South Korea and Singapore.

Speaking no Mandarin, she made her first trip into China while clutching a

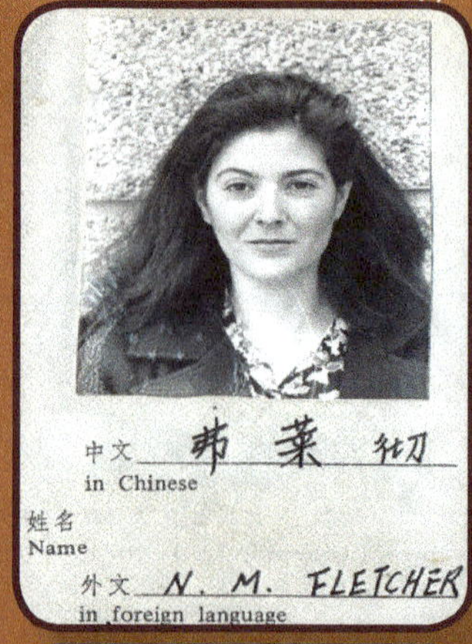

Noël's foreign correspondent credentials in Beijing.

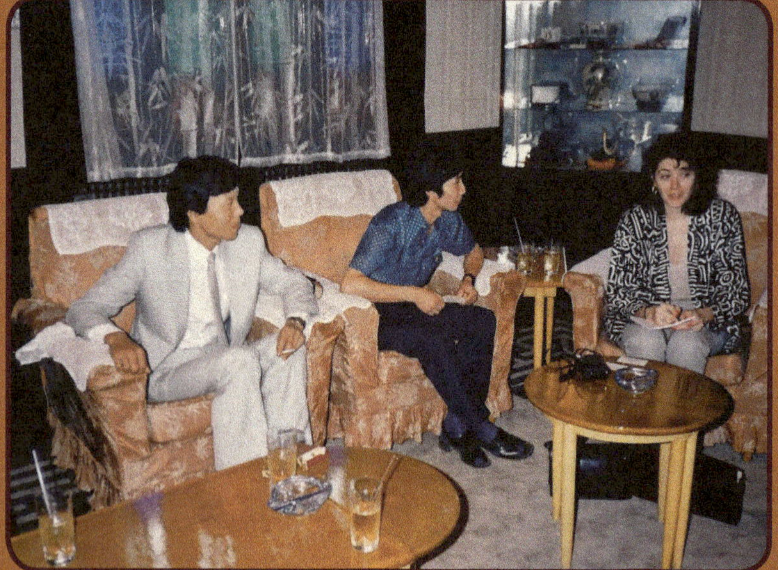

Seated inside the former home of notorious Chief Eunuch Li Lien Ying (Li Lianying), Noël interviews Chinese businessmen in Tianjin (Tientsin). During the last Chinese dynasty Eunuch Li amassed a fortune by taking bribes and selling information. He built this mansion away from Beijing to live in luxury. He died in 1911.

Chinese phrase book. Traveling via trains, hydrofoil, airplanes, and private cars, she conducted interviews for a month before returning to Hong Kong.

She was posted in Beijing as a prestigious "China correspondent" and became fluent in Mandarin. She delved deeper into the art, culture and history of Asia.

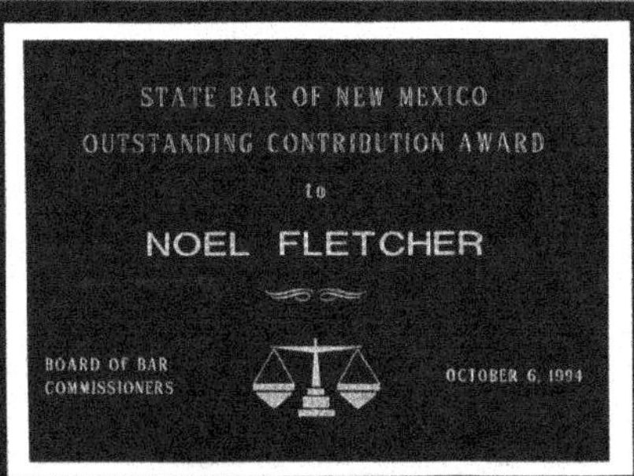

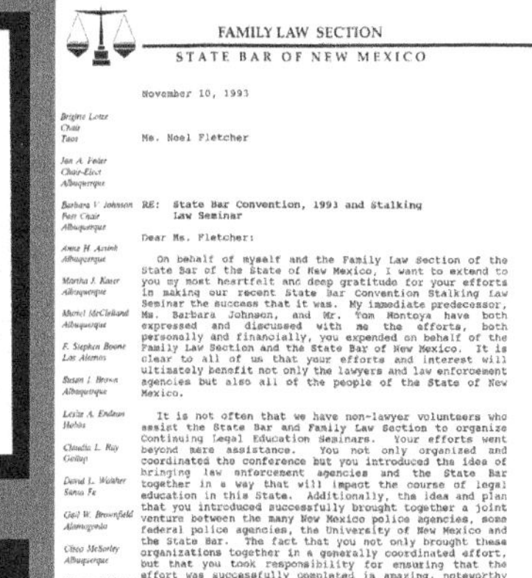

FAMILY LAW SECTION

STATE BAR OF NEW MEXICO

November 10, 1993

Brigitte Lotze, Chair, Taos
Jan A. Feder, Chair-Elect, Albuquerque
Barbara V. Johnson, Past Chair, Albuquerque
Anne H. Assink, Albuquerque
Martha J. Kaser, Albuquerque
Muriel McClelland, Albuquerque
F. Stephen Boone, Los Alamos
Susan I. Brown, Albuquerque
Leslie A. Endean, Hobbs
Claudia L. Ray, Gallup
David L. Walther, Santa Fe
Gail W. Brownfield, Alamogordo
Cisco McSorley, Albuquerque
Thomas C. Montoya, Albuquerque
Stanley A. Read, Portales

Ms. Noel Fletcher

RE: State Bar Convention, 1993 and Stalking Law Seminar

Dear Ms. Fletcher:

On behalf of myself and the Family Law Section of the State Bar of the State of New Mexico, I want to extend to you my most heartfelt and deep gratitude for your efforts in making our recent State Bar Convention Stalking Law Seminar the success that it was. My immediate predecessor, Ms. Barbara Johnson, and Mr. Tom Montoya have both expressed and discussed with me the efforts, both personally and financially, you expended on behalf of the Family Law Section and the State Bar of New Mexico. It is clear to all of us that your efforts and interest will ultimately benefit not only the lawyers and law enforcement agencies but also all of the people of the State of New Mexico.

It is not often that we have non-lawyer volunteers who assist the State Bar and Family Law Section to organize Continuing Legal Education Seminars. Your efforts went beyond mere assistance. You not only organized and coordinated the conference but you introduced the idea of bringing law enforcement agencies and the State Bar together in a way that will impact the course of legal education in this State. Additionally, the idea and plan that you introduced successfully brought together a joint venture between the many New Mexico police agencies, some federal police agencies, the University of New Mexico and the State Bar. The fact that you not only brought these organizations together in a generally coordinated effort, but that you took responsibility for ensuring that the effort was successfully completed is amazing, noteworthy and remarkable. The personal effort and time you must have expended on this task had to be incredible. You must truly be an outstanding person. I very much look forward to meeting you and expressing my thanks to you in person the next time I am in Albuquerque.

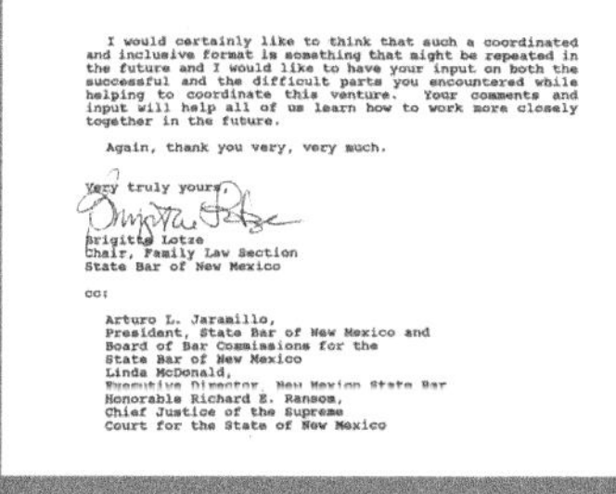

I would certainly like to think that such a coordinated and inclusive format is something that might be repeated in the future and I would like to have your input on both the successful and the difficult parts you encountered while helping to coordinate this venture. Your comments and input will help all of us learn how to work more closely together in the future.

Again, thank you very, very much.

Very truly yours,

Brigitte Lotze
Chair, Family Law Section
State Bar of New Mexico

cc:

Arturo L. Jaramillo,
President, State Bar of New Mexico and
Board of Bar Commissions for the
State Bar of New Mexico
Linda McDonald,
Executive Director, New Mexico State Bar
Honorable Richard E. Ransom,
Chief Justice of the Supreme
Court for the State of New Mexico

Noël experienced a poignant chapter in China's history during the events of the Tiananmen Square Massacre, which took place a few miles from the diplomatic compound where she lived.

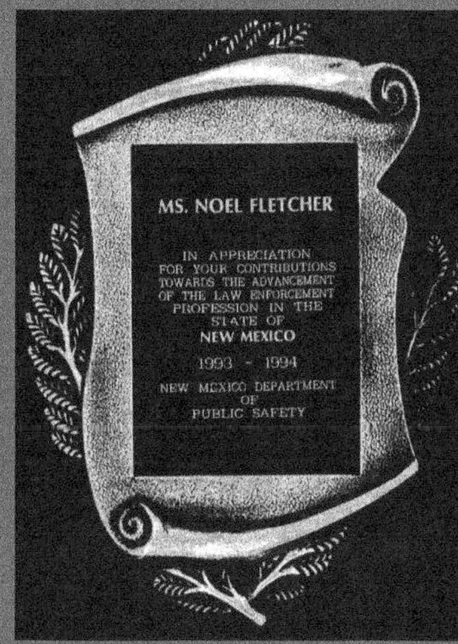

One of the few American women journalists there, she was on the last U.S. flight evacuated from Beijing and returned to China two weeks later to continue reporting. A few months later she left to live in California.

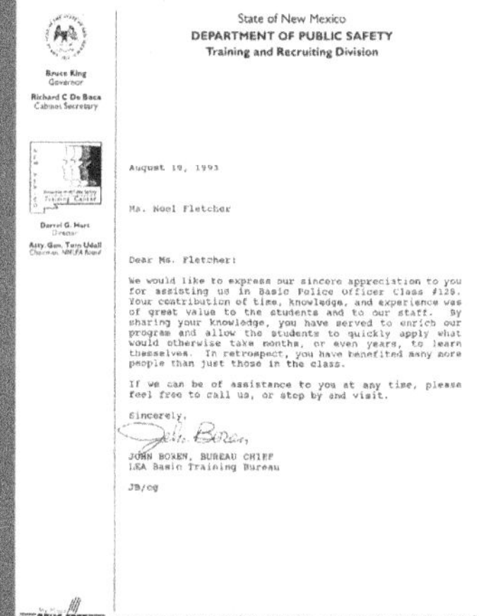

State of New Mexico

DEPARTMENT OF PUBLIC SAFETY

Training and Recruiting Division

Bruce King, Governor
Richard C De Baca, Cabinet Secretary
Darrel G. Hart, Director
Atty. Gen. Tom Udall, Chairman, NMLEA Board

August 19, 1993

Ms. Noel Fletcher

Dear Ms. Fletcher:

We would like to express our sincere appreciation to you for assisting us in Basic Police Officer Class #129. Your contribution of time, knowledge, and experience was of great value to the students and to our staff. By sharing your knowledge, you have served to enrich our program and allow the students to quickly apply what would otherwise take months, or even years, to learn themselves. In retrospect, you have benefited many more people than just those in the class.

If we can be of assistance to you at any time, please feel free to call us, or stop by and visit.

Sincerely,

JOHN BOREN, BUREAU CHIEF
LEA Basic Training Bureau

JB/cg

DRUG FREE — Santa Fe, NM 87505 — NM Toll Free

Two awards and letters are among the accolades Noël received for launching the passage of New Mexico's first criminal stalking and harrassment law, and working to ensure authorities knew how to use the law.

Following a brief bad marriage, Noël moved to New Mexico with her one-month-old daughter and divorced. She realized there was a lack of criminal legal consequences for harassment and stalking. Noël singlehandedly embarked on an effort to create the state's first anti-stalking and harassment law. Speaking to domestic violence groups, gathering political support, enlisting the TV and print media, and testifying before state legislative committees, Noël even helped write the bill that became law – one long afternoon over pizza and coffee in the Bernalillo County District Attorney's office.

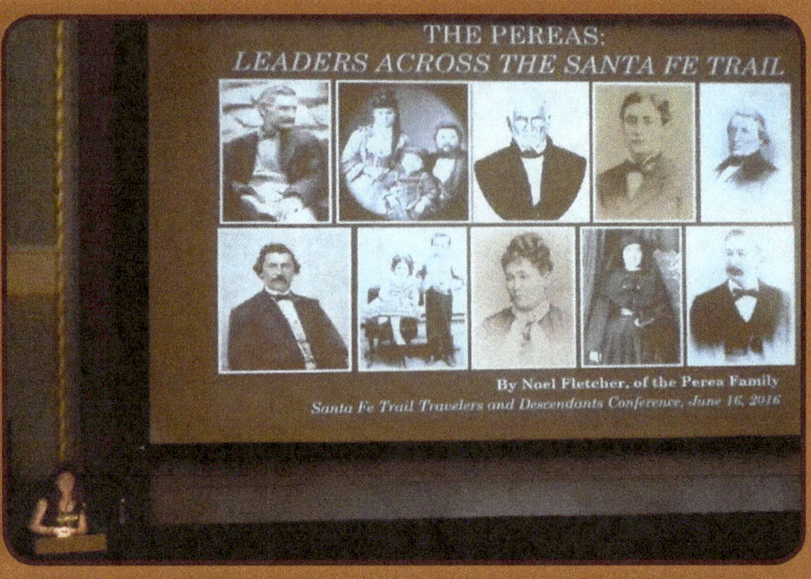

Noël presented information on her Perea family during the Santa Fe Trail Travelers and Descendants Conference in 2016.

Noël enjoys foreign cinema and speaks Spanish, Mandarin Chinese, and some French. She also creates artwork by combining pastels with her pen and ink free-hand drawings.

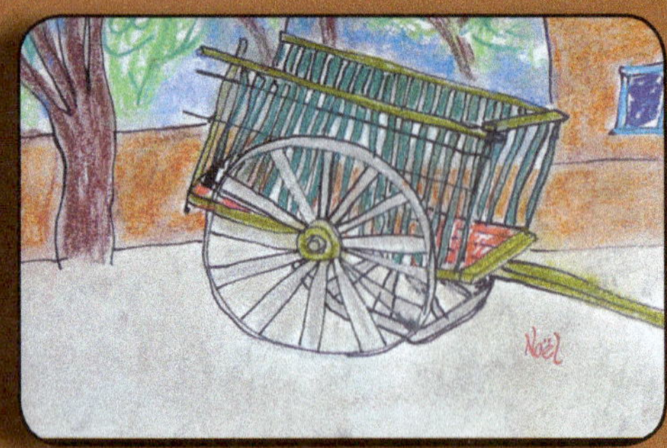

Traditional Spanish cart in Corrales, New Mexico by Noël.

Her work reflects her interests in art, history, and diverse cultures. Her books often involve investigative research. She seeks to blend visual imagery with writing, including her own artwork and historical images.

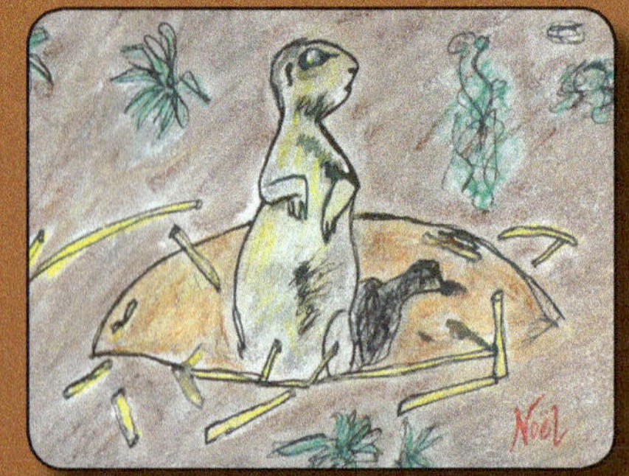

Santa Fe prairie dog by Noël.

Noël's other Books

Captives of the Southwest by Noël Fletcher

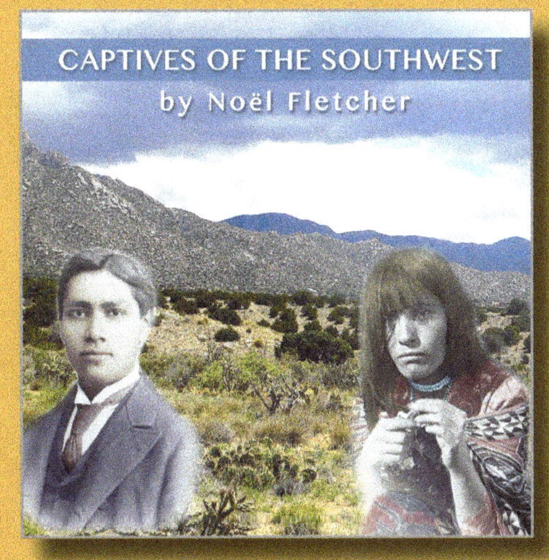

Take a journey into the lives of people who vanished in the Wild West. Explore true stories and eyewitness accounts of the kidnappings and experiences of Anglos, Hispanics, and Native Americans taken captive in New Mexico and the Southwest.

Each chapter takes the reader into a unique setting alongside new casts of characters—including lost settlers, greedy prospectors, elusive desert traders, vigilante lawmen, nomadic tribesmen, courageous women and resilient children. Stunning historical and modern photographs provide vivid glimpses into the life of each captive and the environments they experienced.

Author and researcher Noël Fletcher provides a local perspective and expert analysis for events and stories. Interesting historical details and rare images of key people and places are described.

A rare gem for readers of Wild West history containing gripping tales of adventure, hardship, courage and personal sacrifice. Included are rich illustrations including 115 historic photos, 14 maps, 35 news articles, 40+ modern photos and more.

Pathways in Time: Photo Journeys by Noël Fletcher

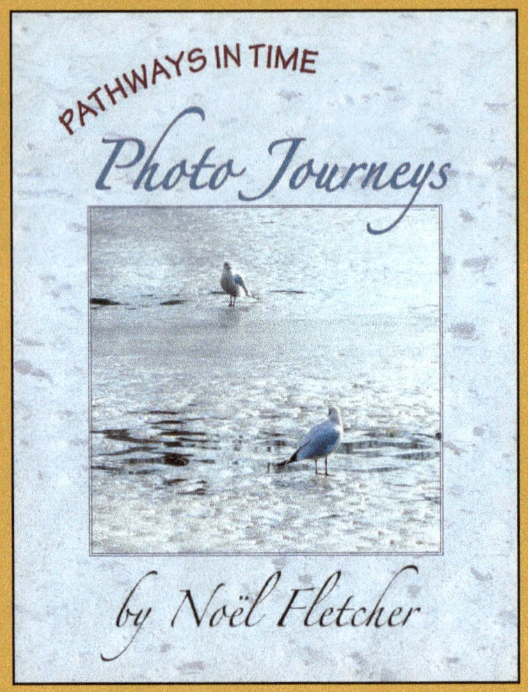

Travel along many roads and witness simple and abstract forms of beauty. Featuring over 160 photos, *"Pathways in Time: Photo Journeys"* shows the wonder of nature such as in rainbows, birds, trees, leaves, raindrops, and the earth.

It also reveals abstract views of architecture, urban settings, and found objects.

Author/photographer Noël Fletcher shows how to find beauty in ordinary life and the world that surrounds us all.

The Strange Side of War *by* SARAH MACNAUGHTAN & NOËL FLETCHER

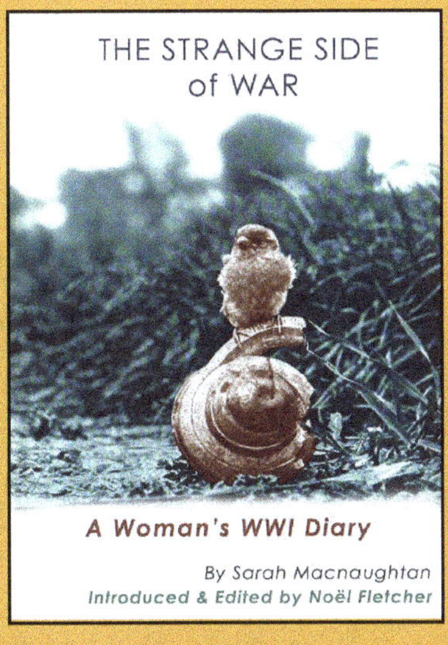

Take a journey across the dangerous battlefields of a world at war. Accompany Scottish novelist Sarah Macnaughtan as she volunteers alongside British humanitarian groups to alleviate the suffering in war-torn lands. Her many adventures tell unique stories of tragedy and triumph, taking readers on an unforgettable journey from the trenches of Belgium to the distant frontiers of Persia and tsarist Russia.

Author/editor Noël Fletcher provides new historical context that brings Sarah's story to life and helps readers to remember the bravery and sacrifice of those who died. Illustrated with 130+ rare photos and propaganda posters from World War I, this important work features historical insights about the people and places involved in the conflict.

Two Years in the Forbidden City *by* PRINCESS DER LING

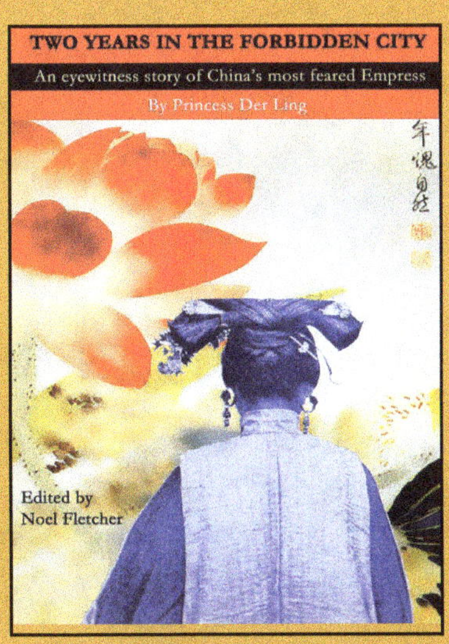

This true story was the first eyewitness account of the Imperial Court written by a Chinese aristocrat for Western readers. It provides an up-close view of the notorious Dowager Empress Tzu-hsi in her final years. Enhanced with rich imagery and additional historical notes, it includes interesting historical details and photos about China's infamous Dowager Empress, the Boxer Rebellion and the Imperial Court. It is illustrated with 100+ historical photographs, illustrations, and paintings from the late 1800s to early 1900s. Author/editor Noël Fletcher that provides context for this book in modern Chinese history.

More Books from Fletcher & Co. Publishers

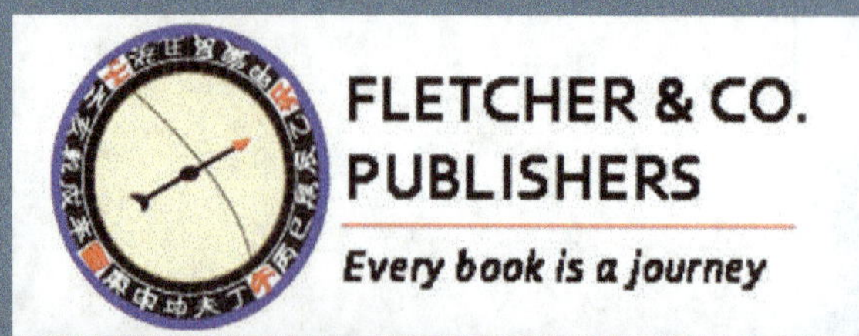

Every book is a journey. Fletcher & Co. Publishers is an independent, art-house publishing company. We use new media and graphic design techniques to transport you into the world of the novel.

Our books aren't just written words. They're experiences: international cultures, art, suspense, history, and adventure.

Watch our video trailers on Vimeo to preview each book, see interesting images, and learn more about our newest releases. Visit us our website to find out about our latest news.

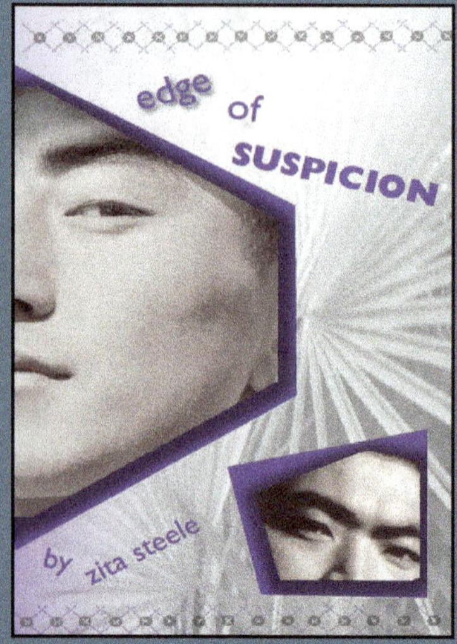

Edge of Suspicion *by* Zita Steele

Justin Moon of South Korea is the world's top private eye. He travels to Singapore to catch an elusive cybercriminal. The pay is lucrative. His client is an attractive blonde CEO. It should be the easiest job in his career. Things get complicated with the arrival of Okada, a mysterious drifter with a mission of revenge. As Moon tries to solve the mystery, he uncovers a tangled maze of deceit. Each new clue leads him in an unpredictable direction.

A deadly game of cat-and-mouse begins. Featuring over 100 photos, *Edge of Suspicion* is both an exciting story and a work of art.

Envoy: Rule of Silence *by* Zita Steele

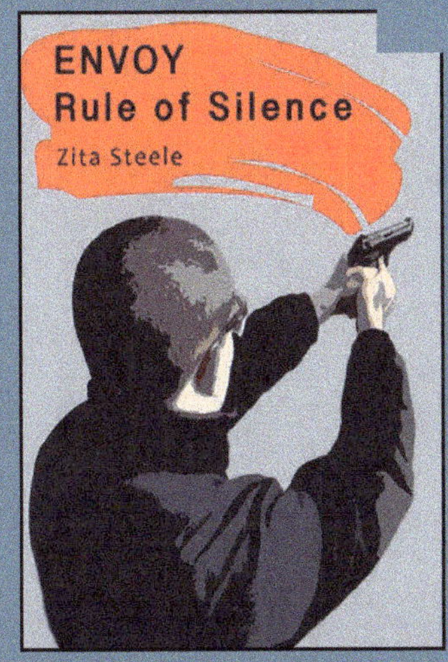

Take a journey into a thrilling world of secrets and lies in modern-day Europe. Polish ex-secret policeman Michal Krynski is tired of working as a double agent for France's security bureau. His last mission - to track down a runaway DJ. As he travels to the strange island of Malta, Krynski plots revenge against the system that ruined his life. Will he catch the DJ or kill him? Zita Steele is a novelist and artist. She writes with an expertise in criminology, cybercrime, and international relations. She creates her own illustrations.

Diné: A Tribute to the Navajo People *by* Zita Steele

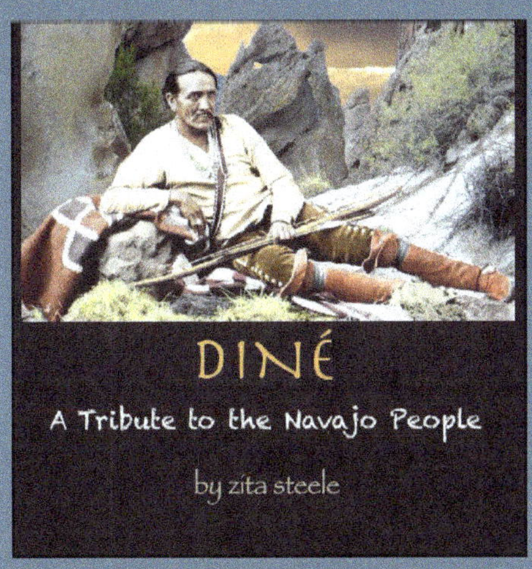

Take a journey into natural freedom and beauty in this tribute to one of America's most vibrant nomadic tribes. Author/artist Zita Steele commemorates the Diné (Navajo) people of the Southwestern United States with a vivid collection of color images. Four chapters honor the Native American tribe's freedom, ingenuity, strength, and joy.

The images create an experience of nomadic life without reservations or borders. The book provides insights into Diné culture and highlights the tribe's vast ancestral roaming territory.

Features include: 40+ original photographs, 25+ photo montages and special introduction by the author and additional artwork.

Erwin Rommel Photographer–Vol. 1 A Survey *by* Erwin Rommel and Zita Steele

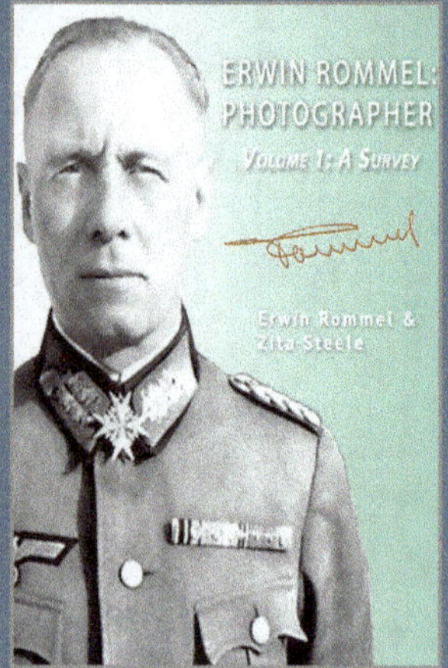

Take a journey behind the camera of a world-famous military commander. Experience WWII firsthand from Field Marshal Rommel's private photo collection, seized by U.S. forces in 1945. View 340+ images, including photos Rommel took during campaigns in France and North Africa and others he collected. Included are Rommel's personal photos of family and friends. The photos are digitally restored for detail. Some are accompanied by Rommel's own handwritten photo captions. Author/artist Zita Steele uses her knowledge of German language and culture, with in-depth research about Rommel and his campaigns, to provide context for the photos. Zita also analyzes patterns in Rommel's photography to shed a light on the artistic personality of this notable military leader.

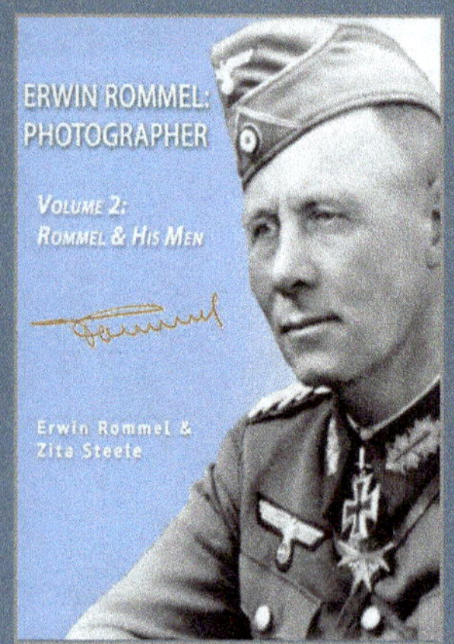

Erwin Rommel Photographer–Vol. 2 Rommel & His Men

by Erwin Rommel and Zita Steele

Experience life on the frontlines with Field Marshal Erwin Rommel. View 200+ images from Rommel's private photo collection, seized by U.S. forces in 1945. Join Rommel as he interacts with his German and Italian troops. See him and his men at work, at rest, and on the move. View Rommel's mementos of his men and military leaders. This book provides a candid view of Rommel as an ordinary soldier rather than a general. The photos are digitally restored and enhanced for detail. Some are accompanied by Rommel's own handwritten photo captions.

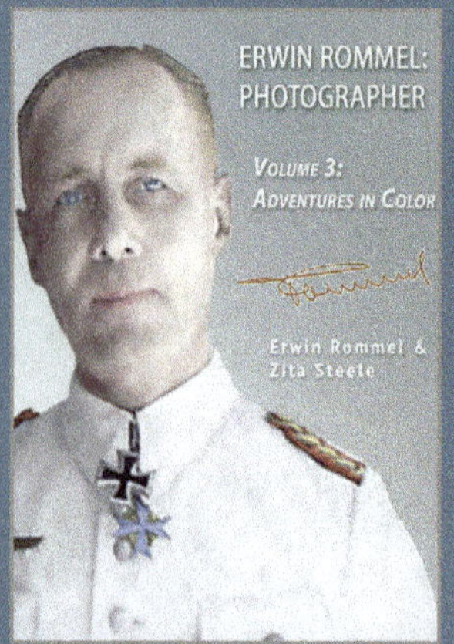

Erwin Rommel Photographer–Vol. 3 Adventures in Color

by Erwin Rommel and Zita Steele

Join Field Marshal Erwin Rommel in WWII through his rare color photographs. View 130 color images from Rommel's private photo collection, seized by U.S. forces in 1945, and a selection of Rommel's hand-drawn sketches of his war experiences. Join Rommel as he travels across vast and colorful terrains, flies a dive bomber plane, drives across desert battlefields and explores North African villages. The photos and sketches are digitally restored and enhanced for detail. Also included are 10 original sketches by Rommel as well as historical facts and analysis.

Lantern of the Wicked *by* CHARLES CLEMENT

In the decadent and dangerous Shanghai of 1929, someone is spying for the Japanese, and the International Settlement's British police are on the hunt. Now, in the midst of the Mid-Autumn Moon Festival, American aviator Jack "Ace" Jordan becomes the prime suspect. A thrilling narrative blending fact, fiction and rare photographs, *Lantern of the Wicked* creates an atmospheric window into the complexity and dark grandeur of the colonial Orient in this gripping historical mystery.

The Spy *by* JAMES FENIMORE COOPER

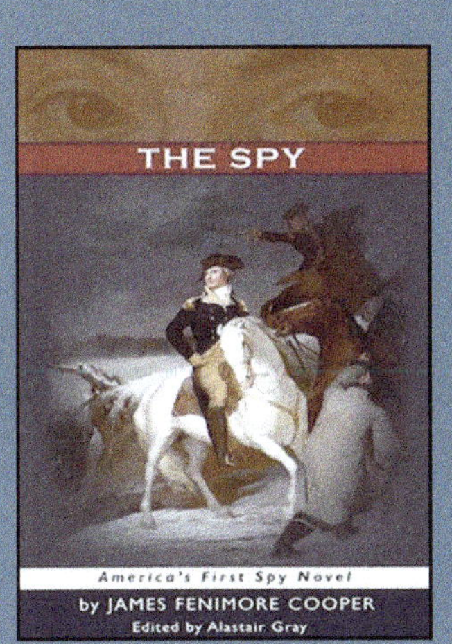

During the dark days of the Revolutionary War, America struggles for nationhood. Meanwhile, in the shadows, a spy is trading secrets of vital importance to the cause – but for whose side? Colonials and loyalists play a game of cloak and daggers in America's first spy novel. Our edition features 30+ color photographs, chapter titles, and illuminating notations, designed to give you a front-seat experience. This was the first major fiction novel on espionage ever written and published in America.

Mystery of the Yellow Room *by* GASTON LEROUX

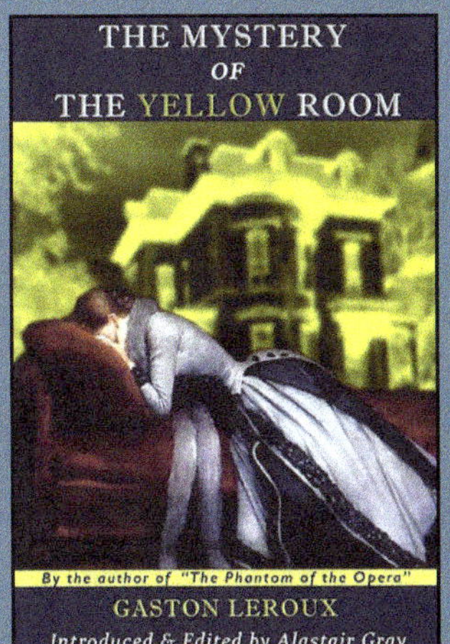

News of a strange crime spreads like wildfire in Paris. Someone has attempted to murder the daughter of a brilliant scientist. But nobody can explain how the murderer got in and out of the locked room of her isolated country home. Only Joseph Rouletabille, an impatient young journalist, has the genius to solve this crime. Written by the author of *"The Phantom of the Opera,"* this novel was published in 1907 as France's reply to Sherlock Holmes. Our edition has adapted text from archaic Victorian to standard English. It also features updated maps and is illustrated with 30+ historical paintings and illustrations from 19th century France.

www.ingramcontent.com/pod-product-compliance
Lightning Source LLC
LaVergne TN
LVHW080320110826
845155LV00026B/169

* 9 7 8 1 9 4 1 1 8 4 0 4 2 *